1 Introduction

Demystifying Modern Slavery: How Offenders Explain Exploitation

> The Government remains committed to ensuring the police and the courts have the necessary powers to bring perpetrators of modern slavery to justice, while giving victims the support they need to rebuild their lives … Illegal immigration causes significant harm and endangers the lives of those undertaking dangerous journeys. This Bill will introduce tougher criminal offences for those attempting to enter the UK illegally or found to be facilitating illegal immigration.
>
> (HM Government, 2021a: 8–9)

Who are the 'perpetrators of modern slavery' the British government is 'committed' to bringing 'to justice'? What harms do they inflict on others? Why do they do it? What might be done to stop such offending recurring? And how, if at all, is modern slavery related to 'illegal migration', its facilitation, and the 'undertaking dangerous journeys'? These are the key questions that we attempt to answer in this book. They are, as we explain below, questions that have, paradoxically, rarely featured in the modern slavery agenda that has played a key part in Conservative politics in the UK over the last decade. The problem of modern slavery received unprecedented political and media attention in the UK between 2012 and 2022. A phenomenon that had barely been mentioned before, let alone counted, was suddenly said to be everywhere, 'hiding in plain sight', a new 'evil', orchestrated by international organized criminals, exploiting the most vulnerable, necessitating new laws, bespoke victim support structures and more targeted approaches to policing and border enforcement.

Despite this unprecedented attention and centrality at policy level, very little is known about those who perpetrate the exploitation modern slavery legislation outlawed. Indeed, much of the rhetoric around modern slavery actually serves to mystify the problem, the use of biblical terms to convey the horrors of exploitation implying that the causes of such behaviour and the motives of most offenders defy social scientific explanation.

DOI: 10.4324/9780429053986-1

Demystifying the problem of modern slavery is a central objective of this book. Through the interpretation of convicted offenders' own accounts of their behaviour, our aim is to make modern slavery sociologically comprehensible. This is not to understate or diminish the significant harms perpetrated against victims of exploitation. Rather it is to show how the choices offenders make are morally legible, if not always forgivable, within the socio-economic, cultural and organizational contexts in which they take place. Understanding the context in which decisions to exploit take place is, from our perspective, the best means of identifying what needs to change to prevent modern slavery from occurring in the first place.

In the pages of this book, we reveal how perpetrators carried out and organized activities that came to be defined as people trafficking, smuggling, labour exploitation and the keeping of another in servitude. We describe, explore and conceptualize the motivations, networks and backgrounds that led to these crimes. We reveal how interdependencies arose between exploiters and the exploited, demystifying how victims become entrapped in modern slavery, as well as why many offenders do not consider themselves to have committed serious offences. Throughout, we illustrate the disjunctions between how offenders conceive of themselves and how they are conceived in modern slavery policy and practice, especially within criminal justice and immigration control contexts.

As we explain in Chapter 2, the few pre-existing primary studies of 'people traffickers' – an analogous group to 'modern slavery offenders' – suggest that the labels applied to those who become convicted of offences involving exploitation often obscure more than they reveal. Most pre-existing studies expose the relevance of the intersection of global inequalities, poverty and migration in shaping the relationships between those who are identified as victims and offenders. They also reveal how anti-trafficking policy tends to mystify these dynamics through references to new, international organized crime threats.

This is also the case in the UK. As we explain in Chapter 2, the modern slavery *agenda* can be conceptualized as the cultivation of a political opportunity utilized by the Conservative Party in a series of attempts to recapture its reputation as the party of 'law and order' – appropriated from them during the Blair years as the Labour Party became 'tough on crime, tough on the causes of crime'. By promising to tackle the threat of 'organized criminals', alleged to be profiting substantially from the trafficking and smuggling of people across international borders, the Conservatives identified a crime problem that appeared imminent, was difficult to refute empirically and which aligned with the immigration fears of a core section of their electoral base. By framing the problem as one of modern slavery, they were also able to encroach on political themes conventionally regarded as strengths of the political left. Exploitation and its redress are the raison d'être of the labour movement. However, in reconceptualizing the extremities of poor pay and poor working conditions as modern slavery, the Conservatives relocated the moral high ground to a symbolic place where they could prevail – crime, border enforcement and immigration control.

"This fascinating book reports on detailed interviews with individuals accused or convicted of trafficking-related offenses, illustrating how and why they landed in work in illicit economies. Overwhelming structural disadvantages are revealed by the victims that resulted in reliance on those who exploit them. Few 'traffickers' are discovered to be 'organized criminals' and many are found to closely resemble those they exploit. An intriguing empirical and policy narrative of how modern slavery has greatly oversimplified the context of what is actually occurring in the environment of human trafficking."

Professor Jay Albanese, Virginia Commonwealth University, Wilder School of Government & Public Affairs

"Broad and Gadd's research is the crucial missing piece in 'modern slavery' scholarship. By investigating the human stories behind the headlines, they skilfully dispel unhelpful mystiques about traffickers. This should be required reading for anyone concerned about trafficking and injustice today."

Emily Kenway, author of The Truth about Modern Slavery

Demystifying Modern Slavery

Who are the perpetrators of modern slavery? Why do they exploit others? What might be done to stop exploitation recurring? These are the questions answered in this book. Reporting on the first primary study of modern slavery offenders, the book depicts the findings of in-depth interviews with people accused of, and convicted for, committing modern slavery offences. The different forms that modern slavery takes are explained chapter by chapter: organized crime, people smuggling, labour exploitation, domestic servitude, sham marriage, the trafficking of adults for sexual exploitation and child sex trafficking. Using case studies to illuminate the perspectives of those deemed perpetrators, we show that few modern slavery offenders conform to stereotypes of people traffickers.

Through an interpretive analysis of offenders' life stories, we reveal the points in the past and present where interventions could have prevented victims from becoming trapped in exploitation. We show that while national governments and international bodies often appear resolute in their efforts to tackle modern slavery and people trafficking, they have also obscured their own roles in compounding the plights of those at the sharp ends of globalization. In racializing the actions of sex traffickers, grooming gangs, and organized criminals, the modern slavery agenda has mystified the roles market dynamics, the absence of workers' rights, and immigration controls play in generating vulnerabilities to exploitation.

This book will be of interest to a wide range of students, policymakers and practitioners concerned with modern slavery, human trafficking, border control and immigration, globalization and inequality, as well as the more discipline-focused criminological audiences concerned with why people commit crimes, what should be done about them and the, often paradoxical, consequences of social control across borders. Given the book's strong focus on narrative, psychosocial and social network methodologies, it will also appeal to audiences across the social sciences concerned with applying these novel approaches to difficult to reach populations.

Rose Broad is a Senior Lecturer at the University of Manchester.

David Gadd is a Professor of Criminology at the University of Manchester.

Routledge Studies in Crime and Society

For more information about this series, please visit: www.routledge.com/Routledge-Studies-in-Crime-and-Society/book-series/RSCS

Demystifying Modern Slavery

Rose Broad and David Gadd

 Routledge
Taylor & Francis Group

LONDON AND NEW YORK

First published 2023
by Routledge
4 Park Square, Milton Park, Abingdon, Oxon OX14 4RN

and by Routledge
605 Third Avenue, New York, NY 10158

Routledge is an imprint of the Taylor & Francis Group, an informa business

© 2023 Rose Broad and David Gadd

British Library Cataloguing-in-Publication Data
A catalogue record for this book is available from the British Library

Library of Congress Cataloging-in-Publication Data
Names: Broad, Rose, author. | Gadd, David, 1975– author.
Title: Demystifying modern slavery / Rose Broad and David Gadd.
Description: Abingdon, Oxon; New York, NY: Routledge, 2023. |
Series: Routledge studies in crime and society | Includes bibliographical references.
Identifiers: LCCN 2022023054 (print) | LCCN 2022023055 (ebook) |
ISBN 9780367149307 (hardback) | ISBN 9781032374864 (paperback) |
Subjects: LCSH: Slavery–History–21st century. |
Human trafficking–History–21st century.
Classification: LCC HT867 .B77 2023 (print) | LCC HT867 (ebook) |
DDC 306.3/620905–dc23/eng/20220602
LC record available at https://lccn.loc.gov/2022023054
LC ebook record available at https://lccn.loc.gov/2022023055

ISBN: 978-0-367-14930-7 (hbk)
ISBN: 978-1-032-37486-4 (pbk)
ISBN: 978-0-429-05398-6 (ebk)

DOI: 10.4324/9780429053986

Typeset in Bembo
by Newgen Publishing UK

Contents

Tables

Acknowledgements

We have had valuable input from many people throughout the research project that informs this book. We would like to thank Mary Bosworth, Paolo Campana and Nicholas Lord for providing valuable advice in the development of the research proposal; our co-investigators Carly Lightowlers and Elisa Bellotti who helped us deliver the wider project of which this book is just one part; Damaris Richards for her help in preparing and managing the research grant; and Joshua Findlay who assisted us to get this book into shape its final stages. Much gratitude is also due to Jay Albanese, Tom Vander Beken, Rozafa Berisha, Floretta Boonzaier, Ella Cockbain, Steve Collett, Barry Godfrey, Emily Kenway, Yenkong Ngangjoh Hodu, Matthew Millings, Jon Spencer and Jon Winterdyk for their insights and suggested readings, many of which we have utilized to strengthen the arguments we make in this book. Thanks are also due to Tom Sutton and Jess Phillips at Routledge for their help with the preparation of this book and their commitment to publishing our research findings.

The research would not have been possible without the funding (ES/R004471/1) provided by the Economic and Social Research Council, whose continued commitment to supporting research on contentious topics is invaluable, nor without the support of the University of Manchester, which provided us with the time and support needed to deliver this pioneering project. We could not have undertaken this research without the access granted by the National Research Council. We are grateful to Elizabeth Heredge for helping us navigate the research approval process. Of course, formal approval is only part of the challenge of gaining access in any research project. We had incredible support from offender managers in prisons and the community throughout this project. We cannot name you here without risking the possibility that our participants will become identifiable. But you know who you are, and we remain in your debt. Marek Musiol provided essential and unwavering support to us in helping to identify prospective participants without breaking any confidences. We cannot overstate how vital your help was and how grateful we are for it. We are also eternally grateful to all our interviewees. Each of you recounted life stories that were personal and sometimes painful to recount. We are grateful for making time to hear what our research was about and for sharing your experiences. We have striven to represent what you told us as faithfully as possible.

We were very fortunate to have the support of a strong network of professionals, practitioners and policymakers who helped us conceptualize this project and overcome the various hurdles its delivery presented along the way. Thank you to Damian Dallimore, Sian Payne, Vicki Charles and Hannah Flint from Greater Manchester Combined Authority; Chris Geneux, Jon Edgerton, Colin Ward, Jim Riley, Chris Nield, Claire McGuire, Debbie Hurst, Declan O'Reilly and Peter Fahy from Greater Manchester Police; Sara Thornton, Katie Lawson and Jenna Teasdale from the Independent Anti-Slavery Commissioner's Office; Olivia Hesketh and Imogen Schon from the Home Office; Viki Hayer from the National Crime Agency; Tina Threadgold (MASH), Phillipa Roberts (Hope for Justice), Paul McNulty (Hope for Justice), Erinma Bell (Chrysalis) and Imelda Poole (RENATE).

All this credit aside, responsibility for the arguments and suppositions made in this book, including any errors, remains with the authors.

Abbreviations

ATMG	Anti-Trafficking Monitoring Group
CPS	Crown Prosecution Service
CSJ	Centre for Social Justice
DTN	Duty to Notify
EC	European Commission
EEA	European Economic Area
EU	European Union
GSI	Global Slavery Index
IASC	Independent Anti-Slavery Commissioner
NAO	National Audit Office
NCA	National Crime Agency
NGO	Non-Government Organisations
NRM	National Referral Mechanism
OCG	Organized Crime Group
ONS	Office for National Statistics
RG	Reasonable Grounds
RNLI	Royal National Lifeboat Institution
SDG	Sustainable Development Goals
SOCA	Serious Organised Crime Agency
TVPA	Trafficking Victims Protection Act
UK	United Kingdom
UN	United Nations
US	United States
VAT	Value Added Tax
WHO	World Health Organization

The central paradox of the 'modern slavery' agenda is that it obfuscates the features of everyday life that make many victims vulnerable to exploitation – the absence of rights and recourse to justice for poorly paid workers, sex workers and undocumented labourers – by scapegoating a new folk devil – the modern slavery offender – who takes the blame for the adverse impacts of the government's own hostile immigration policies and austere economic policies (Gadd and Broad, 2018). As no one in the Labour Party would want to be accused of being 'on the side of the traffickers' – a refrain that Theresa May and her successor Boris Johnson both used as prime ministers to silence opposition – the wider aspects of the modern slavery agenda, most notably the hostile environment policy, passed into UK policy with little resistance, at least until the Windrush scandal and the disenfranchisement of European citizens after Brexit began to expose the institutionalized racism and xenophobia behind what might otherwise have been cast as anomalous system failures (Yeo, 2021).

As Yeo (2021) has documented, what had begun as an accidental policy commitment by Prime Minister David Cameron in the 2010s to 'reduce net migration to the tens of thousands' led to legislation that made it increasingly difficult for foreign nationals who did not have permission to live in the UK, to work, hold bank accounts, gain driving licences, rent properties and access healthcare. These policy manoeuvres were the exact opposite of what organizations committed to eradicating modern slavery would typically advise. Hostile environment policies rendered those living in the most precarious circumstances utterly dependent on cash-in-hand work in the grey and illicit areas of the economy. Indeed, as Kenway (2021), a former adviser to Britain's first anti-slavery commissioner, has explained, this is one of the most unpalatable truths about the modern slavery agenda. While the public have been persuaded to keep spotting the signs in nail bars and car washes, the hostile environment policy has created a situation that:

> Not only pushes undocumented people into riskier parts of our economy but also prevents them from seeking help safely when they experience exploitation ... The practice of involving immigration enforcement in labour inspection and policing ... hands offenders a ready-made tool with which to coerce and control victims because they are too afraid to seek help ... And so they are left with three choices: remain in exploitation, become destitute by running away, or go to the authorities and risk criminalisation.
> (Kenway, 2021: 50 51)

The modern slavery agenda also mystifies British history. It repeats a lie, told infinitum, about Britain's role in the abolition of transatlantic slavery: namely, that this was driven by a uniquely British commitment to instilling human rights and respecting human dignity, while at the same time rendering it unbecoming and unpatriotic to mention the pivotal role of chattel slavery in the growth of the British Empire. As is well documented, slaveowners, unlike freed slaves themselves, were recompensed handsomely by the British government for freeing their slaves (Fryer, 1984; O'Connell Davidson, 2015). They were then able to hire them back as 'forced apprentices' and on indentured labourers – typically from China and India – to ensure a steady supply of very cheap labour from which they were to continue to profit. The contemporary commitment to eradicating modern slavery is thus politically reminiscent of the ways in which 19th-century abolitionism enabled the perpetuation of a capitalistic system of profit-making rooted in the making and unmaking of British colonialism and the persisting legacies of racism and global inequality (Gadd and Broad, 2018). Perhaps as a way to detract from these uncomfortable truths, in the late 2010s, the UK government further expanded its definition of modern slavery to include exploitation within illicit drug distribution chains – 'county lines' drug dealing – into the agenda. In much of the public discourse about county lines, the differences between the exploited and exploiters in drug markets have been over-reified in ways that, arguably, distract from the role structural disadvantages and official drug policies play in sustaining drug markets (Windle et al., 2020; Spicer, 2021).

In short, calls to end slavery, historical and contemporary, have helped build political alliances that have tended to take questions about the systemic features and functions of exploitation off of the political agenda. Through the 2010s, the British public were persuaded both by the government and the 200-plus charities that emerged to tackle modern slavery (Turnbull and Broad, 2020) that it was possible to eradicate modern slavery if enough people came together to oppose it. Campaigns to tackle modern slavery suggested that all those invested in tackling it should feel genuinely proud of their collective endeavour (O'Connell Davidson, 2015). Anyone and everyone could participate in tackling modern slavery by reporting suspicious sightings to helplines or via phone apps, donating to projects that assisted victims to rebuild their lives, or simply sharing publicity about the need to be alert to the signs of modern slavery at work, within schools or on social media.

After a decade of strategizing to end it, however, the British government itself was conceding that the problem of modern slavery had 'not gone away' (Home Office, 2021a: 6). By the 2020s, modern slavery actually appeared to be, at least as viewed via official policy statements and statistics, more pervasive than it ever was. The number of applicants presenting as potential victims to the National Referral Mechanism (NRM) exceeded 10,000 in 2020 (ibid.) – a figure that was over 60% higher than the numbers presented between 2013 and 2016 (NCA, 2019). In the UK, potential victims are referred to the NRM by 'designated first responder' organizations (including police, border officials, local authorities, immigration and several charities) requiring consent for referral for adults, but not children. The referral is then assessed by the 'competent authority' that makes a 'reasonable grounds' decision which means that modern slavery is 'suspected but not proven' (p.3). If the reasonable grounds decision is positive, the authority will gather additional evidence to make a 'conclusive grounds' decision – meaning that it is 'more likely than not' that the person is a victim of modern slavery (ibid).

Why there has been a growth in referrals to the NRM is hard to discern. On the one hand, there is much greater awareness of modern slavery and a vast array of professional designated 'first responders' who are expected to help identify potential victims and refer them into the system. These professionals not only include the police and social workers but also immigration officials and border enforcement, including those working in immigration removal centres. On the other hand, exploitation may well have become more pervasive and entrenched in the UK after a decade of economic austerity. In 2021, 2.5 million families were using foodbanks in the UK, an increase of over 600,000 from the previous year (Trussell Trust, 2021). The initiative was unheard of a decade before. Social services were dealing with a growing number of UK born and foreign national children becoming caught in exploitation (Pearce, 2011) in part because the gains made in reducing child poverty during the Blair/Brown years had been radically reversed. At the same time, the NRM appeared to have become a system working against itself, generating an ever-growing backlog of applicants caught in legal limbos with little hope of securing the official documentation from home countries they had fled the UK government requires of them to evidence nationality, experiences of exploitation, entrapment and victimization (see Chapter 2 for further details on the pending NRM cases).

Successive anti-slavery commissioners in the UK attributed the limited success in reducing the number of people exploited through modern slavery to the allusiveness of organized criminals (Hyland, 2018; IASC, 2021: 153). There is, however, little evidence autonomous of the press briefings of the National Crime Agency to support the political refrain that the failure to convict large numbers of modern slavery offenders lies with sophisticated crime networks with the resources and connections that exceed the combined capacities of Western governments. Nevertheless, in a further twist of the political plot around modern slavery, in 2021 the British Home Secretary Priti Patel attributed the failings of the NRM to 'major increases in child rapists, people who threaten national security and failed asylum seekers' posing fraudulently as victims, and hence 'clogging up [the] modern slavery system' (Home Office and Patel, 2021). As the quote with which we opened this chapter also evidences, much UK government rhetoric about modern slavery, including Patel's unsubstantiated claim, has evoked what Franko (2020) calls the 'crimmigrant other'. The 'illegal immigrant' may only be illegal because they overstayed on a tourist visa or work permit, or because they cannot easily return to a country the government has deemed 'safe'. By conflating the 'illegal immigrant' with the 'foreign national offender', who could have committed any offence however low level, but who might be a people smuggler, a trafficker or even a 'child rapist' or terrorist, references to modern slavery have directed concern towards the potential criminality of all migrants, rendering potential victims of exploitation as suspect as their exploiters.

Numerous Freedom of Information requests, made by ourselves and others, to clarify the number of people referred into the NRM counted as (i) child rapists, (ii) people who pose a threat to national security, (iii) serious criminals and (iv) failed asylum seekers were all declined on cost and/or national security grounds. Whether or not a 'loophole' had been exploited by any 'child rapists and terrorists' as *the Sun* reported it (Cole, 2021), the Home Secretary was seemingly aggrieved that 'in 2019, of those potential victims referred into the NRM after being detained within the UK (totalling 1,949), 89% received a positive RG decision and 98% were released' (Home Office, 2021b: 31). Yet, there is little evidence of widespread abuse of the system. The Home Office's (2021b) own data reveals that in 2018, 79 foreign national offenders were considered by the NRM. A total of 61 of these were deemed to have reasonable grounds to be considered as victims of modern slavery. By 2021, 25 of these had been given positive conclusive grounds decisions, meaning that the government had deemed them to be actual victims of modern slavery; only two cases had been rejected, while the remainder were either undecided and ongoing, or could not be processed further, often because the applicant could not be traced (Home Office, 2021b). In other words, by the government's own accounting, the number of foreign national offenders with legitimate claims to be victims of modern slavery, relative to those making unsubstantiated claims, appeared in 2021 to be in excess of 12 to one.

That some foreign national offenders are also victims is an unpalatable truth that the modern slavery sector has not always drawn sufficient attention to. The ideological work modern slavery discourse achieves obscures this possibility. It involves: positioning the historic 'generosity of the British people' as vulnerable to abuse (HM Government, 2021b: 2); and justifying plans to treat new migrants with considerable suspicion on the basis that the nation is 'open to gaming and criminal exploitation' by organized criminals, among whom modern slavery offenders, people smugglers and traffickers are the most insidious threat (HM Government, 2021b: 3).

In this book, we show that such arguments, overlain as they are with a gloss that rallies those keen to 'protect genuine victims' (HM Government, 2021b: 32), are misdirected. They mystify modern slavery as a problem of evil, foreign national organized crime masterminds in the service of other political agendas. They misread victims' accounts of exploitation exclusively in terms of what has been done to them by offenders without reference to the structural ways in which people are rendered vulnerable to exploitation, or become reliant on prospective exploiters, through economic and legal precarity that could be redressed by the government. Though they sometimes pick and choose from victims' testimonies, official accounts of interventions to 'rescue' victims often misrepresent the complexities of survivors' lives. They rely heavily on intelligence from law enforcement agencies seeking budgets for specific projects (Spencer and Broad, 2012) and are not sufficiently informed by primary research with victims or modern slavery perpetrators: too little of which has been conducted (Albanese et al., 2022). Almost universally, statements about modern slavery – whether offered by politicians, NGOs or law enforcement in press briefings – overstate the differences between victims and offenders. The possibility that the former have found themselves reliant on crime, sometimes like the latter, is rarely contemplated. In so doing, they overlook the systemic nature of exploitation and how it creates hierarchies of vulnerability that make all of us who buy food, clothing, properties and computers in the West complicit with exploitation Many of these hierarchies of vulnerability ultimately culminate in some of the world's most destitute people exploiting each other.

Methodology

This book presents primary research on modern slavery perpetrators in the UK and demystifies how they become implicated in offences against those who are identified as victims by law enforcement. It is unavoidably informed by the perspectives of perpetrators, though these are not presented uncritically or without interpretation. Rather we attempt to explain why the protagonists of what many regard as a pervasive social evil fail to recognize themselves as modern slavery offenders, exploiters or people traffickers. In unravelling the conundrum of how modern slavery happens, we also seek to reveal how severe forms of exploitation can be better avoided, reduced in duration or minimized in their impacts.

The primary data sources for this book are free association narrative interviews (Hollway and Jefferson, 2000; Gadd, 2012) we conducted with 30 people who had been accused or convicted of modern slavery and other allied forms of offending. These allied forms of offending included (county lines) drug dealing, holding people in domestic servitude and facilitating illegal immigration. Participants were recruited primarily through the criminal justice system, typically with probation staff in prisons and the community, making approaches to prospective participants on our behalves before we knew their names or what offences had been committed. Her Majesty's Prison and Probation Service (HMPPS) provided us with 114 reference numbers that were passed to offender managers. Most of the 114 potential cases were not directly approached by probation officers or offender managers. We followed up with offender managers and probation officers a maximum of three times, but frequently received no reply. We were told that 12 potential participants had been deported or discharged before they could be invited to participate. Of the 40 potential participants we know who were invited to participate in the study within the criminal justice system, 13 declined and 27 agreed and were interviewed. The other three participants approached us independently, having read about our research online. All three had previously served prison sentences for offences involving exploitation.

In all those cases where offender managers introduced us to prospective participants, preliminary informed consent to participate in the interviews was secured before we introduced ourselves and with the option to withdraw at any point until the data were anonymized. Given the continuing trend of low numbers of convictions under the 2015 Modern Slavery Act, the prospective sampling frame for our study proved much smaller than we anticipated when we sought funding from the ESRC (Grant Ref. ES/R004471/1). The study and its protocols were approved by the University of Manchester Ethics Committee in 2017.

Both in-person and online interviews took a biographical form. Once some basic demographic information had been collected from the participant, they were invited to tell the story of their life, in their own words, taking as much time as they needed. Some participants started with their childhoods. Others started with the offence for which they had been convicted, or the life events that immediately preceded it. In turn, we used what was disclosed to us to ask further narrative-focussed questions that helped the teller to complete their story, sometimes using active reflection where strong feelings or cryptic expressions suggested there was more to tell but some reticence to tell it.

After each first interview was complete, the audio recording of it was sent away for transcription and returned to us, with places and people anonymized. We checked the transcripts for accuracy, but also to reflect upon what had not been said and which aspects of the participant's life merited more probing in a follow-up interview. In addition to learning more about the life stories and offences committed, we used the follow-up interviews to explore potential contradictions and avoidances, especially in relation to the exploitation and victimization perpetrated. Both of us, David and Rose, would listen to each other's interviews and appraised each other's potential questions in effort to help anticipate the second interviews. We also drafted network maps of the people mentioned in the first interviews to share with participants. Mapping participants' networks after the first interviews enabled us to ask questions in the second interviews about who knew whom and who did what to whom in what contexts. Sketching network diagrams helped us to clarify with our participants the social contexts in which exploitation occurred. It sometimes revealed how arrangements entered into to resolve immediate problems or crises became exploitative over time.

Most of our interviews lasted at least an hour. Some lasted over two hours each, though many were inhibited from lasting longer by the organizational contexts of professional appointments and room bookings in prisons and probation offices. Most participants spoke relatively freely and openly about their lives, though some were guarded and appeared to change their stories substantially in the second interviews, either on reflection or in attempts to iron out inconsistencies flagged by us. The interviews themselves were sometimes challenging to complete, not least because English was not the first language of half of our participants and we had few ways of verifying fluency among those who had told probation officers at the time they gave preliminary consent to be interviewed that they were happy to conduct interviews in English. In two instances we deployed translators. Inevitably, our sample is one primarily of convenience, shaped also by the limitation of conducting fieldwork during the Covid-19 pandemic. Four of our participants were interviewed online.

We did, nevertheless, prioritize interviews with offenders who had committed types of modern slavery offending, such as labour exploitation, that were under-represented in our initial sample. Inevitably though, we have little way of assessing the degree to which willingness to participate skewed what we were told. Table 1.1 presents an overview of the participants in our study. In

Table 1.1 Participant Characteristics

Chapter	Name	Age Range	Gender	Nationality (Ethnicity as specified)	Exploitation Type
Three	Thierry	40s	Male	British (Black)	Facilitating Illegal Immigration
	Mir	40s	Male	Iranian	Facilitating Illegal Immigration
	Alesandro	40s	Male	Albanian	Facilitating Illegal Immigration
	Bob	50s	Male	British (White)	Facilitating Illegal Immigration
Four	John	40s	Male	British (White)	Facilitating Illegal Immigration
	Darius	40s	Male	Romanian	Adult Sexual Exploitation
	Idris	60s	Male	Nigerian (Black)	Criminal Exploitation
	Faizel	30s	Male	British (Middle-Eastern/Asian)	Adult Sexual Exploitation
Five	Rasheed	30s	Male	Pakistani	Purchasing Sham Marriage
	Estelle	30s	Female	Portuguese (African)	Arranging Sham Marriage
Six	Ademola	50s	Male	British (Black)	Domestic Servitude
	Tambara	40s	Female	Nigerian (Black)	Domestic Servitude
Seven	Sammy	40s	Male	British (British Asian)	Labour Exploitation
	Hina	30s	Female	British (Asian)	Labour Exploitation
	Charles	40s	Male	British (White)	Labour Exploitation
Eight	Adam	20s	Male	Hungarian	Adult Sexual exploitation Domestic Servitude
	Sandra	40s	Female	British (Mixed)	Adult Sexual Exploitation
	Andrei	30s	Male	Romanian	Adult Sexual Exploitation
Nine	Reshmin	30s	Male	British (Asian)	Child Sexual Exploitation
	Zahir	30s	Male	British (British Asian)	Child Sexual Exploitation
	Naz	40s	Male	British (British Asian)	Child Sexual Exploitation
	Linda	40s	Female	Zimbabwean (White)	Child Sexual Exploitation
	Susan	20s	Female	British (White)	Child Sexual Exploitation
Not included in this book	Raja	50s	Male	British (Asian)	Labour Exploitation
	Grace	40s	Female	Kenyan (Black)	Sexual Exploitation
	Anton	30s	Male	Romanian	Sexual Exploitation

(continued)

Table 1.1 Cont.

Chapter	Name	Age Range	Gender	Nationality (Ethnicity as specified)	Exploitation Type
	Nina	40s	Female	Slovakian	Sexual Exploitation
	Vicky	20s	Female	British (White)	Criminal Exploitation
	Aron	20s	Male	Albanian	Facilitating Illegal Immigration
	Keith	30s	Male	British (White)	Criminal Exploitation Domestic Servitude

this book, we discuss the stories shared with us by 23 of these participants. The seven cases that are not described further in the chapters of this book are listed at the bottom of the table. For concision, we have had to be selective. Three excluded cases – Grace, Nina and Anton – involved sexual exploitation, which we cover using other examples here to convey the dynamics of distinct aspects of the market. Two cases – Keith and Vicki – had committed offences that fit under the umbrella of 'county lines' offending, but we did not consider these, in and of themselves, to be sufficiently illustrative of the global and local contexts in which drug markets operate. Finally, Raja and Aron were both convicted of offences that involved facilitating the illegal movement of people into the UK, yet both appeared to have been set up by their co-accused. We have therefore prioritized other examples in our chapter on people smuggling.

The Organization of This Book

By way of contextualization, we review the literature about people involved in trafficking and what is sometimes referred to as 'organized immigration offending' in Chapter 2 – situating the few pre-existing empirical studies of traffickers in international and UK policy contexts. Here we also engage with the attempts to estimate how many people have been kept in modern slavery in the UK or trafficked across the world. These vary wildly. We explain that these variations are not merely an artefact of the cleverness of traffickers; the consequences of being caught perpetrating most forms of crime motivate offenders to conceal their misdeeds. With modern slavery and human trafficking, however, there are genuine definitional issues that make such offences difficult to count. These definitional issues can also lead to the plights of victims being misrepresented. Some of the things we are often told, or are implied about victims of trafficking in news stories, police press releases and fictionalized police dramas, are only true of a minority of those subject to exploitation. For example, we often assume that most victims of trafficking have been kidnapped in their home countries, in poorer parts of the world, and then entrapped in slavery in the UK. Although the identification of victims of trafficking is increasingly the job of the world's border officials, very few victims of trafficking are identified at UK borders. Most victims of modern slavery become exploited after their arrival in the UK, not during the dangerous journeys the Borders and Nationality Bill sought to discourage (Hadjimatheou and Lynch, 2017).

We also tend to assume that most victims of trafficking are controlled completely by their traffickers until the police crash down their doors and save them. But this is rarely the case. Few victims are kept hostage, and the vast majority of adults leave exploitation many months before law or immigration enforcement becomes aware of their victimization (Villacampa and Torres, 2019; Cockbain et al., 2022; Lightowlers et al., 2022). From within and beyond Europe many workers do migrate to undertake work for which they know they will be paid less favourably than the indigenous population of the countries to which they have travelled. Those who are not authorized to work in the UK but still wish to come turn to third parties who can assist them with their journeys, with finding work or with loans they need for travel or documentation. Those who are caught providing this assistance are among those who come to be classified as 'modern slavery offenders', 'smugglers' or 'traffickers', the three terms often used interchangeably, though they are not synonymous.

In Chapter 3, we examine the stories of those who are more properly referred to as 'smugglers' because they had been charged with assisting the illegal immigration of foreign nationals with no legal right to be in the UK. Nevertheless, within these narratives the boundaries between smuggling and knowledge of exploitative work were sometimes blurred – the latter more indicative of trafficking. As we show, while people smuggling is a crime that requires some logistical organization, it does not necessarily require hierarchical, mafia-like enterprises. Some of those charged with facilitating illegal immigration might, in other contexts, be regarded as relative 'do-gooders'. Others appeared to be merely repaying favours to those who had helped them, though some were part of enduring profit-making enterprises that were high risk, though not necessarily staffed by 'criminal masterminds'.

In Chapter 4, we continue this theme by focussing on those interviewees we spoke with whose actions most fitted the stereotype of 'organized criminals'. Interestingly, these participants were the ones whose networks most looked like spider diagrams, or bicycle wheels that located them at the centre of diffuse networks that spanned international borders. None of these interviewees fitted the stereotypical image of 'Mr Big' however. While all four had profited from exploitation, these profits were relatively short lived. The high lives they afforded were also difficult to sustain and damaging to family relationships that were interrupted by periods of incarceration, though not necessarily disruptive to criminal enterprises that endured even after arrests were made. In all four of the cases discussed in this chapter, involvement in crime was conducted in the shadows of the men's relationships with powerful fathers who appeared to share their macho beliefs and sexist attitudes,

From Chapter 5 onwards, we turn our attention to specific categories of modern slavery, focussing first on 'sham marriages'. As we explain, what was once regarded as an immigration offence involving EU nationals entering 'marriages of convenience' with non-EU nationals looking to relocate was redefined as a form of entrapment after the implementation of the 2015 Modern Slavery Act. In this chapter, we look at the cases of two offenders who knowingly entered into, or arranged, sham marriages for this purpose, explaining how actions that were cast as highly abusive and exploitative offered solutions to impossible life choices formed amidst destitution at the sharp ends of globalization.

The limits of adopting a binary approach to exploitation that differentiates relatively 'normal' business practices from 'modern slavery' is explored further in Chapter 6, where we consider domestic servitude. It is also addressed in Chapter 7, where we detail the lives of four participants engaged in various forms of labour exploitation within otherwise legitimate businesses. In both instances, we show how the under-regulation of labour markets intersects with immigration regulation that keeps migrant workers on the cusp of a metaphorical line in shifting sands that render them dependent on employers who pay them low wages for long hours.

In Chapter 8 we explore the lives of three people convicted of sex trafficking in the UK, noting the cultural frameworks – 'normal' 'family life', 'an escape from exploitation', 'a comparatively harmless business proposition' – through which they justified their crimes as well as the extent to which they profited from the sex work of economically and legally precarious migrant women. In revealing how collaborations with sex workers are normalized in the lives of those convicted of modern slavery, the chapter challenges the stereotype of the 'evil trafficker' enslaving 'innocent' women and instead notes how the modern slavery agenda imposes a binary distinction on a diffuse industry that is reconstituted hourly, online and in-person, via unregulated financial exchanges and profiteering that take place in the context of largely unpoliced illegality.

In all of these examples, we show how exploitation is embedded in routine aspects of everyday working lives, including the gendered expectations and inequalities these entail, particularly for people dependent on illicit economies. We then take this thesis further in Chapter 9, which perhaps presents the most challenging test bed for such arguments, focussing as it does on the perpetrators of child sexual exploitation, including some offenders assumed to be members of 'grooming gangs'. Here we show how the silence around victim agency in policy responses to both child sexual abuse and modern slavery contributes to the discursive rationalizations perpetrators use to convince themselves that women who are much younger than them and poorly cared for have consented to sex acts in what are otherwise transactional relationships that involve partying, drug use and alcohol consumption. There are obvious parallels between these cases and those that have come to light in recent years involving high profile, wealthy and powerful men who have exploited vulnerable young women in exclusive places where there was a tacit expectation that sex would be exchanged for hospitality. The difference between these high-profile cases and those depicted in

Chapter 9 is that the ethnic origins of the former remain barely remarked upon, while they have become misleadingly definitive of the latter.

Throughout the chapters that follow, few of our participants understood what modern slavery was at the time they committed their offences, and none considered themselves to be 'traffickers'. Their stories are presented collectively here because they had committed offences that were considered at some points of a criminal justice process to amount to something like modern slavery, 'forced labour' or keeping someone in 'servitude'. As O'Connell Davidson (2015: 3) notes, although 'there is no single, precise definition of modern slavery, a series of stock phrases and highly dubious statistics about it are circulated, repeated so often and so earnestly that they have taken on the mantle of incontrovertible truth'. The term is intentionally emotive, ambiguous and hence mystifying. It evokes a historical trajectory that is impervious to the specific global power relationships that fused free enterprise with racism in the colonial past. It obscures the stigma it confers on contemporary victims of exploitation with fears about 'illegal immigration'. It conceals the roles played by global capitalism and border controls in leading some people to turn those working in illicit economies for safe travel, work, documentation and refuge (ICIA, 2020). In other words, ending modern slavery as a political project contributes to an ideological agenda that attempts to side-line critical sociological thinking about the structural and historical causes of exploitation and what might be required to redress them.

For these reasons, it is simply not possible to deduce a common explanation for all forms of modern slavery. What the interview data we present in this book can do, however, is render the perpetration of modern slavery offences more comprehensible. The case studies we present here reveal how modern slavery typically entails a series of events – the processes of recruitment, transportation and control, or exploitation – that take place against a backdrop of structural inequalities, hardships and traumas that complicate the task of demystifying who, among a group of people making a profit from the under-regulated or illicit labour of others, knew they were committing a serious offence, and how those offenders who are also victims of previous exploitation or who become complicit with the misdeeds of others should be held to account.

The essence of our argument is that in order to challenge the political narrative that associates the causes of trafficking with the unparalleled evils of traffickers, we need to engage with those convicted of modern slavery and attempt to understand the circumstances that contributed to their offending. Recognition of the vulnerability of victims has often united the anti-trafficking sector around calls to be uncompromisingly tough in responding to traffickers. What our research shows, by contrast, is that it is the pervasiveness of the structural disadvantages faced by victims that enforce their reliance on those who exploit them, few of whom are 'organized criminals' and many of whom have also faced similar life challenges. This, as we explain in the book's conclusion, is why most modern slavery offenders fail to see themselves in the language of moral condemnation utilized by those most invested in eradicating it. This is why we need to listen to such offenders, even while we disagree with much of what they might have to say, and why reducing the prevalence of exploitation is unlikely to be achieved simply by reiterating the commitment of the government and criminal justice professionals to bringing more 'perpetrators of modern slavery to justice' (HM Government, 2021a: 8).

2 Evil Slave Masters as Political Folk Devils

When unease about the unsettling thunder of mass, unmanageable migration is galvanized politically by the lightning strike of people trafficking, modern slavery discourse redirects the heat from the media storm by casting the government, police, church and voluntary sector as an apolitical alliance conjoined in a battle to reassert admirable national greatness against the forces of organized foreign criminals. Simultaneously, it makes it more difficult to ask pertinent questions – about the role of British commerce in starting and sustaining slavery; about the practices of border control and the demand for illicit immigration services; about the complicity of some victims in their own exploitation; and about the causes of trafficking and the motivations of perpetrators – without appearing to be siding with 'evil slave masters'.

(Gadd and Broad, 2018: 1454)

Introduction

Modern slavery, as a way of framing extreme forms of exploitation, entered into the currency of public debate in the UK at a very particular historical conjuncture. This conjuncture, which reached its zenith in the years just before and after the 2015 Modern Slavery Act was brought into statute, was defined by the referendum to leave the European Union and the UK's prolonged Brexit. These were accompanied by a politics that rallied the British public to choose whether they were on the side of patriotism that claimed to be world-leading, lawful and tolerant or, alternatively, aligned with everything a succession of senior Conservative politicians asserted was threatening the integrity and aspirations of a remerging 'Global Britain'. These presumed threats to the nation centred on the dangers of unmanaged migration and the inconceivable menaces assumed to be posed by foreign national offenders. The potency of the threats modern slavery offenders posed was said to be amplified by the myopia of another set of 'folk devils' living closer to home: human rights advocates, those loyal to the European Union and its commitment to the free movement of people, 'left-wing criminologists and sociologists' and those uncomfortable with the uncritical celebration of British history, including its colonial endeavours.

DOI: 10.4324/9780429053986-2

Drawing on the work of the psychoanalyst Christopher Bollas (1993: 167), we conceptualized the political frenzy into which efforts to combat modern slavery were reconceived from 2015 onwards as akin to a state of denial known as 'violent innocence' (Gadd and Broad, 2018). This way of seeing the world is underpinned by a 'desire to be innocent of troubling recognitions' which, at this particular historical conjuncture, recast those who asked awkward questions about the political and economic causes of exploitation, together with anyone sceptical enough to query whether the UK should really be commended for abolishing modern slavery's transatlantic predecessor, as no less a threat to the nation than people traffickers themselves.

By 2022, sections of the right-wing press in the UK, with much encouragement from some British Conservatives, were depicting those variously attuned to these troubling recognitions as menacingly 'woke' in a succession of desperate bids to retain some moral authority in a culture war the populist right had engendered but could not control. The Home Office's (2021c) *New Plan for Immigration*, which introduced the rationale for the 2021 Nationality and Borders Bill, for example, promoted the assumption that migrants who come to the UK through routes deemed 'illegal' – stereotypically via 'small boats' launched from France's shores – do so because it serves the 'business model' of international 'organized criminals'. These traffickers and smugglers – the two groups of offenders routinely conflated in policy discourses as well as media coverage – were assumed to be profiting substantially. The alleged negligence of the French authorities, together with the misplaced philanthropy of those who mount rescue missions at sea, was presumed to be creating lucrative opportunities for international 'organized criminals' preying on economic migrants seeking better lives in Britain. In response to these largely unsubstantiated claims, the 2021 Nationality and Borders Bill sought to criminalize those who seek to assist migrants at risk of drowning in the sea, placing the UK in contravention of the 1951 Geneva Convention by requiring prospective refugees to apply for asylum before entering the UK's jurisdiction. Paradoxically, the British government also sought to introduce a series of measures that would compound the plights of victims of modern slavery via legislation it claimed would 'break the business model' of 'organized crime gangs'. These measures included: setting 'trauma deadlines' which deny victims of trafficking access to support if they do not share details of their abuse quickly enough, raising the thresholds against which the veracity of the claims of potential victims of trafficking will be tested while reducing the circumstances in which leave to remain will be granted, and disqualifying those victims who have committed crimes or who represent a 'threat to public order' from protection and any right to remain in the UK.

In response, a coalition of anti-slavery non-government organizations (NGOs), represented by the Anti-Trafficking Monitoring Group, petitioned the government alongside the then Anti-Slavery Commissioner, Dame Sara Thornton, to substantially amend the Nationality and Borders Bill (Bulman, 2021). Around the same time, the Court of Appeal quashed the convictions of four asylum seekers who had helped steer dinghies to the UK's shores. The case against the government revealed how the Crown Prosecution Service had been pressurized into using drone footage to depict the defendants as 'pilots' connected to organized criminals and smuggling gangs, when they were merely fellow passengers among many seeking asylum (Dearden, 2021). Donations to the Royal National Lifeboat Institution (RNLI) soared in 2021 as some sections of the public were appalled by the deaths of migrants in the North Sea and the government's endorsement of the far-right rhetoric on 'turning migrant boats back' (Hall, 2021). More diffusely, the ascendency of the Black Lives Matter movement raised awareness of how the British propagated transatlantic slavery and problematized the UK government's desire to preserve historical monuments of infamous slaveholders as celebrated figures in the nation's heritage. The issues resurfaced in January 2022 when a jury acquitted four people who admitted to toppling a statue of Edward Colston in Bristol during the Black Lives Matter protests 18 months prior to criminal damage. Similarly, the resurgence of the #MeToo movement in the aftermath of the murders of Sara Everard and Sabina Nessa drew attention to the pervasiveness of sexual exploitation, challenging the presumption in modern slavery discourse that women are most at risk from a minority of men with foreign origins. The conviction of Ghislaine Maxwell in January 2022 and the 'donation' offered by Prince Andrew to a trafficking charity in recompense to Virginia Giuffre reminded the world that sexual exploitation is not only perpetrated by 'Asian grooming gangs' but also by the white, wealthy and powerful.

Such revelations should really have prompted a debate about who modern slavery offenders are and whether their motives are really so incomprehensible that only a resort to biblical terms – 'evil', 'barbarous', 'heinous', 'slave masters' and 'traders in human misery' – will suffice. In this chapter we begin to redress these questions. We commence with a review of the policy literature, exploring how the problematization of trafficking by the United Nations at the turn of the 21st century inspired US and European Union anti-trafficking policy. We then discuss how these policies formed the backcloth to the modern slavery agenda the UK government was to claim as a distinctively pioneering response that the rest of the world needed to embrace as exemplary. In response, we summarise what is known about the scale of human trafficking globally and the pervasiveness of modern slavery in England and Wales. Against this backcloth, we appraise the sociological argument that concerns about 'trafficking' have been politically cultivated in moral panics that distract from other social problems by displacing anxiety onto the folk devils of the evil trafficker and/ or organized criminal. We conclude by reviewing the few primary studies of those involved in perpetrating human trafficking and modern slavery to assess the salience of the political claims made about them.

Trafficking in International Policy Context

The United Nations' (2000) 'Protocol to Prevent, Suppress and Punish Trafficking in Persons Especially Women and Children' – hereinafter referred to as 'the Protocol' – is part of the United Nations' 'Convention against Transnational Organized Crime'. This defined Trafficking in Persons as:

> The recruitment, transportation, transfer, harbouring or receipt of persons, by means of the threat or use of force or other forms of coercion, of abduction, of fraud, of deception, of the abuse of power or of a position of vulnerability or of the giving or receiving of payments or benefits to achieve the consent of a person having control over another person, for the purpose of exploitation. Exploitation shall include, at a minimum, the exploitation of the prostitution of others or other forms of sexual exploitation, forced labour or services, slavery or practices similar to slavery, servitude or the removal of organs.
>
> (Article 3, Assembly Resolution 55/25 of 15 November 2000)

Despite the shortcomings that are now attributed to it, it was, at the time, a radical definition. It recognized that exploitation could involve the use of fraud or deception as often as physical violence to profit from the labour of others – including sex work – and that such others might be in positions of vulnerability that rendered those who recruited, transported, transferred or harboured them even more culpable. Hence, while it failed to direct standards for victim support and care, the Protocol nevertheless provided a conceptualization of trafficking that gained considerable international traction and was widely adopted as a template for legislation in countries around the world (Anderson and Andrijasevic, 2008; Scarpa, 2020). As of January 2022, there were 190 parties to the Convention against Transnational Organized Crime and 149 signatories. The UK ratified the Convention on 6 February 2006 which, despite subsequent claims to be 'leading the world in tackling modern slavery', was later than some of its near European neighbours. France and Spain ratified the Protocol in 2002. Belgium and Portugal ratified it in 2004.

Arguably, the rapid response of the US to the Protocol had a definitive global impact. In a legislative move that also reflected the combined influence of abolitionist feminist campaigning and the electoral weight of the Christian Right, the 2000 Trafficking Victims Protection Act (TVPA), established under the Clinton administration, defined trafficking as predatory behaviour enacted primarily by migrants against a small minority of 'innocent' victims. Subsequently, as Doezema (2010) elaborates, the Bush administration associated 'trafficking', or more specifically 'sex trafficking', with 'prostitution' including the advertising of sexual services online, engineering afresh the problem of 'sexual slavery' at home and abroad. This set the stage for the US to use combating trafficking as a lever in foreign policy. The annual 'Trafficking in Persons' reports the US produces rank countries according to their anti-trafficking efforts and direct foreign aid accordingly, generating strong incentives to comply among poor nations that receive limited support from the International Monetary Fund and World Bank. Assessments of how well certain countries were doing at tackling HIV, the degree to which they criminalized prostitution and their law enforcement efforts to tackle organized crime and global migration subsequently became proxy measures the US government utilized to assess other countries' commitments to tackling trafficking. In 2004, the Intelligence Reform and Terrorism Prevention Act established the Human Smuggling and Trafficking Centre in the US which, along with the '2003 and 2005 reauthorizations of the TVPA', 'explicitly' directed 'government officials to uncover links between human trafficking and terrorism' (Farrell and Fahy, 2009: 622). In the context of the War on Terror, the connections between Islamic extremism and holding women in sexual slavery became more prominent features in US Trafficking in Persons reports (see US Department of State, 2004, 2020).

Despite this official preoccupation with global security, researchers and policymakers across the world did continue to debate the need for approaches to trafficking that addressed global inequalities, human rights, healthcare, migration and labour regulation. However, the introduction of new criminal laws disproportionately determined how countries cooperated with each other in combatting trafficking that transcended international borders, sharpening the political focus on 'organized crime' (Chuang, 2006, 2014; Gallagher and Holmes, 2008; Goodey, 2008; Segrave, 2009). In 2002, the EU Council Framework Decision on Combating Trafficking in Human Beings advanced a definition of human trafficking that was consistent with both the Protocol and an organized crime model. Within the Framework, trafficking was defined in terms of a chain of events undertaken by connected actors for the purposes of profit. The EU Council Framework required all EU Member States to create or amend criminal laws to render offences 'concerning Trafficking in Human Beings for the purposes of labour exploitation or sexual exploitation' punishable by a minimum of eight years in prison, underlining the presumption that any involvement in activities that lead to trafficking constitutes a very serious offence. Member States were also required to ensure that victims of trafficking received protection and assistance, whether or not they regarded themselves as victims and whether or not they made formal complaints about being trafficked to statutory authorities. Such directives ultimately underpin the notion that the actions of traffickers are so sinister that law enforcement needs always to be ready to break down doors to 'rescue' victims who have yet to realize that they are being exploited (Spencer and Broad, 2012).

Many European countries were also to interpret the requirements of the Framework and the logic of the Protocol as mandates to curb immigration from non-EU countries and to monitor closely the behaviour of EU nationals from former Soviet Bloc, Eastern European accession countries from where traffickers were thought most likely to derive (Goodey, 2008; Krieg, 2009). Subsequent European Parliament Directives were to harness the protection of victims to efforts to pursue and prosecute traffickers. Hence while Article 8 of the European Parliament's Directive 2011/36/EU did not explicitly require victims to support prosecutions in order to receive assistance and protection, Directive 2004/81 grants a temporary residence permit to foreign national victims of trafficking for as long as they cooperate with ongoing criminal proceedings. Such proceedings remain incredibly rare within the EU, limiting the protections available to victims, despite repeated calls for more coordinated and combative forms of law enforcement action against transnational organized crime. The 2021–2025 EU Strategy on Combatting Trafficking in Human Beings, for example, re-emphasizes the need for a comprehensive Europe-wide response that incorporates prevention, protection and the prosecution of traffickers, presumed to be members of

> well-structured and professional criminal networks, operating also inter-nationally. They work with specialised tasks, including recruitment, transport, provision of clients, guarding of victims, or organising accommodation and food for victims. Violence, threats, manipulation and deception are used to recruit and exploit victims.
>
> (EC, 2021: 9)

When trafficking is defined in terms of the activities of professional criminal networks, the logical response is to put forward strategies that involve 'dismant-ling… organised crime structures', the EU's focus until 2025 directed towards 'targeting those groups that are a higher risk to Europe's security and the indi-viduals in the higher echelons of criminal organisations' (EC, 2021: 11).

Modern Slavery Policy in the UK

In the early 2000s the UK, like other EU Member States, responded to the EU Framework Directive by adjusting its pre-existing laws and policies accordingly (Broad and Turnbull, 2019). Prior to the Modern Slavery Act 2015, trafficking-related crimes were dealt with primarily under three pieces of domestic legis-lation in the UK: the Sexual Offences Act 2003, which provided for offences relating to trafficking for sexual exploitation; the Asylum and Immigration Act 2004, which provided for offences relating to forced labour and slavery and ser-vitude; and the Coroners and Justice Act 2009, which established the criminal liability of any person or organization that held individuals in 'slavery, servitude or circumstances involving forced labour', either knowingly or in circumstances where they ought to have known. After 23 Chinese cockle pickers died in Morecambe Bay in 2004, the Gangmasters Licensing Authority (renamed the Gangmasters Labour Abuse Authority in 2016) was established, to provide more effective regulation of British agriculture and fisheries. Following the ratification of the Council of Europe Convention on Action against Trafficking in Human Beings in 2009, the UK established its National Referral Mechanism (NRM) as a response to calls from NGOs to better support victims of trafficking.

It was not until 2010 when a coalition Conservative and Liberal Democrat government was elected in the UK that the virtue of a distinctly British approach to tackling trafficking began to be signalled. While in coalition government, the Conservatives began immediately preparing to win an outright majority, and as Home Secretary, Theresa May was able to make eradicating modern slavery a central feature of the Conservatives' manifesto promise. Some of the momentum for carving out a 'new' approach to what had hitherto been known as human trafficking owed a debt to May's personal commitment to the issues as well as her leadership ambitions. But modern slavery also provided a political opportunity for the Conservatives to re-establish their reputation as the principal party of law and order, effectively challenged the decade before by New Labour's mantra 'tough on crime, tough on the causes of crime'. To recapture the law and order agenda in a context in which domestic crime rates appeared to be falling, the Conservatives in coalition government began to define a new crime problem – modern slavery – to which they would claim to be responding decisively (Bosworth et al., 2018). Attributed to foreign national offenders, this new crime problem played to popular fears about unrestrained immigration that were to define the 2015 general election. It also redefined the issue of the exploitation of workers – the raison d'etre of the Labour movement – as a challenge for law enforcement and border control. This redefinition shifted the agenda away from the need to regulate free-market capitalism, protect worker's rights through unionization and maintain a minimum wage that define the politics of the traditional left and shifted the focus towards the threat of labour-related migration: political ground that parties of the far-right were once again occupying to the detriment of Conservatives seeking re-election. EU migrants who came to the UK looking for work as they were entitled to do while the UK was in the EU were once again conflated in populist political rhetoric and tabloid media reporting with health tourism, undeserving welfare claimants and 'bogus' asylum seekers.

Hence, when the 2015 Modern Slavery Act was introduced it was bookended by two pieces of immigration legislation: the 2014 Immigration Act advanced by the coalition government and the 2016 Immigration Act introduced after the Conservatives won an outright majority in 2015. In combination, the intention of the 2014 and 2016 immigration legislation, and the subsequent 2021 Nationality and Borders Bill, was to create a hostile immigration environment that would encourage those residing in the UK 'illegally' to 'voluntarily go home'. The so-called 'migration crises' of the 2010s were greeted by the reproduction of images of large numbers of migrants crossing borders, on boats and in transient camps, coupled with erroneous claims about the extent to which the UK relative to other European nations was a 'soft touch', taking more than its share of those fleeing the world's war zones. In public debate, migration, human smuggling and modern slavery became conflated in ways that enabled Theresa May and the succession of Home Secretaries that followed after she briefly became prime minister – Amber Rudd, Sajid Javid and Priti Patel – to claim that harsher border controls and greater hostility towards those fraudulently seeking asylum were needed to forestall inward migration to the UK: 'citizens of nowhere', 'left-wing lawyers' and other 'liberal do-gooders' seemingly too ready to welcome them, the brutal travesty of the Windrush scandal notwithstanding.

The hostile immigration environment policy made it much more difficult for foreign nationals in the UK on the periphery of the labour market to seek legitimate employment, and hence increased their reliance on third-party facilitators who would extract a fee for helping them. In this way, the immigration reforms which Theresa May championed were, paradoxically, conducive to enabling forms of exploitation that were quite akin to modern slavery. The right to hold bank accounts and driving licences was withdrawn from irregular migrants. Landlords faced stiffer penalties for providing rented accommodation for undocumented workers. 'Illegal working' became a criminal offence in its own right. And, in the aftermath of Brexit, the population eligible to work in the UK became much more constricted, EU nationals themselves losing their right to live, work and study there unless they had successfully applied for the right to do so. In the absence of legitimate access to employment benefits, bank accounts and healthcare – and with the threat of deportation hanging over their heads if they come to the attention of immigration enforcement – irregular migrants are left with little option but to work cash-in-hand in the grey economy, where they have no rights and little recourse to law.

Such political developments were largely unforeseen by the various NGOs that supported the formulation of the Modern Slavery Act in 2015. In 2013, a collective of anti-trafficking organizations – the Anti-Trafficking Monitoring Group (ATMG) – identified the 'mistaken and perpetuated assumption that trafficking is an inbound immigration problem' (ATMG, 2013: 31). In the ATMG report *In the Dock*, the NGO sector argued that the conflation of trafficking with immigration was largely attributable to unsuitable legislation, leading to unsuccessful prosecutions of traffickers and a failure to effectively identify and support victims. *In the Dock* also recognized the negative impact of anti-immigration discourse in the media and how 'the trafficked person's immigration status can also become the focus of enforcement rather than the exploitation they experienced', fuelling an obsession with asylum seekers assumed to have fabricated their victimization (ATMG, 2013: 45). In response, the ATMG: endorsed an overhaul of the legislative framework addressed to trafficking; its replacement with a single Modern Slavery Act that would facilitate increased prosecutions of traffickers; the appointment of an Anti-Slavery Commissioner; and system change that would ensure those who had been exploited were treated primarily as victims of trafficking or slavery rather than as 'illegal' immigrants.

At the same time, the Centre for Social Justice (CSJ) published their report, *It Happens Here*, which also recommended an independent Anti-Slavery Commissioner and a single Modern Slavery Act because the existing legislative framework 'perpetuated the misunderstanding of modern slavery as primarily an immigration – not a criminal – problem' (CSJ, 2013: 19). The Centre, a centre-right think tank founded by Theresa May's political mentor Iain Duncan-Smith in 2004, also addressed how businesses could become more responsible for redressing exploitation in their supply chains, recommending a Transparency in UK Company Supply Chains Bill which, although not enacted, was reflected to some extent in section 54 Transparency in the Supply Chains provisions of the 2015 Modern Slavery Act. In short, a new consensus was formed, both the CSJ and the ATMG endorsing a crime-based approach to modern slavery that would provide victims with more effective systems of support and to improve prosecution rates.

Seen, mistakenly, as a standalone piece of legislation rather than a core component of the hostile environment policy, the 2015 Modern Slavery Act appeared to reconcile both the CSJ and the ATMG reports with the Palermo Protocol and the EU instruments. The Act recreated offences of human trafficking, slavery, servitude and compulsory or forced labour, replacing the existing criminal offences with a single, unified statute that was much easier to comprehend than the various pieces of legislation that had been amended piecemeal. The Act also

- increased the maximum sentence for those convicted of offences of human trafficking and modern slavery to life imprisonment;
- placed a statutory obligation on the Home Secretary to ensure assistance and support are provided to victims;
- brought into statute the section 45 defence that could, in principle, be used to exculpate victims who had committed criminal offences while being exploited;
- brought into statue the section 54 Transparency in Supply Chains provisions, which require businesses operating in the UK with an annual turnover in excess of £36 million, to create modern slavery statements that report on the action they are taking to eradicate modern slavery in their supply chains;
- established the position of an Independent Anti-Slavery Commissioner.

Home Secretary Theresa May described the Modern Slavery Act as a 'historic milestone' and 'landmark legislation' that would 'shine a light on this hidden crime' (HM Government, 2015). A year later, having become prime minister in the aftermath of David Cameron's resignation following the referendum on EU membership, May insisted the UK was 'leading the world' with its 'efforts to stamp out modern slavery' (HM Government, 2016).

This fanfare was to prove somewhat premature, however. Reporting on the Act just two years after its implementation, the inspectorate report *Stolen Freedom* (HMICFRS, 2017) confirmed that there were systemic problems with the NRM. This included: inadequacies with respect to the support available to victims, stark regional inconsistences in the police responses to modern slavery and little evidence to suggest the new legislation was delivering a substantial number of prosecutions. The National Audit Office (NAO, 2017) report, *Reducing Modern Slavery*, criticized a lack of strategic action from the Home Office and the absence of effective measures and milestones for measuring progress, amidst extensive public spending on policing operations and significant problems evidencing the effectiveness of the NRM in supporting victims. The report concluded that

> until the government is able to establish effective oversight of the modern slavery system as a whole it will not be able to achieve its objective of significantly reducing the prevalence of modern slavery or demonstrate that it is achieving value for money for the resources it applies.
>
> (National Audit Office, 2017: 13)

The first Independent Anti-Slavery Commissioner Kevin Hyland, a former police officer, resigned in 2018, acknowledging these problems and explaining that his role had not been sufficiently independent of government interference to fix them. Hyland was succeeded by Sara Thornton, another former senior police officer, until she announced her resignation in early 2022.

Over the intervening years, the modern slavery sector became progressively more vocal in its criticism of the government's failure to provide adequate care and support for victims. The Anti-Trafficking Monitoring Group's (2018) report, *Before the Harm is Done*, concluded that if government continued with 'wider policies of austerity, a hostile immigration environment and the threats posed by Brexit... the vulnerability of adults and children to exploitation is not reduced and the UK risks contravening its positive obligation to prevent trafficking' (ATMG, 2018: 4). Far from supporting victims, the primary focus of the NRM is on assessing the veracity of victims' claims: an approach to victimhood that would be unacceptable if applied to other conventional crimes and which discriminates against foreign nationals who cannot accumulate the evidence needed to support their claims easily, especially when confined to immigration detention. Consequently, the focus of the NGO sector has expanded beyond simply delivering on modern slavery policy providing support to victims and raising awareness to encompass: actively submitting Freedom of Information requests to a government that is in denial about the ways in which the criminal justice, asylum and immigration detention systems compound the plights of victims; supporting victims who are not recognized as such by the state; mounting legal challenges in individual cases where victims are unduly criminalized, detained or threatened with deportation; and contesting the compromising of victims' rights in newly proposed legislation (Anti-Slavery International, 2021; Joint Committee on Human Rights, 2021). Part of the bind that the NGO sector has found itself in, however, is its reliance on subcontracting arrangements with government and fundraising activity with the public and corporate donors that rest to some degree on claims-making about the scale of modern slavery and the presumption that the pervasiveness of victimization is driven by the activities of a substantial number of traffickers acting with impunity. Such claims-making, as we will show in the next section, has proved difficult to substantiate. The number of modern slavery offenders successfully prosecuted in the UK remains small despite the sustained intensification of law enforcement activity in this area.

Internationally, few have been persuaded that the UK's approach to modern slavery is 'world-leading' and superior to the UN Protocol, US TVPA or EU Framework on 'trafficking'. A review of how the UK's approach has been received in other countries where exploitation is pervasive highlighted that the terminology of modern slavery has 'negative historic undertones and risks stigmatising survivors as "slaves" especially in former colonies' (ICAI, 2020: 1). Moreover, the UK government was castigated for its unsystematic approach to understanding and evaluating the impact of interventions and its reluctance to share data with external partners or the public. In sum, the UK had merely 'encouraged other international actors to adopt' its particular approach to modern slavery 'rather than drawing on the experience of those who had been active on modern slavery issues for much longer' (ICAI, 2020: i–ii). To date, only one country – Australia – has embraced the UK's approach (HM Government, 2019: 7). The Australian Modern Slavery Act 2018 builds on the UK's Transparency in the Supply Chains provisions, improving upon them by requiring public bodies to report on the measures they are taking and creating a government-run and funded repository of modern slavery statements. Canadian legislation, in the process of development at the time of writing, is also focussed primarily on the supply chain, the UK's criminal justice-come-immigration approach now garnering more critical global scrutiny. Following lobbying from the British government, the Sustainable Development Goals (SDGs) set out by the United Nations General Assembly in 2015 did include the eradication of modern slavery. But the SDGs explained modern slavery as the products of historic inequalities, perpetuated by economic disempowerment and global labour market structures, rather than the outcome of individual actions or the products of organized crime. While the UN moved 'modern slavery... out of the realm of criminal justice' (Geringer-Sameth, 2015; see also UN University, 2021), on the global stage the UK's narrow focus on 'illegal immigration' was rendered explicit with the appointment of Jennifer Townson as the UK's 'Migration and Modern Slavery Envoy' in October 2019.

Estimating the Pervasiveness of Modern Slavery from 'the Tip of the Iceberg'

Efforts to estimate the size of the problem are an enduring feature of anti-trafficking and anti-slavery policy all over the world. Many policy prefaces begin with the presentation of statistics containing estimates of the number of slaves globally or nationally, before declaring that those counted represent the 'tip' of a metaphorical 'iceberg' that symbolizes the 'true volume' of undetected exploitation. Capturing the the total volume of something as difficult to define as 'trafficking' and/or 'modern slavery' may not even be possible. Regardless, it is certainly the case that the secreted and enduring nature of trafficking and modern slavery perpetrated against populations that are often on the margins of society – often mischaracterized as '*hiding* in plain sight' – makes it harder to measure using the kinds of victimization surveys routinely deployed to measure the 'dark figure' of other forms of crime perpetrated against individuals, typically by visiting a random selection of households.

The Global Slavery Index (GSI) is one of the best-known attempts to quantify modern slavery internationally, though its primary purpose is to capture how well the different governments of the world are responding to the problems of human trafficking and modern slavery. The Walk Free Foundation, which commissions the GSI, was founded in 2010 by Australian billionaire and philanthropist Andrew Forrest whose fortunes derived primarily from the mining industry and whose daughter had been moved by the plights of sexually exploited orphans in Nepal (Gallagher, 2017b). In 2014, the Foundation attempted to collect data on three key variables: (1) the degree of vulnerability to slavery in different countries, (2) the prevalence of slavery in those countries and (3) the responses of government, law enforcement and NGOs to the modern slavery to be found within those countries. As Gallagher (2017a) reports, Forrest shared a perspective with Microsoft founder Bill Gates. Gates had invested much of his personal fortune in eradicating global diseases and thus wanted evidence of the impact of his own philanthropy. Forrest similarly considered it important to be able to quantify how his philanthropic investment in the Walk Free Foundation was eradicating modern slavery.

Estimating the prevalence of different diseases and the mortality rates that derive from them is, however, a much simpler task than estimating the scale of modern slavery and its relation to government interventions. There are universally agreed classifications in public health and medicine, and the definiteness of outcomes (i.e. life or death) is more self-evident. Indeed, transatlantic slavery was perhaps a simpler phenomenon to quantify than modern slavery. In the 19th-century America, 'slaves' were a legal category and 'slave-owners' routinely took stock of their property. Modern slavery, however, is 'something quite different', for it is a problem 'to which no international legal definition is attached' (Gallagher, 2017a: 93). As we have seen in the development of international and national policy approaches, many different relationships can be classified as modern slavery and those who do become trapped in one form or other of it can struggle to know for sure when it began and when it has truly ended. Modern slavery, as defined within the GSI,

> seeks to encompass under its expansive umbrella a raft of exploitative practices and a myriad of victims: from the schoolgirls abducted by Boko Haram to the abused maids of diplomatic households in London and Washington; from orphanage tourism in Cambodia to the recruitment of child soldiers by the so-called Islamic State. Even the authors of the Index have recalibrated their conception of 'modern slavery' from year to year, which makes comparison between their own reports a challenging exercise. That recalibration may also help to explain the extra ten million slaves uncovered between the Index of 2014 and that of 2016 (perhaps more convincingly than the proffered explanation that this dramatic increase reflects improvements in the methodology).
>
> (Gallagher 2017a, p. 91)

The GSI's method is notoriously difficult to comprehend. Surveys are conducted primarily by the polling company Gallup, though other methods of estimation are also used. In December 2017, the Foundation's website reported that within the last three years, 25 surveys were conducted 'engaging more than 28,000 respondents in 52 languages'. While this may sound ambitious, these surveys only reached around 470 participants – aged 15 and above – who claimed they or someone in their immediate family had been forced into labour or marriage within the past five years (Gallagher, 2017a). This number of participants is, in statistical terms, too small a sample from which to make prevalence claims generalizable to the population of the world.

Indeed, the GSI does not attempt a sampling frame from which such generalization would be possible. First, participants are accessed through an omnibus survey using simple random-route procedures to select households, begging the question as to how access is secured to those who do not live in domestic properties or whose presence is coveted by cold-calling interviewers. Second, not every country is sampled. Instead, the prevalence estimates in the index are 'extrapolated to countries with an equivalent risk profile' (Walk Free Foundation, 2016: 8). These risk profiles are themselves not uncontentious and are based on providing an overall score informed by measures of 'civil and political protections', 'economic, health and other social rights', 'personal security' and 'refugees and conflict' (p.96). The measures used to inform these variables are in most, but not all, cases reasonable proxies for poverty and human rights, but not necessarily for modern slavery. Hence, as Gallagher (2017a) points out, a country's vulnerability to modern slavery as measured by the index can seemingly be reduced by increasing the use of mobile phones, reducing the incidence of tuberculosis and curtailing the ownership of guns. By way of contrast, measures of 'corruption' – which might better predict the scope for exploitative labour practices – are excluded from the GSI's vulnerability scoring (p.97).

The questions used to identify victimized participants in the GSI are no less methodologically suspected (Larsen and Diego-Rosell, 2017). In 2016 these asked:

1. Have you or has anyone in your immediate family ever been forced to work by an employer?
2. Have you or has anyone in your immediate family ever been forced to work by an employer to repay a debt with that employer?
3. Have you or has anyone in your immediate family ever been offered one kind of work, but then were forced to do something else and not allowed to leave?
4. Have you or has anyone in your immediate family ever been forced to marry?

(Walk Free Foundation, 2016: 163)

While the questions are provided in many different languages, it is unclear to what degree participants' understandings of having been 'forced' are clarified, since the term could be variously interpreted as involving 'coercion' – as the concept of modern slavery presumes – or being 'pressured' which, though undesirable, might not amount to enslavement. This matters because many people who are not coerced into employment feel they have little choice but to undertake undesirable work to support themselves and their families. Likewise, the religious taboos and legal prohibitions on sex and having children outside of marriage in some parts of the world mean that some people feel they must ultimately marry, but this does not necessarily amount to being 'forced' in a way that amounts to modern slavery. Nor is it clear how knowledge – however vague – of what has happened in one's immediate family – however large – is incorporated into the statistical estimates that follow from such responses, the survey's counting rules assuming that participants know for sure if a 'spouse, child, parent or sibling' has been 'coerced' into 'forced labour' or 'did not consent' to 'marriage' in 'the five years preceding' (ibid).

Such methodological shortcomings lead ultimately to conclusions that are highly counter-intuitive. Despite the human rights protections afforded by being a member of the European Union, Italy, for example, scored worse than both Vietnam and Singapore in the 2016 GSI, even while the Foundation itself reported on the specific ways in which debt bondage generates the markets for sexual slavery and domestic servitude of women in South East Asia. Despite these anomalies and methodological shortcomings, the Walk Free Foundation articulated its claim that in 2016 '45.8 million people' were 'in some form of modern slavery in 167 countries' with absolute confidence (Walk Free Foundation, 2016: 8). The impact of this over-claiming, as Gallagher (2017a) explains, has been more insidious than is often realized. Such statistics have been uncritically reproduced by governments and NGOs alike to underline the urgency of the problem, also perpetuating a philanthropic colonial discourse. This discourse perpetuates the 'belief that slavery is all about bad individuals doing bad things to good people' (p.110), alongside the notion that bad people derive principally from those countries where governments, typically in former colonies, are deemed to be failing. It thus distracts our attention from the troubling recognition that these countries, where labour is under-regulated and people are vastly underpaid, produce the 'goods and services' that are primarily consumed by wealthy westerners living in countries where national prosperity derives from a history of global exploitation and trade agreements that keep former colonies in a state of economic dependence (p.102). The dubious implication inferred by those who uncritically accept this rhetoric is that good countries are those that are doing the utmost to weed out bad people and that it is wise to be able to demonstrate this through messages that emphasize the scale of victimization alongside estimates of how many modern slavers have been caught and how many are still at large.

This, in a nutshell, is one of the ways the drivers of modern slavery have been conceived within UK policy. In the absence of credible survey data on modern slavery victimization, in 2013 the UK's Home Office Chief Scientific Adviser, Bernard Silverman, attempted a new method of assessing its prevalence. This method involved analysing the overlaps between cases that come to the attention of the police, local authorities, NGOs, the National Crime Agency (NCA) and other enforcement and regulatory bodies (including the Gangmasters Licensing Authority and the UK Border Force) (Silverman, 2014). Principles used to esti-mate the size of fish populations were deployed to estimate the dark figure of modern slavery. With fish populations the method works as follows: you catch a set number of fish, mark them before returning them to the lake and fish again to see how many marked fish you recapture relative to the number of unmarked fish. One can then estimate the size of the total population of fish within cer-tain degrees of statistical confidence. Silverman's 'Multiple System Theory' applied the same principles to measuring modern slavery while allowing for the more complex permutation that the cases identified can be known to – or marked by – several different sources or organizations. Applying these untested principles to the 2,744 potential cases of modern slavery officially recorded in 2013 – many of which would have been mere outlines – Silverman estimated that the NCA was aware of around 20–30% of the modern slavery intelligence known to other bodies and the public. From this, he deduced that the potential dark figure of modern slavery cases unknown to law enforcement in the UK in 2013 was between 7,000 and 10,000 cases. Adding this dark figure to the 2,744 cases that had already been recorded in 2013, Silverman suggested that the actual prevalence of modern slavery in the UK that year could have been between 10,000 and 13,000 cases.

Though widely cited as a 'fact' by government, Silverman was explicit that this estimate was very 'tentative, because the modelling included assumptions which (though plausible) cannot be easily verified and uses data that inevitably has limitations' (2014: 1). The methodology was further criticized by Whitehead et al. (2019) who ultimately found the approach too unreliable. Most problem-atic to the estimate is its reliance on the 2,744 intelligence reports. Intelligence reports are pieces of information that merit further investigation and are thus, by definition, not necessarily proof of a crime, let alone grounds for arrest. Some intelligence reports are simply mistaken interpretations of legitimate behaviour. Typically, they are incomplete intimations of a crime in which the identities of suspects and victims are often unknown. These intimations can overlap with other similarly vague grounds for suspicion that may have been reported to the police who decide if there are sufficient grounds to investigate further. Even if it were possible to count only that intelligence that was veri-fied, we would then need to know whether it referred to a single incident or an enduring pattern of criminal behaviour, as well as whether the offence was historic or contemporary, before we could quantify it within any meaningful estimate of the prevalence of modern slavery. Consequently, Silverman's (2014) 10,000–13,000 estimate refers to an indecipherable mix of people who might or might not have been victimized in 2013 as well as those who might have been being victimized many years prior in cases the police typically refer to as 'historic abuse' (Lightowlers et al., 2022). His estimate made presumptions about how various official bodies were sharing intelligence in the UK at that time, presumptions that were not tested then and would not have continued to apply post the implementation of the 2015 Modern Slavery Act, when information sharing between official bodies became more commonplace.

Despite these considerable shortcomings, Silverman's estimate was subsequently revised twice. In what may well have been a thinly veiled bid for greater investment, the estimate was first inflated by the Head of the NCA, Will Kerr on the spurious basis that because the police had become aware of more cases, the dark figure must be proportionately bigger. The reverse ought to have been the case (Grierson, 2017). To the extent that it is meaningful to talk about a dark figure of modern slavery unknown to law enforcement, one would expect this to have become proportionately smaller as government bodies have become more invested in sharing intelligence, and the public have been encouraged to report suspicions about modern slavery crimes. In 2020, the CSJ also revised Silverman's estimate upwards, via an analysis produced by a company called National Data Analytic Solutions. They calculated a nationwide estimate of 99,469 potential modern slavery victims in the UK (Centre for Social Justice, 2020). Their questionable methodology used police data of potential victims identified by West Midlands Police to arrive at a final figure, deemed by the authors to be a 'significant under-estimate', 'by extrapolating the number of victims based on the proportion of the population covered by West Midlands Police compared to the overall UK population, which is 23.7 times larger' (p.21).

In the interim Silverman (2020) revisited the 2014 methodology and rearticulated the limits of an approach that was in the infancy of its development. He recommended that future estimates utilize statistical models that anticipate the lack of a baseline 'ground truth' in modern slavery data, inconsistencies in its recording and the reluctance to share it between organizations (p.692). The Office for National Statistics (ONS) has since attempted to collate various sources of modern slavery data in the UK, while acknowledging that 'the data sources cannot be used to measure the underlying prevalence', only 'a better understanding of the nature of the crime in the UK than is possible from any data source individually' (ONS, 2020a: 3). The report rightly attributes some increases in modern slavery cases known to the police to improvements in official recording and notes how increases in the number of individuals referred into the NRM can be explained in terms of more victims becoming known and consenting to referral. But the ONS has been unable to surmount the criticisms social scientists have made of previous attempts to count modern slavery. As Whitehead et al. (2019: 11) conclude: making an 'estimation of the number of people not seen is intrinsically difficult ... perhaps the attempt to do so should be abandoned'.

Offenders and Victims in Official Statistics

In the absence of a credible estimation of the dark figure, official statistics about modern slavery cases known to law enforcement have to be read with considerable caution, not least because any growth in the number of victims detected, suspects arrested, or prosecutions brought are likely to have been shaped by enhanced policing in this area as much as any change in the pervasiveness of exploitation or any intensification in the activities of traffickers. In 2013, UK police forces recorded just under a thousand intelligence reports of modern slavery offending (Silverman, 2014). By 2016, this had tripled to just under 3000 (HMICFRS, 2017). In August 2021, there were said to be at least 3,335 live police investigations ongoing in the UK, the police having recorded 8,730 modern slavery offences over the previous 12 months (HM Government, 2021c). And yet, while prosecutions for trafficking and modern slavery offences generally rose between 2010 and 2020 (when the progression of many legal cases was stalled by the pandemic) their absolute number remained small (shown in Table 2.1). In 2016–2017, for example, 295 modern slavery charges were brought to courts in England and Wales (CPS, 2017). This compares with 93,590 prosecutions for domestic violence offences in the same year. Convictions for modern slavery offences were, inevitably, rarer still. The latter appears to have fallen from around 71% of cases brought to court in 2010–2011 to 61% of cases brought to court in 2016–2017, the year after the 2015 Modern Slavery Act was brought into statute. By comparison, 76% of domestic violence cases resulted in a conviction in 2016/17.

Moreover, these figures for offences prosecuted after 2015 include offences that are *flagged* as being 'related' to modern slavery, inflating the totals beyond what would be counted if the focus was only on prosecutions and convictions directly under the 2015 Act (see Table 2.2).

In fact, the 2021 UK Annual Report on Modern Slavery (HM Government, 2021c: 19–20) reveals that that 'the number of prosecutions peaked in 2017 at 132, decreasing to 68 in 2019' – despite a widening of the definition of modern slavery to apply the law to forms of exploitation not initially envisaged, such as 'county lines' drug distribution and 'sham marriages'. Convictions secured under the 2015 Modern Slavery Act peaked at 40 in 2019 and fell to a low of 10 in 2020. Given that some offenders will have been convicted of several charges brought under the Act, one might anticipate the number of offenders with convictions to be still lower in both these years. The average custodial sentence for those convicted under the 2015 Modern Slavery Act was 36.2 months (p.20), just over 3 years, suggesting sentencers were not confronted with many offenders whose crimes were so grievous as to merit the life sentences provided for in the 2015 Modern Slavery Act.

Victim-focussed data does not tell a compellingly positive story either. Table 2.3 shows the data recorded across the annual modern slavery reports, where this information is available, from 2013 to 2018.

In 2019, responsibility for the NRM statistics moved from the NCA to the Home Office, who no longer provided complete overviews of the annual number of victims referred to the NRM as the NCA had done. Instead, the focus shifted to decisions made:

Table 2.1 Outcomes of Completed Prosecutions for Flagged Modern Slavery Offences

Prosecutions	2010–2011	2011–2012	2012–2013	2013–2014	2014–2015	2015–2016	2016–2017	2017–2018	2018–2019
Convictions	73	94	99	155	130	192	181	185	219
Unsuccessful	30	48	40	71	57	103	114	99	103
Total	103	142	139	226	187	295	295	284	322

Data sourced from Office for National Statistics (2020b).

Table 2.2 Prosecutions and Convictions under the Modern Slavery Act, England
and Wales

Year	2017–2018	2018–2019	2019–2020
Prosecutions	115	82	67
Convictions	19	14	36

Data sourced from IASC (2020: 63).

> The Single Competent Authority made 10,608 reasonable grounds and
> 3,454 conclusive grounds decisions in 2020. Of these, 92% (9,765) of rea-
> sonable grounds and 89% (3,084) of conclusive grounds decisions were
> positive. Of the 2020 referrals, 8,665 are awaiting a conclusive grounds
> decision.
>
> (Home Office, 2021d: 1)

Precise details of how the system was working for victims became harder to
ascertain as the Home Office reports became less exacting:

> *Around* 8 in 10 referrals made in 2019 are awaiting a 'conclusive grounds'
> decision (8,429) compared to 38% of referrals made in 2018. Just 26
> referrals from 2019 were awaiting a 'reasonable grounds' decision when
> this data cut was taken, whilst 10% of referrals made in 2019 have received
> a negative reasonable (1,064) or conclusive grounds (90) decision. Whilst
> *around* 7% of referrals made in 2019 have received a positive conclusive
> grounds decision so far, this is a result of the current length of time taken
> to make conclusive grounds decisions.
>
> (Home Office, 2020: 5, our emphases)

For individuals who do not consent to being referred to the NRM, their
experiences can be brought to the attention of authorities through the Duty
to Notify (DTN) provision of the 2015 Modern Slavery Act. The DTN provision provides anonymous information about each potential victim of slavery,
including gender, nationality, the type of exploitation and where that exploitation is thought to have occurred. For people under 18 or those who consent,
this can also include their date of birth, name, the names of other potential
victims and the perpetrators' names. Public authorities have a statutory duty
to make DTN submissions while other organizations, for example charities
working with potential victims, are encouraged to but are not compelled. As
DTN submissions have increased, so has the potential for the double counting
of those that do not include names and birth dates, with the consequence that
DTN statistics do not provide a reliable measure of changes in the pervasiveness
of modern slavery (ONS, 2020a).

Table 2.3 NRM End of Year Statistics

Year	Total Number of Referrals	Positive Conclusive Grounds Decisions	Negative Reasonable and Conclusive Grounds Decisions	Pending Decision (Reasonable or Conclusive Grounds)	Suspended Cases	Withdrawn
2013*	1,745	819	776	19	64	67
2014*	2,340	834	924	470	54	58
2015*	3,266	674	768	1,662	87	75
2016**	3,805	635	962	2,053	64	91
2017***	5,145	665	1,049	3,273	34	124
2018****	6,993	1,151	1,617	3,867	109	248

Data sources *NCA (2016); **NCA (2017); ***NCA (2018); ****NCA (2019).

The overall number of people being considered by the NRM exceeded 12,000 for the first time in 2022 (Home Office, 2022). In 2018, the last year for which the UK government released data from which meaningful annual comparisons could be easily deduced, over half of the cases in the NRM – 3,867 of 6,993 – were still 'pending', that is, they did not secure negative or positive conclusive grounds decisions within the year. The number of pending cases is indicative of a backlog that has grown as the pace of processing claims has not kept up with the rate of new referrals. With additional training for Border Force, UKVI and other statutory agencies, it is likely that more of the metaphorical iceberg of modern slavery is being observed by officials charged with tackling modern slavery than in the 2000s and 2010s. The imprecision with which modern slavery statistics are now presented makes it impossible to deduce what changes in the returns of the NRM actually mean. These figures were already difficult to interpret because they have never differentiated victimization that has occurred within the year from that which is historic. The length of time between exiting exploitation and reporting can vary considerably by exploitation type. Police data suggests that it averages around two years between exploitation ending and reporting to the police for labour exploitation offences. In domestic servitude and sexual exploitation cases, the time between exploitation and reporting to the police. It averages around 18 months between exploitation ending and reporting to the police (Lightowlers et al., 2022).

Folk Devils and Moral Panics

Rises in the recorded number of victims can therefore be products of changes in the administration of many official practices. The political attention given to modern slavery and the resources and training given to those obliged to detect and record it can, in turn, contribute to a self-fulfilling prophecy and deviancy amplification that suggests the problem is getting worse or all pervasive. This is the view of many social scientists (see e.g., Weitzer, 2007; Keo et al., 2014; Ellison, 2017; Howard, 2017). From the perspective of those influenced by Cohen's (2002: 1) concept of a 'moral panic' – defined as when 'a condition, episode, person or group of persons emerges to become defined as a threat to societal values' – the efforts to imply trafficking and slavery are bigger 'problems' than can be reliably demonstrated are suggestive of a demonizing logic that benefits miscellaneous interest groups. The concept of moral panic does not require that the problem be totally fictional – 'based on fantasy, hysteria, delusion and illusion' – only that both the 'extent' of it and its 'significance' be 'exaggerated' (Cohen, 2002: viii). Few social scientists would deny that trafficking happens or that there are people who traffic others. But when depicted as an all-powerful foreign enemy armed with global organized crime connections to rival the collective power of international policing and border controls, the figures of the trafficker and modern slavery offender begin to be cast as folk devils in morality tales that approximate Cohen's (2002) formulation. As Howard (2017: 15) argues:

> In spreading what is effectively an assuring morality tale, the dominant discourse of criminality de-politicises the structural relations that engender

exploitative work and mobility in the first place. It thus diverts attention away from the real power-holders in the story – from those who really should be targeted with critique. The 'folk devil figure' therefore serves a purpose, but its purpose is a nefarious one: to naturalise the injustices and inequities of the wider political economy.

Importantly, this usage of the concept of a moral panic exceeds Cohen's classic conceptualization in that it is more deliberately anticipatory of a crime threat that – unlike the disorder perpetrated by mods and rockers and British seaside towns – is very rarely seen first-hand. It is thus more ideological, and hence more racializable, in the sense Hall et al. (1978) conceived it in their analysis of the moral panic over 'black muggers' that gripped Britain in the 1970s. In this vein, the tragedies victims of exploitation suffer, as Weitzer (2007) has observed in the US, are retold by opinion formers in order to maintain an enduring 'moral crusade' that dissipates through successive news cycles. By connecting trafficking and sexual slavery in particular to other serious global problems – terrorism, arms trading and child pornography – moral entrepreneurs distort and amplify problems caused by structural inequality in under-regulated markets rendering them reducible in public debate to an 'unqualified evil'. The combination of 'exaggerated, unverifiable or demonstrably false' statistical claims with 'horror stories' of victims subject to the most severe forms of exploitation serves 'to alarm the public' in order to 'justify draconian solutions' (Weitzer, 2007: 448). Ideologically, it also sidelines those who might speak for those most at risk of exploitation, such as those who work to support migrants' rights or sex worker advocates in favour of a small number of ideal victims whose cases are identified as typical of the 'unqualified evil' law enforcement choose to present as exemplifying their work (Doezema, 2010; 2005; Agustín, 2008; 2006).

As we explained in the first part of this chapter, international policymaking about trafficking in the 21st century has often been driven by a migration-crime-security frame that has stifled alternative foci on human rights, migrants' rights and workers' rights (Goodey, 2008) in favour of the apparent 'rescue' of young women being exploited in the service of organized crime groups (Agustín, 2007). In the UK, politicians have, as O'Connell Davison (2015) has argued, tried to harness the 'positivity' some people feel about 'saving' victims of slavery to distract from the brutality of highly restrictive immigration policies. As the definition of modern slavery has widened to include more crime types, it was 'wheeled out by politicians, media pundits and campaigners in discussions on anything from prostitution to child labour to illegal immigration to female circumcision to begging to organ-trading' (O'Connell Davidson, 2015: 2–3). The 'new abolitionism' that fictitiously marries hostility to migrants with saving victims of trafficking thus conjures up a moral panic in the ideological service of keeping questions about why some types of violence, injustice and exploitation perpetrated by 'evil' foreign national offenders are classed as slavery and others like enforced immigration detention and removal, sanctioned by the state are not. In turn, the consensus built around the celebration of 'happy endings' for trafficking victims distracts from 'the social structures that limit the options open to people, thereby generating unenviable choices and cramping the space for self-expression' (O'Connell Davidson, 2015: 205). Tackling modern slavery has thus become 'a celebration of the existing status quo' in which a virtue has been made of being hostile to 'illegal immigrants' (O Connell Davison, 2015: 12). As Young (2007: 131) argued, in many Western countries the figure of the 'immigrant' has become a scapegoat 'like no other' used to 'mobilise prejudice' that can magically 'explain away problems inherent'.

> For he or she is an alien other, a carrier of problems into the First World rather than a group who are most blatantly exposed to the problems inherent in the First World.
>
> (Young, 2007: 131)

Modern slavery discourse extends this logic by invoking a set of references that conflate the criminal with the migrant – what border criminologists call the 'crimmigrant other' (Bosworth and Guild, 2008; Aas, 2011). In the context of the public alarm about foreign national offenders, this logic ultimately demonizes those populations most vulnerable to exploitation – undocumented and irregular migrants – alongside their potential exploiters.

Empirical Studies of Traffickers

Who are these exploiters? While there is an extensive body of literature on human trafficking and modern slavery, there is a dearth of first-hand research with the perpetrators of these crimes. We discuss relevant studies of people implicated in specific types of exploitation in each of the chapters that follow. Here, however, it is pertinent to note that the few primary studies of those deemed 'traffickers' reveal a population whose motives are much more morally comprehensible than the discourse of 'evil' conveys, and whose relationships with potential victims tend to commence as collaborative solutions to predicaments caused by global inequality, immigration restrictions or both.

Across Europe, relationships between migrant labourers and those who need their crops harvesting rely heavily on intermediaries, some of whom become classified as 'traffickers'. Howard's (2017; 2019) ethnographic research in Benin, Nigeria and Italy with workers, employers, intermediaries and other labour market facilitators reveals a complex set of interdependencies between people working against a 'political economic backstory' that structures their experiences unduly simplistically in terms of victim/perpetrator binaries. Tomato farmers in southern Italy, for example, rely heavily on migrant intermediaries – the *caporali* – who broker other migrant labourers known to them. While a few *caporali* do take advantage of opportunities for exploitation, their reputation as 'traffickers' imparted by European law enforcement is ill-justified. Rather the *caporali* are essential for ensuring tomatoes continue to be harvested in a world where the profit margins to be made from farming are miniscule in European countries where indigenous workers cannot contemplate accepting lower pay.

> The tomato harvest simply could not take place if caporali were not able to organise the labour gangs and co-ordinate with the farmers … Unlike most migrant workers, they speak Italian and can thus communicate with the farmers; while, unlike the farmers, they speak various west African languages and can thus communicate with the workers. Without this intermediary function there would be no harvest, and no money for anyone. Everybody knows this; and this is why workers implore their bosses to hire them … Yet the caporale's relative power in this economic field is close to zero. The rules of the game are fundamentally set by the global retailers. Collectively, these retailers take €0.83 out of every €1 made from the sale of tomato-based supermarket products to Western consumers … This means that, of the €0.17 remaining from every €1 sale, Italian industrial transformers take around €0.10, while the farmer, the caporale, and the migrant worker, are left to fight over €0.07 between them.
>
> (Howard, 2017: 13–14)

Mai's (2010) auto-ethnographic study of Albanian and Romanian 'sex work agents' also reveals the limits of the victim/exploiter binary as a frame for capturing the dynamic nature of the relationships that become classified as sex trafficking in Europe. These relationships often involve the mixing of business and romance in order to tell convincing stories to families back home and border enforcement. While acknowledging the techniques of neutralization used by interviewees to avail themselves of guilt, Mai's research revealed considerable agency among Eastern European sex workers who had migrated to the West to overcome enduring structural inequalities and poverty in their home countries. At the beginning of their migration journeys, sex work was mostly undertaken by women in return for security, logistical support and respectability derived from being with a pseudo male partner. In hindsight, some female sex workers came to regard themselves as exploited by male agents who had lied to them or started working with other women. Meanwhile, the men often felt they had honoured informal agreements, where they provided essential services in otherwise volatile illicit markets that were difficult for undocumented women who could speak the host country's language to navigate alone. As one Albanian man at risk of being criminalized as a 'trafficker' in Italy argued:

> I helped her as a friend, I did not ask her money … only to give me back the money I had given her for the trip. Maybe in the future I would have asked her to give me half, but not at that stage, when they arrested her … and me … I did not want to get myself into this kind of things, but she had already escaped from home and got in trouble with guys in Albania. She kept calling me in Greece, asking me to help her find a job there … she had already worked as a prostitute in Albania … she was not doing well … her

Evil Slave Masters as Political Folk Devils   39

family … they were all poor; if it weren't for me they would still be eating raw fish … I brought her to Italy. She knew what she was going to do, we were in agreement from the very beginning, I did not lie to her.

(Mai, 2010: 27)

While discovering violence and coercion in a small numbers of cases, Petrunov's (2014) interviews with 12 traffickers in Bulgaria also confirms that comparatively consensual forms of recruitment into sex work are the norm and that female sex workers typically negotiate what share of their earnings will be divided with male brokers before migrating. Similarly, Marcus et al. (2014: 323), in their interview-based study of sex workers and pimps in the USA, exposed a two-way power dynamic between sex workers and those who facilitate their work. While the facilitation of sex work could become violent and controlling, this was rare, the majority of pimps maintaining positive relations with sex workers because it was the key to maintaining a profitable business. Zhang's (2011) study of those working in Mexican sex markets also found that most pimps had little interest in enslaving the women they had introduced to sex work. Men who profited from women's sex work knew they needed to maintain at least functional relationships with sex workers in order to avoid drawing unwanted attention to themselves from law enforcement and health workers and they typically moved on once debts they were owed had been recouped.

In poorer parts of the world such collaborations are also in evidence, though the brutality of the exploitation they give rise to in the absence of choices that provide any hope of a better life are stark. Keo et al. (2014) examined the backgrounds of traffickers in Cambodia using a combination of documentary evidence and interviews with 91 detained alleged 'traffickers', defined there as anyone found to be facilitating sex work. Around three quarters of those convicted for trafficking in Cambodia were women, among whom there is 'scant evidence that trafficking … involves organised crime' (Keo et al., 2014: 204). Typically, there was a process of negotiation between eventual perpetrators and victims within which both parties attempted to work together to make a basic living. Likewise, the ten women imprisoned in China for internal child trafficking that Shen (2016) interviewed were 'largely peasant farmers and migrant peasant workers – China's most disadvantaged social groups' (68–69). All but one was illiterate and only one had a previous criminal history. All perpetrated child-trafficking with help from their spouses or other family members in order to make money upon which their relatively impoverished households were reliant.

How gradations of disadvantage drive exploitation in countries multiply divided by the legacy of colonialism is perhaps most evident in India. Sen and Nair (2004) interviewed 160 people implicated in internal child trafficking within India, much of it for the purposes of sexual exploitation: a vast social problem there given how many children live amidst severe social deprivation, which they and their parents were desperate to escape. The study's sample consisted of similar numbers of male and female traffickers, the vast majority of whom had prior involvement in the sex industry themselves: many as victims of child sexual abuse. Some had also worked as brokers, pimps or brothel owners in what had been a 'family business' they had inherited. Child exploitation was often undertaken in collaboration with victims' family members from very poor areas who hoped to secure money and a better life for their children as they moved to bigger cities. Choi-Fitzpatrick's ethnography *What Slaveholders Think* (2017) also addresses enduring social inequalities in rural India, alongside the economic hardships now facing those who were once able to sustain comparatively comfortable lives that benefitted from the deference of bonded labourers. Many slaveholders described the bonds they had with those enslaved as loyally familial and deferential. They were thus shocked when their authority was challenged, noting how new labour laws threatened long-standing localized customs from which they had long benefitted. Though in contravention of 'federal and international laws', bonded labour was largely consistent with long-standing 'local norms' (p.161) that normalized debt bondage by landowners and landlords through a moral 'sense of obligation and gratitude' (p.44) articulated by indentured labourers upon whom they were irreconcilably and economically dependent. While landowners were struggling to remain competitive in a global economy in which the profits to be made from farming were being driven down, India's rural labourers became conscious of their exploitation, to the considerable annoyance of their masters, now regarded as 'slaveholders', who felt themselves to be the real victims of globalization and to have been betrayed by workers attempting to assert their autonomy.

Discussion

Two decades since it re-emerged as a political issue, the landscape of anti-slavery policy and practice remains fraught with tensions and blotted with failures that appear more systemic than anomalous. This is nowhere more evident than in the UK where legislation meant to protect the vulnerable became part of a hostile environment policy that made the lives of irregular migrants all the more precarious. Internationally, cultivation of concern about trafficking, buttressed with spurious statistics, has enabled political agendas to be engineered that attribute exploitation to a new 'evil' orchestrated by organized crime groups that include people traffickers and people smugglers. The few primary studies of 'traffickers' suggests such offenders are not reducible to the 'folk devils' evoked to condemn their actions. The rest of this book investigates whether the same applies to modern slavery offenders in the UK, by reporting on the first primary study of them.

3 People Smuggling

When, in October 2019, the British police confirmed that 39 people had been found dead in the back of a lorry in Essex, the UK's media moved rapidly to diagnoses that were unwarranted. Speculation about organized crime groups from Bulgaria (Osbourne, 2019) was supplanted by commentary about Chinese 'snakeheads' (Smith et al., 2019), until it was revealed that the deceased were actually Vietnamese nationals, ten of whom were teenagers (BBC News, 2019). While a few journalists exposed how climate change, political encouragement and acute inequality have motivated Vietnamese migrants to undertake perilous journeys to the UK for many years (Rugman, 2019; Wright, 2019), the contribution of European immigration policy to the victims' reliance on smugglers went largely unremarked. Instead, the then British Prime Minister, Boris Johnson, demanded in parliament (Hansard, 2019a) that Robinson's fellow 'traders in human beings' be 'hunted down and brought to justice', engendering news coverage that emphasized the threat posed by a 'global ring' of 'evil' smugglers and 'traffickers' headed by a 'Vietnamese gang lord' (Duggan, 2019; Robinson, 2019). In turn, Johnson's Home Secretary, Priti Patel, promised the House of Commons (Hansard, 2019b) a 'ruthless' response as the driver – a 'Northern Irish' (aka British) national called Maurice Robinson – was charged with murder.

In this chapter we ask how plausible this conceptualization of smuggling as a component of an organized, transnational 'evil' empire of trafficking actually is. We begin by outlining the ways in which smuggling and trafficking are differentiated in domestic and international law, before reviewing the few empirical studies of people smugglers. We then analyse four case studies extracted from the 30 life-history interviews we have conducted with people convicted of immigration and modern slavery offences in the UK. Our research reveals how men who presented as helpful 'fixers' with problems of their own came to be criminalized as smugglers and traffickers. Our conclusion highlights what is missed when those implicated in immigration crimes are cast either as 'evil' or conversely as 'heroic saviours' – as some of the academic literature has it – and calls for public debate that attends to the reasons why immigration offences become organized in the ways they do before reaching for the reductionism of some organized crime narratives.

DOI: 10.4324/9780429053986-3

Distinguishing Smuggling from Trafficking

In international and domestic law, human smuggling and people trafficking are discrete crimes. Both were defined in the United Nations (2004) *Convention against Transnational Organized Crime*, signed in 2000, but in the European Union they have become increasingly conflated, especially since 2014 when the crises in Syria and Libya, in particular, caused millions of people to seek refuge in Europe. The Convention's 'Protocol against the Smuggling of Migrants by Land, Sea and Air' defines the 'smuggling of migrants' as:

> The procurement, in order to obtain, directly or indirectly, a financial or other material benefit, of the illegal entry of a person into a State Party of which the person is not a national or a permanent resident.
>
> (United Nations, 2004: 54–55)

In contrast, the UN Convention's 'Protocol to Prevent and Punish Trafficking in Persons, Especially Women and Children' defines 'trafficking in persons' as:

> The recruitment, transportation, transfer, harbouring or receipt of persons, by means of the threat or use of force or other forms of coercion, of abduction, of fraud, of deception, of the abuse of power or of a position of vulnerability or of the giving or receiving of payments or benefits to achieve the consent of a person having control over another person, for the purpose of exploitation.
>
> (United Nations, 2004: 42)

So, while smuggling and trafficking both usually involve movement, they are not the same. People actively consent to being smuggled. They typically seek out smugglers to help them travel across borders and enter countries when governments deny them a right to do so. The smuggled typically, but not always, pay smugglers for their assistance. And it is possible to breach anti-smuggling laws while acting benevolently. In 2018 in Greece, three Spanish firefighters working for a humanitarian aid organization were prosecuted for smuggling offences after they attempted to rescue migrants from drowning in the Mediterranean, though they were later acquitted (Dolz, 2018). By way of contrast, people cannot, as the law defines it, genuinely consent to be trafficked. Trafficking, by definition, involves exploitation and does not necessarily involve illegal entry into another country. If they have not been forced to travel, trafficked people will have agreed to be transported or recruited for some form of work, but they will have done so either under false pretences, or because they or their families have been threatened, or because they or their families are so indebted that they were left with little choice. The trafficked person's agreement does not equate to consent in the eyes of the law, as it is not freely given.

In practice, however, smuggling and trafficking are not always so easy to distinguish. Smuggling often leaves the smuggled vulnerable to exploitation, not least because 'the majority of smuggling ventures constitute underground exchanges of service against payment in the absence of licit options to migration' (Nicot and Kopp, 2018: 225). Traffickers typically exploit the vulnerability of a person whose migration journey has been forestalled, and nation states, as we show below, place a key role in forestalling migration journeys.

The Reconfiguring of Smuggling as European Security Threat

Within the European Union, anti-smuggling policy was slower to develop than anti-trafficking policy, the latter of which has been understood as a pressing security issue. Likewise, across Europe, migrant rights organizations are generally less closely aligned with law enforcement than anti-trafficking NGOs have been. Put more critically, 'there is no anti-smuggling industry, no well-funded organizations focused on scrutinising responses and holding States to account' (Gallagher, 2017b: 2). At a political level, things are changing, however. In 2014, the European Union identified countering smuggling as a strategic priority. Thereafter, the European Agenda on Security (European Commission, 2015a: 4) included in its remit the 'fight against transnational organized crime and terrorism, smuggling of migrants and trafficking in human beings' enabling enhanced communication, intelligence sharing and coordination of neighbouring countries across the EU. At the same time, the European Agenda on Migration (European Commission, 2015b: 2) acknowledged how 'misguided and stereotyped narratives' obscure 'the inherent complexity' of forms of migration and stressed the importance of understanding its 'root causes'. But in calling for a 'halt' to 'the human misery created by those who exploit migrants', the agenda also became more deterrence focussed. In defining smuggling as a problem caused by 'smugglers' – 'most of whom', it was assumed, were 'not based in Europe' (p.8) – the EU was able to shift its focus towards reducing 'incentives for irregular migration', stepping up 'action against illegal employment of third country nationals' (p.9) and dismantling the 'ruthless criminal networks' and 'highly profitable business' in which smugglers were presumed to be engaged (European Commission, 2015c: 1).

Thus, improved international coordination and cooperation with regard to 'voluntarily' returning migrants to countries of origin outside the EU came to be defined as a measure of 'progress' with respect to efforts to counter both smuggling and trafficking (European Commission, 2019a). In turn, search and rescue missions, especially in the Eastern Mediterranean where many lives are lost as people seek to reach Europe from Libya, have been replaced by deterrence-based border controls. Operation 'Mare Nostrum', which began in 2013, exemplified the life-saving capabilities of coordinated efforts in assisting those in desperate and risky situations at sea, was terminated in 2014 as some European leaders, under pressure from the far-right and anti-migration lobby groups, concluded that it incentivized the pursuit of hazardous migration journeys, placing a drain on the state (Travis, 2014). Its successor,

Operation Triton, focussed instead on border patrol and anti-smuggling tasks (Campesi, 2018), while Frontex, the European Border and Coast Guard Agency, was rebranded by Dimitris Avramopoulos, the European Commissioner for Migration, Home Affairs and Citizenship, as 'exactly the European response that we need for the security and migration challenges of the 21st century' (European Commission, 2016: 1). In 2019, Frontex's remit and budget were widened to include assisting member states to conduct 'identity and document checks', to enhance their 'border surveillance and return operations' and to 'protect their borders and ensure the security of European citizens' (European Commission, 2019b: 1). Long-standing attempts to create a 'Fortress Europe' by linking migration to terrorism (Albrecht, 2002: 1) have thus been given a further boost as security and control policies initially focussed on trafficking have extended to include smuggling and potentially all irregular migration. In this context, the compromising of human rights through stricter border controls has become justified as an acceptable price to pay for the avoidance of catastrophic danger (Whitty, 2011; Aas and Gundhus, 2015).

The Politics of Immigration Control in the UK

Before Brexit, the UK played a key role in advocating for a more constrictive European Union migration policy that prioritized border security over humanitarian interventions. Before the referendum on European Union membership, the then Prime Minister David Cameron advocated for greater restrictions on immigration in a bid to avoid Brexit. At the same moment, his then Home Secretary, Theresa May, was also championing new legislation to control immigration alongside new measures to combat modern slavery. The decade before, the New Labour government led by Tony Blair and Gordon Brown owed some of its electoral success to its capacity to position itself as tough on both immigration and crime, and its willingness to cast 'bogus asylum seekers' and 'economic migrants' as pressing social problems in the context of the EU's enlargement to incorporate eight Eastern European countries (Gilroy, 2004). And their agendas were in large part established primarily, though not exclusively, by Conservative governments before them; governments that came to see immigration from former Commonwealth countries Britain had colonized as a 'problem', but whose cheap sources of labour it had depended heavily upon to rebuild infrastructure damaged during the Second World War (Hall, 1980).

People smuggling has been redefined successively in UK law in terms initially brokered under Section 25 of the 1971 Immigration Act. This legislation established what we colloquially think of as smuggling as one of two infractions: (a) 'Assisting Unlawful Immigration to Member State' and (b) 'Facilitating Entry by Asylum-Seekers to the UK for Gain'. In these contexts, those deemed 'smugglers' are guilty of either (a) facilitating entry in the UK among those with no legal right to come there or (b) profiting from prospective asylum seekers who may, of course, have a legal right to refuge in the UK that has yet to be determined. Human trafficking, under Section 2 of the Modern Slavery Act 2015, by contrast, occurs when a person 'arranges or facilitates the travel of another … with a view to [that person] being exploited'. In law then, the smuggler can be someone who charges another with a legitimate claim for asylum to help with their journey. This helper-cum-smuggler can easily become a trafficker if they have an understanding that in charging the person whose journey they are facilitating they are rendering them dependent on people who will exploit them. This means that some smugglers become traffickers, either wilfully or inadvertently.

Inevitably, there are few people with interest in defending those smugglers who do inadvertently contribute to trafficking and some politicians who find a stake in obscuring the distinction. Because smuggling exposes the exclusionary power of the state, some politicians prefer to cast smugglers as traffickers. As Zhang et al., observe

> Using smuggling facilitators as scapegoats of tragedies that can arise from migration enforcement and control measures exempts states from their role in creating the conditions that lead to the emergence of smuggling as a practice.
>
> (Zhang, Sanchez, and Achilli 2018: 222)

At least two of those found among the 39 dead in the lorry discovered in Essex had fled deportation centres in Europe – one in the UK and another in the Netherlands (Badshah, 2019; Martin et al., 2019) – though nowhere did anyone make a connection between the risk of being sent back home empty-handed and the migrants' willingness to pay for the services of smugglers. Less than a year before, the former Home Secretary, Sajid Javid, fronted a royal naval expedition to seize 'smugglers' boats' thought by some commentators to have been staged in anticipation of his decision to run for prime minister. Javid explained that the purpose of his mission was to discourage migrants from travelling across the North Sea by dingy and to send a message to 'gangs … preying' on those who should have claimed asylum in France by 'selling' them a 'false prospectus' (Dearden, 2019). Ten months later the UK's National Crime Agency was reporting an increase in the 'number of migrants being smuggled into the UK in containers and lorries' and 'increasing use of higher risk methods of clandestine entry' (Gallagher, 2019). It is hard to imagine that the introduction of invisible imaging technologies to detect the body heat, breath and heartbeats of stowed-away migrants in lorries at the Dover/Calais border (Armitage, 2018; Shoal Collective, 2017) did not bear some relation to the decisions of those who transport undocumented migrants – or even the risks calculus of some undocumented migrants themselves – to utilize refrigerated containers for the purposes of smuggling. Too often the condemnation directed at the assumed callousness of profiteering smugglers prevents the question of how border control practices encourage smuggling from being asked. It is therefore important to clarify why smugglers do what they do. What are their motives? How do they appraise the morality of profiting from facilitating irregular migration? This is a question that we attempt to answer in this chapter.

Studies of Smugglers

Opportunist Immigration Offenders

Curiously, few British Home Secretaries ever refer to their own department's study of 'Organised Immigration Offenders', though it remains one of the most in-depth pieces of research on convicted smugglers and traffickers conducted in the UK. Webb and Burrows (2009) interviewed 45 convicted 'organised immigration offenders' – 25 of whom were smugglers. Their study revealed an industry organized more often through 'word of mouth' (p.14) than hierarchically organized crime groups. Typically, those convicted of transporting migrants illegally across borders perceived their action to be morally defensible, low risk and lucrative, with payments made in cash. Smugglers and traffickers were sometimes hard to differentiate in terms of motives and modus operandi. This was because those convicted of trafficking were less likely than smugglers to accept the criminal label they had been given, some traffickers having been former 'victims' of trafficking themselves (p.16) and others explaining that young women who had asked them for transport had subsequently cultivated stories of exploitation against them to benefit from legal protections in the UK.

Most were in their 30s and male, and while they came from many regions of the world including the UK itself, participants from the Balkans predominated. Most had worked for small-scale operators reliant on peer and family connections and some had learnt from their experiences of being former illegal immigrants. Migrants' journeys were brokered through 'friends, relatives and local networks' (p.14) including places of worship – in their countries of origins: people who had connections in the UK are who had previously helped 'family members and close associates' (p.21). Most of the migration networks were organized around distinct ethnic minority communities, but some ran 'in tandem with, legitimate business activities' such as 'solicitors and legal advisors', 'language schools' and 'travel, employment and accommodation services' (p.22). Conceived as providing a form of help, alongside legitimate service providers, those who were convicted for facilitating the entry of illegal entrants into the UK often 'felt they could justify their actions' and did 'not accept the intrinsic wrong in what they were doing' (p.2).

> Smugglers claimed the credit for cutting down on asylum claims; assisting people in the realisation of their goals; contributing to a reduction in labour shortages; and ultimately increasing tax revenue. Within the 'source countries', emigration was considered a reasonable and normal ambition. It was maintained that many smugglers were revered by the clients and communities that they served.
>
> (p.28)

Of course, there were also biographical reasons why participants had been drawn into smuggling that connected to their own backgrounds and aspirations.

> Many of those interviewed had been motivated into entering the 'profession' by the prospect of easy money coupled with poor employment and financial prospects arising from a lack of skills, lack of English, illicit status or criminal record. Some had given up low-paid jobs to enter the market. Some had certainly entered the market from other criminal activity including forgery, fraud and other forms of smuggling … Some respondents, particularly drivers, claimed that they had not realised they were taking part in illicit activities. Others claimed that their involvement was tenuous, for example that they had merely sub-let accommodation to friends or associates and were not aware that the premises would be used for prostitution or other illicit activities.
>
> (p.27)

Morally Righteous Snakeheads and Coyotes

Such findings about the absence of hierarchical organization in people smuggling are echoed in the works of US scholars. Zhang and Chin (2002) interviewed 129, unconvicted Chinese smugglers recruited for their study through snowball sampling methods. Often referred to as 'snakeheads' to denote their place at the top of winding migration journeys, those who help to smuggle Chinese citizens into the US are typically 'ordinary citizens' who form 'temporary business alliances' able to deliver 'highly specialized' services, navigated primarily through 'one-on-one contacts' (p.1). Those Zhang and Chin interviewed were predominantly but not exclusively married men in their 30s or 40s, holding green cards or citizenship in the US and typically self-employed, often with legitimate retail businesses of their own. Their peers usually regarded them not as organized criminals but as 'upstanding', 'decent' and 'reliable people' (Zhang and Chin, 2015). What united them was their willingness to take risks, often only for a few years, with a small circle of family and friends, to make money through 'moonlighting' as smugglers. How much they made depended upon the roles they played; roles which were 'precariously assembled', organized temporally by brokers and substitutable (Zhang, 2013:129). They included: 'recruiters', who would introduce those looking to travel to 'coordinators'; who could assist them in finding a 'transporter' who could help them get onto a ship, plane or to safe house; 'document vendors' to provide false papers, and/or bribe 'corrupt public officials'; as well as 'guides', 'crew members' and 'enforcers' (who maintained order among those being smuggled) and 'debt collectors' (who would detain illegal migrants until smuggling fees had been paid). Zhang and Chin found that most individual smuggling groups lacked the ability to respond to disruptions posed by law enforcement border controls. Hence, they formed temporary alliances, brokered through 'dyadic interactions' that ensured that the smuggling 'enterprise as a whole' responded 'collectively and effectively to uncertain market conditions' in ways that could be financially 'favorable … to individual entrepreneurs' (Zhang and Chin, 2015: 229). Because their work was 'task-orientated' (Zhang, 2013: 126), most snakeheads perceived smuggling to be 'non-predatory' and 'at worst' a 'legally ambiguous' (Zhang and Chin, 2002: 25–26) means of earning an 'honest living' that enabled them to reduce unemployment and send remittances back to family in China (p.19).

A similar conclusion was reached by Sanchez (2014) in her study of those referred to as 'coyotes', who assist migrants across the Mexican border into Arizona. Sanchez's study is based on the qualitative analysis of court cases against 66 men and women charged with human smuggling-related offences, open-ended interviews with 'smuggling facilitators, their families and clients' and a period of participant observation in 'restaurants, beauty parlors, money-wiring businesses, food stands, bars, parking lots of detention facilities and open-air markets' where she had 'conversations with individuals who had been involved in some aspect of smuggling, either as border crossers or as facilitators' (p.10). Like Zhang and Chin, Sanchez found little evidence of 'powerful criminal interests' at play in a market that was 'comprised of independent facilitators who assist one another … on a sporadic basis, and without criminal intentions' (p.69). These facilitators tended not to identify as smugglers or 'coyotes'. They did what they did to access 'supplementary resources within a community that' was 'unlikely to ascend socially or economically' (p.69), for an income that often proved 'unreliable, inconsistent or even delusive' (p.88).

Profits, when they were made, were typically recycled into the community immediately, meaning that little wealth was accumulated. Often those facilitating smuggling were raising funds to support their own border crossings. Others saw opportunities to improve their own 'social status' by helping community members 'perceived as vulnerable or in need' (p.81) or to pay back 'favors others had done for them during their own migratory journeys' (p.87). Sanchez revealed smuggling to be a highly gendered activity, with tasks like 'desert treks, driving, security enforcement, etc' typically 'performed by men', while women – though 'central to the success of every migrant's journey' – undertook lower-paid tasks such as 'recruitment, coordination, the provision of room and board and the execution of financial transactions' in order to supplement other precarious sources of income (p.104). For these women, engagement in smuggling was a less socially stigmatizing means of staying financially afloat than engagement in prostitution or selling drugs. It could also facilitate family reunifications that these women felt a duty to support and which enhanced their status in communities that tended to regard it as women's responsibility to maintain family ties.

Trusted Handlers and Social Obligation

This depiction of smugglers as enterprising and often benevolent is echoed in Maher's (2018) 18-month ethnography of smuggling from Senegal across the

Mediterranean. Her study revealed the significance of trust between migrants and those who facilitate their travel; trust which is usually carefully negotiated when migrants first embark upon clandestine journeys, but which becomes harder to establish during the latter legs of complex journeys. Maher found that in Senegal most migrants were 'familiar with their handlers', 'more likely to call them a friend (*ami*) than a criminal' (p.36) and grateful for the assistance and protection they, unlike state officials, offered. Many handlers were migrants who expressed 'solidarity' with 'their human cargo' (p.42). Their operations were small-scale and the prices they charged were often determined less by how much they thought they could exploit fellow travellers and more by the degree of social proximity between the two parties. This social proximity determined the degree of moral and religious duty handlers felt to ensure prospective migrants' safe passage.

> Handlers and boat owners quickly and efficiently sized up candidates, depreciating costs for friends and charging more from those who seemed to possess the means and less from those who did not. For migrants, knowing someone was crucial … If a migrant knew the handler, he could petition for a reduced fare. Migrants could, and often did, try to claim social proximity by referring to common origins, distant relations, or religious fraternity.
>
> (p.42)

Prices could also fall as more passengers were amassed – and those with a history of failed travel attempts were sometimes offered places for free – but this could mean waiting for weeks until all the seats in a boat were filled. Those who sailed the ships could not easily be cast as profiteering predators either. Many were fishermen who 'quickly realized that their passengers were ultimately ignorant of what it would mean to sit in a boat for seven to eight days' and who felt obliged to teach them how to survive (p.46). Of course, the more migrants progressed with their journeys, the less social proximity there was between them and the subsequent handlers with whom they had to negotiate. At this point, costs sometimes increased as the risks of the journey escalated and the chances of being turned back by border patrols increased. These increased costs were usually passed back to the migrants' families back home, committing the migrants more fully to perilous journeys in the hope of being able to secure employment and repay their relatives once they reached their final destinations.

Militia Groups and Localized Network on the Outskirts of Europe

Of course, the discovery that smugglers in particular places see themselves as morally attuned brokers does not rule out the possibility that there are some dangerous players operating elsewhere in the global market. Campana's (2018) network analysis of transcribed phone records wire-tapped by the

Italian Anti-Mafia Prosecutor's Office in Palermo suggests just this possibility. The phone records Campana accessed concerned people smuggling between the Horn of Africa via Libya. Campana analysed the structure of a people-smuggling network that had continued to operate after a major tragedy in which 366 migrants drowned off the coast of Lampedusa. The vast majority of actors within the smuggling network studied were men in their early 30s, working along the smuggling route, but with a minority based in other Western European countries, Canada and the Middle East. Campana's analysis revealed the degree to which segmented and localized illicit activities contribute to smuggling into Europe. Because migrants tended to pay for each leg of the journey separately, higher-level smugglers tended to operate independently and in competition with each other, contracting out to smaller operators with access to cars, boats or properties, for example. When journeys went wrong, migrants were turned back or people died, the reputations of these higher-level organizers could be tarnished. Some were keen to highlight they had paid compensation to the families of victims in order to make reparation and rebuild trust.

Some, but not all, of these higher-level smugglers were embedded in groups involved in organized kidnappings for ransoms or militia groups supported by corrupt officials in charge of Tripoli-based detention centres. These centres are, of course, the major transit zones for migrants seeking to enter Europe and ones that European governments have been accused of supporting, before and after the collapse of the Gaddafi regime, through their investment and collaboration with the Libyan coastguard. By curtailing the flow of migrants across the Mediterranean, responsibility for reinforcing the European Union's borders has been effectively pushed back to North Africa where militias are known to profit from the torture of migrants held in inhumane detention facilities (Amnesty International, 2017; Sunderland, 2019). In other words, providing migrant transport, which was once 'recognized as a normal and legitimate economic enterprise' in sub-Saharan Africa that followed 'established social norms' has, under pressure from European governments, become a criminalized enterprise, pushed 'out of the public gaze, sometimes beyond the geographic bounds of "humanity", making the unspeakable possible' (Brachet, 2018: 28).

Indeed, as Sanchez's (2020) case analysis of the 'facilitation of migration in Libya' reveals, 'the labelling of mobility facilitation strategies as migrant smuggling and their criminalisation responds to EU-dictated migration enforcement and control measures' (p.1). It is these control measures that have 'fostered the emergence of often unequal and abusive interactions among these actors that put human lives at risk' (p.2). As Sanchez surmises:

> To refer to people's mobility strategies along the lines of smuggling, trafficking or 'modern day slavery' as it has occurred in the case of Libya is inaccurate and simplistic, for neither term reflects the complexities of people's experiences, and obscures the vast continuum of strategies migrants

and those behind their journeys employ in their attempts to achieve multiple kinds of mobility.

(p.1)

Sanchez explains that militias do sometimes play a part in these journeys, not least because non-state organizations that can command a capacity for violent practices inevitably become part of the picture of facilitating migrant flows in regions where toppled governments leave behind brutal structural inequalities. Nevertheless, most facilitators of migration in Libya are 'ordinary people', including women and children, who share languages, places of residence or countries of origin with those trying to travel. Most facilitators offer help for a fee: some in order to offset the cost of their own journeys and others to overcome acute poverty and desperation in the places they live. Those who live in areas where people are in transit rely heavily on the seasonal trade migration brings for income. Some are young people who choose to work facilitating migration because the alternatives – facilitating the smuggling of arms and drugs – involve greater brutality. Some of those who sail the migrant boats coastguards routinely return to shore do so in order to pay off debts accrued on their own journeys. Few make massive profits, for while the facilitation of migration journeys does 'involve the circulation of significant amounts of money', much of this is spent on an 'accumulation of small transactions that allow for the survival of the marginalised' (p.24), with bigger amounts more commonly spent on the bribing of officials.

Case Studies

In accessing participants for this research, the lists we received (detailed in Chapter 1) included those who had facilitated illegal entry into the UK. Sometimes we were able to ascertain that such offenders were not necessarily modern slavery perpetrators before we agreed to interview them. For example, in one instance, a man convicted of facilitating the illegal entry of a non EU national had secured false papers to enable his wife to join him in the UK. Knowing this, we did not pursue an interview with this man. In most instances, however, it only became possible to detect whether migrants had paid to travel during the interviews with those convicted of immigration offences, and even then it was not always clear whether such payments constituted or contributed to subsequent exploitation. As we show in what follows, what was clear, was that few of those involved in facilitating the illegal entry of migrants from outside the EU considered themselves to be complicit in exploitation, and while it would be stretching it to cast all such facilitators as irreconcilably altruistic, their motives were rarely exclusive economic.

Thierry: Inadvertent Smuggling

Not everyone who facilitates the illegal entry of people into the UK does so knowing they are committing an offence. Thierry, for example, was a 40-year-old man from Burundi and had emigrated to Britain aged 22. Thierry had given a lift to the fiancé of a family friend – Michelle – whose engagement party he had attended. When Thierry and his wife first got to know Michelle – a singer in their church – she was pregnant. As a mentor in the church, Thierry had helped Michelle come to terms with being an unmarried mother, dissuading her from staying with the child's father, whom he knew was being unfaithful. When Michelle subsequently announced that she was marrying a Congolese friend from her childhood who was now living in France, Thierry advised caution but attended the new couple's engagement party in Belgium. Thierry paid three hundred euros to the groom for hotel rooms by bank transfer and, encouraged by Michelle, drove over to France, taking his car on the ferry, so he could pick up some cassava on the way and share petrol costs with a friend who was also attending.

After the party, Michelle asked Thierry if he could give her, her daughter and her fiancé a lift back to the UK. Thierry agreed but when they arrived at French immigration their vehicle was stopped for ten minutes. At this point Thierry and his friend accused the officials of 'racism' and began 'shouting', Thierry assuming the officials were 'the same' as others who stopped him for no reason at UK airports. The officials explained that Michelle's fiancé was travelling on a stolen identity document and took Thierry and his friend away for questioning. No charges were ultimately made against the friend despite searches of his computer. The fiancé returned to France and Michelle and her daughter were allowed to continue their journey. Thierry, however, was charged, because he was the driver and thus accountable for his passengers. In court, it was suggested that the money he had paid the groom for the hotel room was suspicious and that his accusations of official racism were an attempt to distract from his own guilt.

With his car impounded, Thierry had to travel the length of the UK to fight his case, putting a strain on his family and business. An advisor at the immigration service immigration officer encouraged him to give evidence against Michelle, but he felt obliged to protect her, even though she 'disappeared' and cut all ties with his wife and family. Rather than prolong the expense and risk a higher sentence, Thierry pled guilty to the charges of facilitating the illegal immigration of a non-EU national, offering no explanation to the court for what had happened. During a year in prison, he resolved that 'God' was 'testing' his strength. His reasons for going to the engagement party were partly informed by a sense of Christian duty to help a woman from his congregation, as well as a familiarity with crossing borders. Thierry had often travelled to France, Germany and Belgium to catch up with friends he had known as a student and had previously given lifts back to other passengers without their being problems. These friends were mostly other young men he had known in Burundi and Congo as a student, before he sought asylum in the UK.

Back in Burundi, Theirry's family had been an influential one: his father a diplomat who had twice fled with his wife and children across national borders late at night – when Thierry was 16 and 19. The first time was after the assassination of the Burundian and Rwandan presidents, events which are taken as the beginning of the Rwandan genocide by the Hutu against the Tutsi. Border crossings then were made sometimes by car, and sometimes on foot, amidst gunshots in the forest, and without papers.

At the age of 22, Thierry was studying in Congo when Tutsi soldiers apprehended him and a Burundian cleaner who serviced his accommodation. Both men were accused of being Hutu soldiers, and the cleaner was shot dead, but because he was multi-lingual, Thierry was able to conceal his ethnicity. Thierry became a refugee and was granted British citizenship. He met his wife – a Congolese airhostess – when travelling back to Burundi. Thierry undertook two degrees and secured a professional job in the health service, but encountered enduring racism in the UK, despite concerted efforts to 'adjust'. As a student, he was sometimes refused service in local pubs and people would steal his drinks to cause a conflict that would see him thrown out. Two decades later, there had been vandalism to his car, bananas thrown in his garden and racist comments written in the snow outside his house. A lack of interest from the police led him to install CCTV cameras in effort to find out who was harassing him and his family. And when he had tried to fly abroad, he had been detained at the airport for reasons he believed to be connected to his racial profiling. This was why Thierry said he reacted angrily to the accusations made by immigration enforcement at Calais. Understandably, he did not consider himself to be a people smuggler.

Mir and Alesandro: Social Obligation and Wilful Obliviousness

Other participants convicted of facilitating the unlawful entry of non-EU nationals also invoked a sense of obligation to others, though they did so in ways that implied either considerable naivety or a degree of self-deception. Mir, for example, was an Iranian man in his 40s serving a sentence for facilitating illegal immigration. He maintained his innocence throughout the interview, saying that he had no knowledge that a woman had been hiding in the bunk above the cab of the lorry he was driving from Calais to Dover and explaining that he was a 'family man' with 'kids' and that he had 'never been in trouble' and would not risk going to 'prison for anything like that'. Mir had undertaken numerous unskilled jobs in the UK – 'always working, working' while trying to learn English – before becoming a self-employed lorry driver with various reputable companies: a job he had also held previously in Iran. As a driver based in Britain, Mir transported second-hand electronics, vehicle parts and refrigerated foods between Iran and Europe – 'anyone wants it, you know, I'll do it because

I'm driver', 'if anyone pay me, I'll work for it'. Often his work was casual, and he took opportunities to earn extra when asked to add to his load. This is what had happened on the journey which led to Mir's arrest and conviction for people smuggling.

Rather than 'go empty' on his return from France to the UK, Mir took a job transporting 18 pallets of lettuce, so he could 'make some' extra 'money'. As he recalled it, he had become aware that some of the lights on the side of the trailer were not working and therefore had stopped three times to 'try to fix' them but could not because there was 'heavy rain' and 'snow'. His last attempt had been at midnight and he now assumes – or rationalizes – that he must have failed to lock his cab while attempting the repair, because unbeknown to him a woman had 'jumped in, in the cab' and climbed in the bunk above where resting drivers normally sleep. Mir said he failed to notice the woman because: 'These people is so professional. They know what they're doing'. But as he approached the next checkpoint the police pulled him over and discovered the female stow-away. Mir explained that he did not know the woman and was 'innocent', only later discovering that the woman's uncle had paid nine hundred euros for the journey to 'two guys' who were 'smugglers'. However, the police investigation revealed that the stowaway was the girlfriend of a friend of Mir's: a man who had helped Mir to pass his UK lorry-driving test. At trial, a jury presented with phone evidence connecting the two men, convicted Mir, despite his not guilty plea, presumably because they assumed it could not be a coincidence that a woman who was a friend of a friend managed to sneak into his lorry many miles from the point where he collected the lettuces.

Similarly, Alesandro, an Albanian man in his mid-40s, was serving a three-year sentence for facilitating the illegal entry of 11 Albanian men into the UK. A decorated soldier who had been granted asylum in the UK after the end of the war in the Balkans, what Alesandro described as a 'good' life in England, had actually been incredibly hard, though better than the curfew-like conditions under which saw his family 'persecuted' as 'kulaks' – land-owning peasants – by the communist Albanian state until the Balkan war. Having smuggled himself across the continent by dingy, then by train and lorry, almost starving, Alesandro was then detained in an immigration centre upon arrival. Once granted asylum, he travelled to London where his late grandfather had previously found safety and served as a member of the London-based Free Albania Committee. There, Alesandro undertook casual jobs in the construction industry for about £90 a day, but his employment became increasingly casual as he suffered – for a decade – with acute depression and PTSD, thinking constantly about the friends he had seen killed during the war, the dismembered children he had tried to save, and the families back home who were left in acute poverty after he left. He explained that a patriotic 'promise' to 'help each other out' during the war when close comrades had been killed had not been honoured after the war, as the wives and children of the war dead were left starving while others got rich, including, it seems, a former Prime Minister of Kosovo.

In London, Alesandro became indebted by £2000 to a man from his former hometown – a plasterer whom he had worked alongside – who lent him money to send to his brother who needed private heart surgery back in Albania. When the friend asked Alesandro to take one of his young relatives who spoke no English to go and collect a lorry load of clothes, Alesandro sought assurances that it was nothing illegal. However, he appeared unwittingly to reveal that he knew he was not only collecting clothes having first turned up at the lorry, checked 'these people, Albanian in the back', and learning they were all men coming for work, 'for example for builder' and that none were trafficked. It was when he returned, after 'two three minutes … come back to collect [the] clothes' that the police arrested him for facilitating the illegal entry of eleven Albanians apparently hoping to enter the UK before the border was closed by Brexit. One of these passengers in the lorry subsequently alleged that he had been kidnapped. Implying it had all been an honest mistake, Alesandro said he had to trust that his friend had not deceived him. The friend, he explained, had sworn on the Koran in the presence of his family. Alesandro also surely owed him a debt of gratitude – if not also actual money – for providing the loan that had saved his brother's life. Moreover, Alesandro explained, he had much sympathy for the Albanians who were stowed away in the lorry whom he regarded as like him; people who came to the UK for a better life, to reunite with family and to work. Alesandro saw his imprisonment as unjust for reasons that were in part contradictory. He denied any prior knowledge of the lorry's cargo, while explaining that what he did was 'for human rights, for help people' 'with no work' 'to cross border' and 'make some money'. Either way, his imprisonment had come at a considerable cost. It had left his wife living alone to cope with a terminal illness. It had also rendered him at risk of deportation at the end of his sentence.

Bob: Smuggling as Enterprise

Unlike those who suggested they had never intended to smuggle anyone, Bob admitted to being part of an international enterprise that facilitated illegal immigration. A British man, in his early 50s, serving a four-year sentence for attempting to facilitate the illegal immigration of nine adults and one child from Sri Lanka. Bob had taken the job after his 'mate', Pete, whom he had met in prison while serving a sentence for actual bodily harm on a former partner, had introduced him to a Sri Lankan next-door neighbour – Sly. Sly offered to help Bob out of his financial predicament and introduced Bob to the 'main boss' – Maj – a 'nice fellow' and not 'gangster' – who had seen 'an opportunity to make a lot of money'. Maj was a respected businessman in the UK's Sri Lankan community and had his own shops that employed Sri Lankan workers. Maj explained to Bob that 'the Asians and stuff, they all stick together and their family all put money together', paying £15,000 per person for the journey into the UK, which they can repay by working for £300 a week. 'They come to this country and they'd work for, like, a year, more or less, and then that's it …

After, basically a year, they're free'. Following the retirement of a driver – who had 'probably made over half a million pound in six months' driving weekly van loads of migrants from Calais to London for Maj – Bob was offered the vacancy at £20,000 per week. Bob agreed to drive a lorry containing fitted kitchens to London where the kitchens were refashioned to create coffin-style spaces people could fit in. He then drove the lorry over to Paris, with Maj, going for lunch with him while the lorry was loaded up out of his sight. An initial stop and search by armed police with a drug sniffer dog on the French side of the Calais border found nothing, except a suspicion-arousing light on in the back, which Bob now thinks had been fitted to reassure a child passenger he was unaware was on board. However, once the lorry reached the British side of immigration controls, Bob was made to open the backdoors revealing twice as many passengers as he had been told: seven men, two women and, to his dismay, an eight-year-old girl. Some of the passengers 'were just upset and quiet, really', though most were later granted asylum. Maj who had pled guilty received a sentence that was only a few months longer than Bob's, despite apparently making millions of pounds from the enterprise.

Explaining why he decided to take a job that his daughters had disowned him over and his son said he should have known he could never get away with in the longer term, Bob focussed his story on 'guilt' he still felt for abandoning his three children when he left their mother for another woman some 15 years prior (aged 36) and the enduring 'depression' this guilt left him with. The affair was 'when things started going downhill', Bob mixing cocaine and alcohol and 'getting nicked' a lot because his new partner would make malicious accusations against him. Following a prison sentence for assaulting this woman, Bob's drug use became 'reckless', with 15-hour 'sessions' of drinking alcohol, consuming cocaine and driving. He financed his substance use through illicit driving work: being the getaway driver for Pete – the man who invited him to consider the smuggling job – when he had stolen crates of alcohol from shops. Bob was also the getaway driver for a sex worker who would 'clip' high-paying clients, stealing thousands of pounds from them without offering a service. 'Ashamed' to discover he had, in the course of this driving work, colluded in robbing someone of their life savings, Bob began ruminating on how little he had done for his own children, now adults, and how he had let his 'family down':

> I wanted to help my family out. I wasn't in … a good financial place at the time, and I felt like I've let my family down, my kids, financially and I wanted to have a chance to – that would be a chance to earn a lot of money.

His own father, a drink-driver and domestic abuser, 'belittled' Bob for looking 'daft', reinforced Bob's teachers' assessments that Bob was a 'naughty boy' and 'not a very good listener and learner'. At school, a teacher who was subsequently convicted for child sexual abuse offences routinely caned Bob with a long board compass. He was only beginning to realize that this had paved the way, not only for his failure at school but also for a lifetime of substance dependency that followed from having very low self-esteem and making poor choices, including the unforgivable mistake of 'leaving' his 'family'. Bob's decision to undertake people smuggling was thus motivated by a desire to provide a financial fix for his many years as an absent father and poor provider in the expectation that this would alleviate the guilt behind his depression.

Discussion

When the UN Protocol against the Smuggling of Migrants by Land, Sea, and Air was drafted, those countries that signed up to it were divided on whether the non-criminalization of those making illegal border crossings would alleviate or accentuate organized crime (Nicot and Kopp, 2018). Today, with most countries in the West criminalizing 'the facilitation of illegal entry, whether done with the aim of making a profit or not', anyone who offers 'assistance to people on the move – including in some instances humanitarian assistance provided to asylum seekers when no other options are available to escape war and persecution' – risks a conviction for smuggling (Nicot and Kopp, 2018: 223–224). And yet, as Agnes Callamard, a Special Rapporteur of the Human Rights Council, has highlighted, 'Smugglers and traffickers are an integral component' of the movement of people exercising their rights to life:

> 'without them, refugees and migrants are generally unable to navigate the barriers many States erect to deter entry' and which 'purposefully funnel … migration flows into more hazardous terrain' … 'The intensification of border controls traps both States and migrants in a vicious circle in which increasing numbers of border deaths lead to calls to "combat" smuggling and increase border patrolling, which forces refugees and other migrants to use more dangerous routes using smugglers' services'
>
> (United Nations, 2017: 5–6)

In pointing to 'criminal gangs and illicit business networks' who expose 'unfortunate migrants on precarious journeys', Western governments detract from their complicity in the exploitation and deaths of those who attempt such journeys (Zhang et al., 2018: 7). As we have tried to show through these use of four case studies, those convicted of smuggling offences in the UK are not always part of these criminal gangs, and to the extent that they are connected to 'organized crime', they are often small-bit players, agreeing to help to repay favours (Mir and Alesandro), out of a sense of duty (Thierry) or to get themselves out of a financial fix (Bob). While some smugglers like Bob (and John, depicted in Chapter 4) are part of semi-professionally organized groups working for profit across borders, they – like those who provide more casual assistance to fellow migrants for compassionate reasons – are rarely totally devoid of principles or empathy for those they help to cross borders (Aziani, 2021). None of the people smugglers we interviewed intended to trap people in exploitation. The people whose migration they helped facilitate were people whose journeys were otherwise blocked by Western governments. In some cases, the smuggled were people like the smugglers. They were men who had fled from war, stigma, shame and poverty who wanted to work and build decent lives for themselves and saw nothing wrong in helping others to do so. In this context, those who end up facilitating illegal entry rationalized that what they were doing was not immoral, even if they too accrued some personal benefit from it. Sharing travel costs (Theirry), making a bit on the side when undertaking low-paid work (Mir), helping someone who has helped family members of one's own in dire need (Alesandro), looking to raise money in a hurry for one's own children (Bob) were all motives for facilitating smuggling in the case studies we have presented in this chapter – miscellaneous blends of altruism, profit and mutual obligation all playing a part. Only one of these participants – Bob – stood to make anything approaching a large sum of money from facilitating the travel of migrants, and after serving four years in prison, even he had not been paid.

The banality of these motives needs to be brought into public debates that are so easily misdirected towards manhunts for criminal masterminds to detract from tragedies that are products of the impossible choices many migrants face when border controls are designed to render crossings perilous. Smugglers work to surmount such border controls, while state actions to thwart them generate vulnerabilities to trafficking, as migrants become ever more desperate and the costs of facilitating their travel increase. Some – but not all – of those involved in smuggling facilitate travel knowing that would-be migrants have to undertake low-paid or illicit work, but like Bob they assume this is a fair price to pay for a better life. One reason for this is that some of this low-paid work is comparable to work previously undertaken by the smugglers themselves. Often though, the facilitation of illicit migration is not so well orchestrated. Because the desire for a better life is shared by virtually all migrants, many take calculated risks and proactively negotiate deals with those who can offer them travel. In the countries from which both the smuggled and those who do the smuggling often originate, trading offers of help to cross borders has become, by necessity, a way of life, and the 'right thing to do' for people in trouble, poverty and at risk of violence.

There is little compelling evidence to suggest that many smugglers operating in Europe actively set out to prey on the vulnerable, but plenty of evidence to show that those who have spent all they have entering a European Union country unlawfully will continue to seek out people who can help them complete their journeys. Some of these helpers undoubtedly take foolish risks, while others are tempted by the prospect of 'easy money'. If our own case studies are anything to go by, most are likely to be naïve about immigration law and how diligent they need to be in determining whether debts accrued by migrants they assist can be readily repaid. Some inevitably reappraise what they want in return – or regret agreeing to do favours to friends with few questions asked – as they only realize belatedly the significant risks they are taking. But there is no getting away from the fact that the demand for such helpers, facilitators and fixers derives from the enforcement of border controls and the closure of routes of passage used by previous generations of migrants. Casting smugglers as 'evil' and committing to hunting them down is a means of conjuring folk devils and moral panics (Cohen, 2002). As we have shown in this chapter, these folk devils bear little resemblance to the reality of smuggling and misdirect attention away from important questions about why smuggling occurs and how the politics of anti-immigration sentiment are implicated in tragedies where migrants lose their lives.

4 Organized Criminals?

With the signing of the United Nations Convention against Transnational Organized Crime in Palermo, Italy, in December 2000, the international community demonstrated the political will to answer a global challenge with a global response … Arrayed against these constructive forces, however, in ever greater numbers and with ever stronger weapons, are the forces of what I call 'uncivil society'. They are terrorists, criminals, drug dealers, traffickers in people and others who undo the good works of civil society. They take advantage of the open borders, free markets and technological advances that bring so many benefits to the world's people. They thrive in countries with weak institutions, and they show no scruple about resorting to intimidation or violence. Their ruthlessness is the very antithesis of all we regard as civil. They are powerful, representing entrenched interests and the clout of a global enterprise worth billions of dollars, but they are not invincible.

(Annan, 2004, foreword to the Convention Against
Transnational Organized Crime: iii)

Those deemed responsible for human trafficking and modern slavery are frequently depicted, as in the quote from the former Secretary-General of the United Nations, above, as 'organized criminals', working internationally for vast profits, much like drug dealers and terrorists, to undermine the safety and freedoms governments provide to their populations. The dominant construction of human trafficking (discussed in Chapter 2) enshrined within the Palermo Protocol depicts traffickers as evil, foreign national criminals who profit extensively from undermining the integrity of national borders and threatening international security. The re-emergence of human trafficking as a global policy priority has relied heavily on the cultivation of concern about the dangers assumed to be posed by unscrupulous and powerful 'Mr Big' mafia bosses who have ruthlessly acquired the resources needed to challenge the security of independent nations.

In this chapter, we consider the organization of activities that amount to modern slavery, the extent to which those involved in these activities can be perceived as 'organized criminals' and the ways in which their networks of

DOI: 10.4324/9780429053986-4

acquaintances facilitate criminal activity. First, we consider the portrayal of human trafficking and modern slavery as a type of organized crime in international and national policy. We then review what is known about those convicted of organized crimes before discussing how it manifested in our sample. The case studies in this chapter illustrate the stories of four men – those of our participants who presented with the characteristics of organized criminals were all men – who have spent their lives working between legitimate and illegitimate markets. We show how the legacies of influential and successful fathers, enterprising approaches to masculinity, and paternalistic and macho attitudes towards women and family life influenced much of what they did, as did the opportunity to make 'easy money' in high demand and loosely regulated economies. But we ultimately question the veracity of the stereotype of 'Mr Big', all four participants revealing that the profits of their exploits were short-lived and that their involvement in cross-border criminality became unsustainable as their lives became destabilized by drug use, law enforcement interventions and deteriorating relationships with family and partners. We also question how useful it is to depict all those involved in cross-national criminal networks as uncompromisingly ruthless or unscrupulous – the four men whose stories we present in this chapter all regarding themselves as 'fixers' of other people's problems, at least until things went wrong and the risks associated with the absence of safeguards to protect vulnerable people travelling or working illicitly became all too apparent.

Serious and Organized Crime and Human Trafficking: Policy Development

The role of organized crime in human trafficking became of particular concern to policymakers in the 1990s with the ending of the West's 'Cold War' with the Soviet Union (Woodiwiss and Hobbs, 2009). Then, the 'threat from an alien and nebulous enemy', epitomized in the stereotype of Russian mafias looking to enter new Western markets, began to draw the attention of security services and political leaders (ibid: 106). The United Nations Convention against Transnational Organized Crime, signed in 2000, emphasized the 'political will to answer a global challenge with a global response' (United Nations, 2004: iii). While setting out definitions for Transnational Organized Crime, the Convention also included the Protocol to Prevent and Punish Trafficking in Persons, Especially Women and Children, presenting human trafficking as 'one of the most egregious violations of human rights' (iv). The Protocol formed the basis for legislation and problem framing in most countries, including the US and the countries of the European Union. In turn, national and international bodies prioritized approaches that put national security before the human rights of the exploited in what became conceived as a series of 'battles' or 'wars' with serious and organized crime.

The EU's approach focussed on the identification and measurement of the threat posed by organized crime groups. Europol's first report named organized crime as its major challenge and defined trafficking in human beings as one of the most threatening components of it (Europol, 2000). EU–wide 'organized crime threat assessments' began to be produced in the early 2000s. The 2017 Europol Serious and Organised Crime Threat Assessment (Europol, 2017) subsequently identified trafficking in human beings and human smuggling as 'key priorities' and asserted that organized crime groups (OCGs) involved in the drugs trade were diversifying into human trafficking markets in which shadow networks of international accomplices could mount a serious challenge to the capacities of law enforcement and the integrity of nation states. In practice, the assessments failed to provide an effective basis for national policymaking or a better understanding of the trafficking of people. In the absence of a convincing evidence base to support their claims, some academic commentators concluded that the function of the Europol Serious and Organised Crime Threat Assessments was primarily political, their real goal being to change the international landscape of policing and border enforcement (van Duyne and Vander Beken, 2009).

The global and European focus on organized crime also found effect in the UK with the first conference on the subject hosted by the Police College in 1993. In the decade that followed, organized crime became an increasingly prominent UK policy issue. The White Paper 'One Step Ahead' (Home Office 2004: iii) identified organized crime as 'big business' causing 'untold harm on our streets [and] damage to our communities'. The then (Labour) Home Secretary, David Blunkett, highlighted how the ease of international travel and developments in technology had the potential to expand the reach of organized crime. In response, New Labour government introduced a package of organized crime-related legislation. This included the Proceeds of Crime Act 2002 and the Serious Organised Crime and Police Act 2005, the latter of which led to the establishment of the Serious Organised Crime Agency (SOCA) in 2006.

The UK's political agenda shifted further to wards 'organized immigration crime' following the Morecambe Bay tragedy in 2004, when 23 undocumented Chinese labourers drowned. Two years later, when the Home Secretary Charles Clarke was forced to resign following the release of 1,023 foreign national prisoners with seemingly no consideration given to deporting them, the Conservatives, in opposition, began to reposition themselves as the only party able to control immigration and redress the threats to national security the mismanagement of foreign national offenders could engender (Balch and Geddes, 2011). As incoming Conservative Home Secretary from 2010, Theresa May located anti-trafficking work squarely within the context of organized crime and as the key to combatting illegal immigration, proclaiming: 'the transport and exploitation of vulnerable men, women and children by predatory organised criminal groups is something that no civilised country should tolerate' (Home Office, 2011: 3). The National Crime Agency duly expanded and was awarded enhanced intelligence capabilities to disrupt the threat posed by OCGs. The 2015 Modern Slavery Act created a post of

Minister for Modern Slavery and Organised Crime, and although the 2014 Modern Slavery Strategy (Home Office, 2014) acknowledged that opportunistic perpetrators working alone are responsible for some modern slavery activity, its emphasis was placed squarely on serious and organized crime as the driving force behind the trafficking of people.

By 2018, modern slavery and human trafficking had become a central focus of UK's Serious and Organised Crime Strategy. This defined organized crime as 'individuals planning, coordinating and committing serious offences, whether individually, in groups and/or as part of transnational networks' (HM Government, 2018: 11). In the introduction to the 2020 NCA Strategic Assessment, the case of the Essex lorry disaster (described in Chapter 3 of this book) was used to illustrate the need for a response that tackled 'high harm, high impact offenders who exploit the vulnerable through modern slavery', though those who died had mostly paid to be smuggled and were not trafficked (NCA, 2020: 1). The Serious and Organised Crime Strategy and the NCA Strategic Assessment nevertheless linked human trafficking and modern slavery with 'mass migration and economic imbalances' which create 'a pool of vulnerable people (at home and abroad) who may be exploited' (NCA, 2020: 17). Modern slavery and human trafficking perpetrators, it was assumed, 'are most likely to operate in organised groups or networks' that are 'driven by profit' (NCA, 2020: 22).

Organized Crime Groups or How Crime Is Organized?

Academic opinion on the threat posed by organized crime has been rather more critical (Edwards and Gill, 2002; van Duyne and Vander Beken, 2009; Albanese, 2012). Some argue that the illusiveness of 'Mr Big' seems always to justify the ramping of security to resolve imminent threats to the future of democracy rather than any serious questioning as to whether mafia bosses exist (Kleemans, 2014). The definition of what counts as organized crime is so loose that it can readily be found everywhere. As Paoli and Fijnaut (2006: 311) explain, in their critique of EU policy on organized crime:

> if three people only are sufficient to form a criminal organisation, one might justifiably ask if the (alleged) increasing presence of these entities in the illegal arena really represents a major innovation in regard to the past and the threatening menace.

Others suggest that the expansion of international security cooperation across borders risks has had the unintended consequence of forcing what might otherwise be small-scale, illicit enterprises to find ways and means of becoming more organized in order to circumvent the additional security and meet the demands of local markets. This, as Reuter (1983; 1985) argued, is something those involved in transnational crime did not always have to do. In the 1980s, most criminal groups in the UK operated locally to avoid the risk of detection.

Few had the means to manage enterprises that spanned larger geographical areas, while opportunities to profit could be found locally. Hence, as Hobbs' classic ethnographic research illustrated, most crime problems – especially those involving the international trafficking of illicit drugs across physical and virtual borders – need to be understood locally because transnational activity is shaped by the demands of particular communities, in particular places that rely on networks that are close to them. The interface of the local with the global – the glocal – determines the 'commercial viability' of much illicit business activity and whether expansion is viable (Hobbs, 1998: 417).

> Organised crime is … 'Local at all points'. Unlike previous eras, con-temporary organised crime with its emphasis upon drugs, fraud and counterfeiting, simultaneously occupies both the local and global. Further, these criminal activities offer the possibility of moving from one sphere to another … [C]riminal career trajectories no longer are limited to spe-cific, often stereotyped geographic locations of some urban 'underworld' … Drug networks in particular constitute: '… continuous paths that lead from the local to the global, from the circumstantial to the universal, from the contingent to the necessary' (Latour 1993: 117). Networks are the media through which individuals and groups move between the local and the global, but this does not indicate the kind of structural determinism suggested by many writers on organised crime.
>
> (Hobbs, 1998: 419)

There is reason to ask if the same is also true with respect to trafficking in people. While the modern slavery agenda has presented the public with an image of 'outsiders', namely transnational, ethnically charged mafias, infiltrating 'open, democratic societies' (Kleemans, 2014: 33), it is 'the involvement of insiders and the ways in which societies create and promote organised crime oppor-tunities themselves' that has been most 'neglected' (p.34). This is obviously so in relation to the purchase of goods and services supplied by exploited workers but is probably also the case in relation to the illicit movement of people. This activity ultimately requires actors with knowledge of the stop-off points and final destinations to arrange transport, accommodation, safe passage at border points and work, if debts need to be repaid. The implication of this is that we have to look more closely at how legal markets and illegal markets intersect, for as Paoli (2002: 59) argues: 'Parallelism between legal and illegal markets has fre-quently led to the conclusion that the supply of illegal goods and commodities is carried out by collective actors similar to those present in legal markets'. The same is probably no less true of the trafficking and smuggling of people. Put bluntly, it is much cheaper and simpler to fly from Europe to the UK with a low-cost airline if you have the right to do so than to pay a smuggler, buy false papers, hire a dingy or secure a place in the back of freight lorry. We thus need to ask both how illegal markets in people trafficking become organized and who the actors are who fill the gaps in these markets.

Researching Organized Criminals

As Hobbs (1998: 415) explains this dual focus necessitates methods that grapple with the life histories that produce people, most frequently men, who have the 'flexibility' and 'innovative engagements with the market' needed to operate 'within multiple, interwoven networks of legitimate and illegitimate opportunity' and hence succeed in 'bad business'. To date, criminologists have tended to approach this challenge quantitatively through the secondary analyses of criminal records and case files, by asking if those involved in organized crime are similar to more general career criminals. This research is largely inconclusive in its findings. Kleemans and De Poot (2008) found that 72% of their sample had been previously engaged in criminal activity, while 28% did not. Vere van Koppen et al. (2010) found that 40% of those with convictions for organized crime were adult-onset offenders without any previous convictions. Francis et al. (2013) confirm a mixed picture. Some of those involved in organized crime had similar criminal career trajectories to generalist offenders, but others had no previous convictions.

The very small number of qualitative studies do suggest there is, nevertheless, something distinct about those serving prison sentences for organized crime offences. Vere van Koppen and De Poot's (2013) in-depth interviews with 16 people serving sentences for organized crime offences in Dutch prisons found that most only entered organized criminal activity in later life. The specific social ties, opportunities and mobility needed to facilitate engagement in organized crime are not readily available to younger people. Becoming a business owner was important to all interviewees, but only some had established businesses with illegal intentions at the outset. Some had drifted into illicit activity as pressures to profit from larger sums of 'easy money' collided with the opportunities to do so. For others, the 'residue' of traditional masculine cultures, in which men's engagement in sharp business practices was relatively unconstrained by the law and by obligations to women and children, formed the basis for their engagement with serious and organized crime (Hobbs, 1997): sometimes on a sustained basis, but at other times as a casual means of making money quickly when circumstances required it, or as a means of forging new business relationships with other enterprising men.

Here we want to focus on those within our sample of 30 offenders who appeared to most closely approximate the stereotype of the organized criminal or 'Mr Big'. By virtue of the nature of the offences and definition of organized crime, all 30 participants in our sample could be – and sometimes were – considered organized criminals when charges were brought against them. As we have discussed in other chapters, the stories most of them told about their lives revealed this to be something of a fallacy. In choosing the case studies for this chapter, we drew on the social network maps developed from the interviews. The following four case studies are those that ally most closely with transnational organized criminal activity. They include individuals who profited from multiple forms of criminality: men variously involved in the illicit movement of goods, drugs, people and/or money across international borders who worked at the interface of legitimate and illegitimate markets.

Case Studies

John: Jack of all Crimes, Master of None

John was a white British man in his late 40s, serving a 20-month sentence for facilitating the illegal entry of Vietnamese nationals into the UK. Though he had a legitimate business in the care sector, John had been persistently involved in criminal activity since his childhood. In total, he had served 21 years in prison. Between the ages of 5 and 11, the house John lived in facilitated 'predominantly criminal activities', orchestrated by his father who was a 'renowned bank robber'. As he recalled, it 'was not a bad life cos we had money' – 'we never used to like want for nothing'. Dad was his 'hero' and 'best mate', just 16 years his senior, known and 'respected' by 'everyone' for what he 'was into', a man no one would 'mess' with and a father who would give his son a 'good hiding' to 'discipline' him, though never to 'hurt' him. It was only after John's father was sentenced to 20 years in prison that things 'went downhill'. Then, John became an uncontrollable 'little bastard': 'breaking into houses, pinching off family members', 'fighting', truanting, even committing his own armed (with a broken bottle) robbery – while his mother was having to sell off everything: 'the house ... cars ... gold' to make ends meet. Unable to handle John, his mother agreed with social services that he – but not his younger brother and sister – should go into institutional care.

The hurt of this decision was barely evident in the first interview with John, the story moving rapidly onto the positive time he had in care. In the second interview, it became more apparent that his mother's rejection of him had been exceedingly painful and that he had not spoken to her or his siblings for 35 years. Against this backdrop, John said he 'loved' being in care, 'it was better than life ... I would a chopped me little finger off with a spoon to stay there'. Relocated to the countryside, until he received a four-year custodial sentence at the age of 16 for a grievous assault, being in care, John claimed, 'turned' his life 'around', the 'holidays' and outdoor pursuits better than anything he had enjoyed before. Allegations of sexual abuse against one of the care home's workers – a 'top guy' – had not changed John's view, for he had a 'mad time' being 'easily led' by the older lads – burgling pubs, shops and schools. This ended abruptly when John, already a heavy drinker and a cannabis smoker of several years, decided to rob the residence of a party he was at, before smashing a champagne bottle across the head of a man who tried to stop him. The victim was saved only by a 'hundred' stitches to his head.

Only after another four-year prison sentence did what John regarded as a 'normal life' resume. This meant returning to the estate on which he was raised and working actively as a member of a gang involved in the selling (but not consumption) of ecstasy in nightclubs, turf wars against rival illicit drug 'firms', and factories and violent protection.

Money was easy. Because back in them days … that's when our reputation really come a bit fierce because … there was violence.

Having re-established his 'reputation' as his father's son, John secured a 'nice car' and a 'beautiful girlfriend' with whom he 'fell in love straightaway'. His criminal work was, nevertheless, both relentless, keeping him busy four or five nights a week, and 'exciting': telling the doormen of famous nightclubs to let them in or they would not be working for much longer, being part of a 'bad firm' with an infamous 'top man' who kept a kind of order, and stealing the profits and products from rival gangs involved in the selling of drugs. Marriage to his girlfriend, with whom he had two children – both born while he was in prison – and a stepchild, did little to change John's lifestyle: 'it's just been criminal activities all the way through', 'mad robberies, shit like that, woundings', and neither did a stab wound beneath the heart or being shot at ('It was them or us'). One five-year prison stretch commencing at the age of 24 for possession of a firearm was followed by a couple of years doing semiskilled manual work with his father-in-law and then a five-year stretch in custody for robberies – motivated by the desire for 'nice' clothes and a car.

Upon release, John pursued legitimate work in a bid to go straight, working with his wife delivering a 24-hour call-out service for people needing hands-on care. This work was terminated when a seven-year sentence was imposed for armed robbery on a rival drugs firm. By the time this sentence concluded, John was a grandad, his daughter having had her first child. This, John said, 'changed' his 'life completely', though seemingly not completely enough. He went straight for seven years and 'cut' himself off from some of his long-standing criminal acquaintances, until the temptation of 'easy money' was presented in the form of bringing foreign nationals across from Paris with 'no questions' asked.

Specific details of these people's smuggling operations emerged across the two interviews, in ways that were not without contradictions. The idea for the trips came when John was hooked up with his 'white-collar criminal', cousin and some old friends. The offer of £7,000 per passenger for bringing some Vietnamese people back was too good for John to turn down – it was 'pure greed', after all he had been 'running drug dens' and 'risking' his 'life' for far less. A van was hired by someone else and collected with a pre-programmed satnav. On the first trip, a 'French black guy' appeared on the street in Paris to let three Vietnamese passengers in, and John and his female accomplice dropped them off at a hotel in London. The journey passed without incident through the Eurotunnel, securing – in one version – John 'the easiest £21,000' he had 'ever had', though 'split' three ways – but, in another version, a crime from which he ultimately 'didn't bloody make anything'. Either way, there was, John said, no reason to feel bad. All the passengers were 'male adults' who 'sounded like they were happy … laughing and joking in the back', who hugged him in gratitude that they 'finally' arrived in London, though he 'couldn't understand a bloody word they said'. Admittedly, John had heard in the news about 'sex trades and shit like that', but his 'conscience was clear knowing that it was just all male adults' who 'had their own mind', or so he had been 'told'. If it had not been 'adult males' he would have never done the job, because:

> Women and kids sometimes can't make their own choices. And … I wouldn't want a choice to bring them over and if there was kids. I wouldn't [2]. I don't think me conscience would have been able to – knowing what you hear on the news and what you see.

The third of these trips was arranged at the 'last minute' to collect four passengers – who unbeknown to John had fled when another vehicle organized by his cousin had been seized the week before. On reflection, John thought, this cousin probably knew him to be the 'kinda person' tempted by 'easy fucking money'. A stop at English passport control at Calais ultimately saw John, and all those implicated in planning the three journeys, charged and convicted for facilitating the illicit entry of non-EU nationals. As John remembers it, his passengers were simply released in France when the van was stopped by border control, though it was later reported that a 'pregnant' woman was among them, rather undercutting John's principled commitment to only assisting men who had chosen to come for work and paternalistic aversion to smuggling 'women and kids' who can't always 'make their own choices'. John was thus relieved that his dad understood why he did what he did. However, his wife was less forgiving. Post-conviction, speaking to her on the phone made John feel like someone had 'died'. He struggled to conceal his emotions, knowing that his 'fierce' reputation might be compromised if other inmates spotted how much the sentence was 'breaking' him.

Darius: No Income Tax, No VAT

Darius was a Romanian man in his mid-40s serving over three years in prison for conspiring to arrange the transportation of people for sexual exploitation. He expected to be deported on the completion of his sentence. Darius was the only child to two influential parents, his father – who died of a heart attack when he heard Darius had been sentenced – was a high-ranking and respected military officer during and after the Ceausescu years, and his mother was formerly a senior figure in government goods distribution for the communist regime. Consequently, the family had 'money, everything' during the communist times. 'Now', after the collapse of communism, Darius felt it had become more difficult, at least for people like him, the sons of former elites, to get ahead: 'it's more hard … after forty years … work … you don't have money enough for decent life, not for luxury life': something Darius appeared to yearn for but denied he had secured, despite police claims to the contrary.

As a teen, Darius claimed, he had been vocal in the 'revolution', leading street protests that anticipated Ceausescu's demise, though he provided little detail of his activism. After leaving school, Darius secured a job within an antiriot police unit. The work was often tedious, consisting of long periods of quiet punctuated with emergency calls, while a blind eye was turned to more routine crime matters. The job came to an abrupt end, however, when Darius was convicted by a military court for perpetrating grievous assaults on a 'mafia' family – involved in running casinos and debt collection – who had threatened his family. Darius served nine years in a Romanian prison for assaulting nine people from this mafia family. He nevertheless regarded his time in prison in the UK, following his conviction for conspiring to traffick people for the purposes of sexual exploitation, as far more degrading. In prison in the UK he felt he was treated as 'not human': 'I feel now dead person [3] … [At] night when I stay in my cell … I cry'.

Upon his release from his first prison sentence in his early 30s, Darius sold a flat he owned in the city and relocated to a smaller town, where he invested in a business building play areas. This proved hugely successful, both economically – netting him a profit of £70k in the first year – and in terms of raising his profile, creating a network of acquaintances involved in international transportation. Over the next 12 years, Darius reinvested his profits in a distribution company that could transport goods between Romania, Germany, Austria, Italy, Hungary and the UK, while living in Italy, Germany and the UK. Just before he was arrested, the business employed almost 100 workers, who loaded the vans and delivered parcels to distribution centres in each country. Parcels were weighed, checked that they were not drugs, and paperwork was kept, reducing liability at customs: though Darius was never stopped there. People were never transported, though Darius knew at least five firms in this line of work to whom he passed enquiries. His legitimate business veered into illegitimate realms, however. 'Most people, they want to send money', without incurring transfer charges or attracting attention from the governments of the countries where it had been made and tax, presumably, had not been paid. 'In Romania everybody works with the cash'. It was not unusual for Darius' customers to ask him to move £200k in cash from one country to another for which he charged a 10% commission, though he did not consider this 'money laundering'.

Darius also became a broker for other services of questionable legitimacy. He helped Romanians secure cheaper car insurance by supplying false addresses in Scotland. He was involved in renting and subletting properties, buying and reselling flight and ferry tickets and providing payment for adverts on grey economy sales sites like VivaStreet. Most of the business was done on an 'ask no questions' basis. People would approach Darius for travel tickets on Facebook Messenger or WhatsApp. He would establish their desired price and would hold reservations in their names until the payment was secured. There could be as many as 2000 enquiries a day, most of which were handled by Darius' wife, from whom he was at least temporarily estranged. Financial transactions made online were processed, however, to an account in his elderly mother's name (with money transferred through a petrol station chain) largely so that it was safe for him to inherit the profit when his mother dies without having to share it with his wife should they divorce.

Darius had become a VIP user on VivaStreet, having previously used the site for his transport company. People could approach him and ask for a code that would enable them to pay for adverts debited from his account, presumably in return for upfront cash. Initially, this had been for mobile phones or cars, but at least six adverts were for 'massage' services, the women's 'husbands' and 'boyfriends' having transferred him £250 for each advert. Darius did not see it as his 'problem' to check what was being sold from his account, maintaining that 'VivaStreet does not promote prostitute, it's massage and escort' and definitely not 'the trafficking', for which he was convicted alongside five other men, three of whom he did not know at all. Only one was a friend (from whom he sourced spare car parts and insurance) and he had met another in the gym and had helped him hire a flat for him and his wife (who was also prosecuted for sex trafficking). Darius said he also did not know the sex workers he was alleged to have trafficked, none of whom provided witness statements. Darius explained that he did know a 'thousand' women involved in prostitution – most of whom were friends of male friends, and some he hired: 'yes I know it's prostitute. What is the problem if I pay? ... I pay on legal site'.

Darius was insistent that he was not involved in trafficking and that evidence of his association with sex workers was not the same as exploitation. Prostitution was part of the party life he had enjoyed while establishing his distribution business in Italy and the UK. When Darius was away from Romania, there were sometimes parties for birthdays and Christmas hosted by Romanians who enjoyed the same tastes in food and music: 'twenty, thirty, forty, fifty person staying, music, this is normal'. Some of the men would bring their wives or girlfriends. It would have been rude to ask which of the 'girlfriends' were 'prostitutes', he explained. Darius expected to return to his 'ex-wife' upon his release: 'I stay with her, normal', his relationship with his 'girlfriend' ending once his capacity to buy her luxury goods was curtailed by imprisonment.

Idris: Dealing with the Destitute

Idris was a preacher in his mid-60s, who had left a life of international drug trafficking behind him 17 years prior to the interview. Though many of his criminal convictions were for possession of drugs, he had served an 18-month prison for drug trafficking: offending that had entailed the exploitation of sex workers and other vulnerable Nigerian people who transported illicit substances on flights upon which Idris was also a passenger. Typically, these women also carried forged European passports in Idris' name that he used to expedite his departure from international airports. As Idris explained, the women often had 'aged parents or there are younger ones and, you know, poverty and all that'. He recruited these 'destitutes' by promising to 'change' their 'life' for the sake of 'just one trip'. However, he also knew some women and their partners were liable to become 'hooked' on the drugs he supplied them with and hence dependent on the income they accrued from working for him as drug couriers.

Born in Nigeria in the 1950s, Idris' family was comparatively privileged. His father worked with 'white men' as a senior civil servant in the British colonial administration, and the family benefitted from a quality of life his contemporaries did not have. Both Idris and the administration 'loved' his father. Aged ten, Idris was moved from his family home to live with his father's cousin in a rural village to experience a traditional Nigerian life. The separation left Idris with an emotional 'scar', though it also offered new freedoms. Idris' 'uncle' was also a cannabis dealer who 'loved' Idris 'so much' that he shared his marijuana with him, putting 'pot' in his mouth, despite the prohibitions of Idris' mother.

This freedom did not last long. The advent of the Nigerian Biafran war caused Idris, aged 13, to be engaged first as a child spy and then as a child soldier in three years of brutal conflict. Boys living destitute lives were forced by Biafran forces to share their intelligence, which was used to 'bomb' the Nigerian army. Idris witnessed children who had been caught spying 'slaughtered' and women being raped by men and boys during the war, activities he claimed never to have perpetrated though he did have to kill as a soldier. When the war ended, Idris was admitted to a boarding school ran by former combatants for child soldiers. In the absence of counselling or the chance to return to family, marijuana use was no longer 'enough'. Idris began using heroin.

Upon leaving school, Idris joined the police and was rapidly promoted to police inspector. Corruption and drug use among officers were rife at this time, a legacy that supported Idris through a criminal career that spanned into his late 40s. Intervening to protect a banker who was being threatened with violence by police officers for a driving offence provided the opportunity for a dual career, Idris assuming a clandestine job by day in a bank (under the pretence accepted by his police superior that he was studying), while continuing to work for the police by night. Idris' heroin use became habitual at this time, as did his engagement in fraud. He became an expert at forging signatures and would take a commission from signing company cheques brought to him by a third party. When the fraud was spotted Idris was arrested, but he bribed someone to get the case dropped and continued working at the bank until a fellow officer spotted him there, prompting his resignation.

Needing 'quick money' to repay a drug dealer he was indebted to, Idris migrated to India, where he knew heroin to be sourced. Idris registered as a university student but rarely studied. He brought heroin back to Nigeria to pay off his debts, but he then continued this venture with the daughter of a lawyer whose family had been overseeing the production of heroin in rural India for generations: a young woman 'who spoke fluent English like' Idris and who 'loved' him 'so much'.

Back in Nigeria, Idris was approached by desperate West Africans looking for work, because they needed money or had sick parents or children. Some were 'prostitutes' Idris recruited in the five-star hotels he frequented and where transactions were completed. Idris told the prostitutes they were 'beautiful', deserved better and promised passports and enough money to secure a flat or buy second-hand cars if they would travel with him. Others were simply 'fools' he knew from school – desperate men who were envious of his wealth – and who offered to run 'errands'. A few were off-duty police officers who became Idris' 'bodyguards'. Idris fixed their problems by making them his couriers and carriers in a business that widened to include credit card frauds and the international distribution of heroin and cocaine. Customs agents, immigration officials, passport issuing services and travel agents were all within Idris' employ to smooth the journeys of drug couriers. False documents were bought from Sri Lankans, both for travel and to assist purchases made on 'stolen' credit cards that tourists sold for $1000 – enabling goods valued at up to $10,000s to be bought and resold – before the original owners reported the cards missing 48 hours later (and hence with no cost to the 'victim'). Drug couriers who looked similar to the people whose passports and visas Idris obtained were actively recruited. And some were successful enough to be able to start up business of their own: 'if someone brought two hundred grams of cocaine to India, they could go back' to Nigeria 'with one kilo of heroin'.

Idris explained that some men in Nigeria were so desperate for drugs they offered him sex with their wives: an offer Idris said he always declined, handing over the drugs for free to these men as well as to some destitute students who needed to raise funds to return to Europe. Idris insisted that he had never forced a woman to sleep with him, but at the same time he explained that 'a girl you wanted to sleep with, you give her free drugs for some time, even if she was with another boy. But … if you don't give, she will even say she was ready to do anything'. Idris had been violent to women though. He nearly killed his girl-friend in India after she 'flirted' with another man to secure some cocaine. Idris called her a 'prostitute' and beat her in the street in front of other people in a fit of 'jealousy'. Idris also inflicted a severe 'beating' on the 'junkie' daughter of a wealthy Nigerian he caught stealing from him. And some of his 'girlfriends' also carried his drugs and money for him in case the police came looking. Though one woman had directed blame at Idris when she was caught smuggling drugs in a European airport, Idris explained it should have been obvious to her – like the other couriers he used – why she was travelling on a passport that was not her own. He and she were arrested and imprisoned for this offence.

On another occasion, Idris, then in his mid-30s, was caught travelling with two women with whom he had swallowed drugs in order to bring them into Italy. As usual, he had travelled with several passports – typically concealed in the underwear of women he travelled with – and a stamp, destroying evidence of where he had travelled from, to generate the appearance, at passport control, of having arrived from a European country. But one of the women – who had a child of her own – failed to get her story straight and was subject to an ex-ray, leading to Idris' detection. Hence, by his 40s, convictions for drug trafficking were expediting the collapse of Idris' business, not only because they limited the trips he could make but also because he had to contend with his own des-titution and dependency on heroin upon his release. Idris almost killed himself swallowing heroin he was concealing from the police and spent years living rough in India and Europe. Friends disowned him, he suffered acute depression, made multiple attempts to kill himself and sometimes heard voices informed by the guilt of having made a 'mockery' of his father's name and disgraced his mother. Idris turned his life around when he committed to sharing the gospel in order to save others from 'addiction'.

Faizel: Mixing Business with Pleasure

Faizel was a British citizen in his mid-30s serving a five-year sentence for conspiracy to traffick for the purposes of sexual exploitation. Born to an Iranian father – who was a well-educated socialist and journalist – and a Pakistani mother – whom he regarded as lucky to have married such a 'decent' husband – Faizel came to the UK with his mother and brother aged four on a tourist visa in a bid to reunite with his father who had secured refugee status. Faizel excelled at school, but his studies were seriously disrupted by health complaints, diagnosed later as Crohn's disease. The problems with his bowels affected Faizel's confidence at university, and he struggled to form relationships with women. A paternalistic cousin, who was a successful businessman, treated Faizel to a session with a Thai escort in a five-star hotel, as his first sexual experience. Although Faizel 'didn't connect' emotionally with the woman, it inspired him to seek out other Thai escorts. He developed a pseudo-friendship with another Thai woman and learnt a little about how she booked and worked with clients who hired her to provide sexual services and the rates of commission (30%) that she paid to her agent.

In the course of making another booking for a male friend, Faizel got talking to a 'highly intelligent' and well-educated entrepreneur from Dubai – who was 'only in his early 30s'. This man offered Faizel the opportunity to share a web platform with him and recruit his own Thai sex workers. Aged 18 or 19, Faizel approached a number of Thai sex workers he was acquainted with and recruited five to the new website. Faizel pitched his marketing at American businessmen travelling to London. He also hired, online, a technician from India who worked to ensure the business' website was not thwarted by Google's algorithms, which can make escort websites difficult to find.

Poor attendance and performance at university prompted Faizel's father to give him an ultimatum: either return to his studies or move out. So Faizel withdrew from the business, registered at another university and agreed to marry a Pakistani woman his parents introduced him to, though she never moved to the UK. After his attempts at running a catering business faltered, Faizel approached his friend's girlfriend – also a Thai sex worker – to ask if she would help him re-establish his escort business. She declined the invitation but introduced him to her husband, Zahir, a much older man.

Zahir let properties to Thai sex workers who were recruited through a Thai woman, known as 'Alice', who travelled to Thailand frequently on behalf of various London-based agencies. Zahir was taking commissions for up to 15 Thai women who paid him rent on the ten properties which he owned alongside debt repayments amounting to £35k per woman for support with their migration to the UK. Zahir agreed to work with Faizel for a 50/50 cut of the commission of his own escorts and any women Faizel recruited, the business growing to around 25 workers. This netted Faizel £9000 a month for a few months before the pair were arrested for the offending described below.

Faizel became intimately involved with Ratina, a Thai 'escort' 15 years his senior who took a 'big liking' to him. Once they had sex, Ratina claimed Faizel as her 'boyfriend' to the other Thai escorts, demarcating him 'off limits' to them. This, Faizel had since realized, was a form of 'blackmail', for Ratina threatened to 'discredit' him among the other women if he did not agree to an 'emotional' relationship with her. Having agreed to the relationship, Faizel became obliged to sign a new tenancy agreement for Ratina after she was evicted from the property in which she had been living.

Faizel explained he had 'learnt very early on' that:

> These ladies don't work for you. They're working for them. They can turn around at any point and say, right, can you take my pictures down from your site. So, the minute you act like any bit of a dickhead, that's it.

And, at least when he first started the business, most of the women did not see themselves as completely exploited, some maintaining relationships with several men who paid their rent and remittances, leaving them to keep the 'extra' cash they earnt from other clients.

> Every girl was confident, feisty, aggressive, you know. They were pretty much living the life they wanted to live. You know, they had their designer handbags and these rich financers or part time boyfriends, you know. They're sending a decent money back home and they were … – not 100% – but they were half doing what they'd set out to accomplish.

Faizel regarded it as his responsibility to provide good marketing that involved distinctive webpages with sophisticated photos and profiles that established more personal relationships with clients that would secure repeat custom for the women. He also saw it as his job to hire-in security on the rare occasions it was needed for the women's protection. Hence, despite his conviction for trafficking, Faizel did not feel

> sorry for any of them, not one bit. I – I won't ever do it again, and part of the reason I did it is because of that kind of mutual understanding … I make a little bit, but you make a lot. And that's – that's what I've always been happy with. I didn't want to make a lot and they make a little bit or nothing. I was only ever happy with – I'd take 30% commission and out of that 30%, I'll use 20% to market you and I'll pocket 10%.

There were, however, more vulnerable women working in the business who were unable to pay their debts to Zahir and Alice, including one Thai woman – who Faizel neglected to name – who had become trapped in sexual exploitation. This woman had travelled to the UK with her ex-husband, a government official 20 years her senior, an arrangement having been made to deposit borrowed money (temporarily) in a bank account to demonstrate their eligibility for a UK visa.

After they arrived in the UK, the woman's husband returned immediately to Thailand, while the woman was greeted by Zahir and Ratina, who told her that if she saw four clients a day she would be able to send £500 a month home and earn £100 a week for food, until the £35,000 she owed Zahir had been repaid. The woman had also to cover the costs of web services and getting photographs taken, as charged by Faizel. Although earning well initially, when her income dropped, the woman became 'depressed' and a 'psychological mess'. Zahir blamed her lack of custom on being 'fat', though Faizel explained part of the problem was that the woman could not speak 'a word of English', possibly because she had learning difficulties. The woman's income remained too low to satisfy Zahir, who started 'bothering' her daily for money, forced her to advertise on a public website, assigned men to monitor her, shouted at her and threatened her, retained her passport, made her fearful that the police were coming for her and ultimately tried to arrange for her to be subject to a sham marriage in order to recoup the money he believed he was owed. Another sex worker took the exploited woman to the police, where the two women explained how Faizel had tried to help them secure the custom needed to pay off the debt to Zahir.. Yet, this attempt to exculpate Faizel inevitably incriminated him. Post his conviction, Faizel had no remorse for being involved in what he defined as marketing escort services. He was pessimistic about his future, however, noting that he cannot have children, is likely to get cancer and is unlikely to be ever able to sustain an intimate relationship.

Discussion

These four case studies reveal men engaged in loosely organized networks that facilitated serious crimes. Along with acquaintances, family or friends each man had profited, directly or indirectly, from the exploitation of others. Three of them – Darius, Idris and Faizel – depicted criminal activities in which they were centrally organizing forces, and all four made use of family reputations and connections to take advantage of opportunities to make money quickly. They did so by variously facilitating the sale of sex, laundering money and transporting undocumented migrants. They did not see themselves as traffickers. Instead, they regarded themselves as 'fixers' of other people's problems: men who could find logistical and technical solutions when called upon by those to whom they owed favours. They also rationalized that they were the saviours of destitute people in need of work and money, though this was largely a secondary justification to personal pecuniary goals.

While the events they described were largely in accordance with the definition of organized crime – necessitating three people engaged in ongoing serious crime for profit – the stories they told suggested relationships between offenders and victims that were typically interdependent and, at least on the surface, consensual. This makes their accounts hard to reconcile with the unscrupulousness typically imputed to organized criminals and was a large part of the reason these four participants could not see themselves as irreconcilably 'bad' men.

The Vietnamese migrants whom John transported had paid for journeys he believed they had wanted to take, the first arrivals apparently delighted to make it to London. The sex workers for whom Darius arranged travel were, from his point of view, like any other tourist or friend of a friend, their line of work none of his business. The people who approached Idris for work were desperate for money – they carried drugs and passports for him and with him to secure better lives for themselves. The 'escorts' who worked with Faizel accepted the 'going rates' of commission in order to repay the debts accrued in making their journeys, many of them having been poorly paid sex workers in Southeast Asia before they migrated to the UK. Within these contexts, John, Darius, Idris and Faizel considered themselves to be entrepreneurs, occasionally straddling the line of legality but not unscrupulous exploiters. Though their lives had become entangled with those who were not always able to afford the journeys they had signed up for, swallow the drugs they were paid to transport, or sell sex to men who wanted more than just a massage or escort, all four men continued to regard themselves as relatively competent fixers of problems, albeit too easily swayed by the allure of 'easy money'.

In truth, all four struggled to think beyond the surface level consent secured from victims. While they saw the dire straits faced by the destitute people they were 'helping', they did not fully appreciate how the inequalities – structured by gender, undocumented status and substance dependence – rendered those people's choices far from free and consensual. Rather they were firm believers in making your own luck in life and taking a chance, with who you know as much as what you know. The clandestine nature of the four men's work meant they heard few dissenting voices. They played their cards close to their chests and shared their plans more often with likeminded male acquaintances than female partners. John, Darius, Idris and Faizel seemed to have convinced themselves that they had provided helpful solutions to the challenge border controls present to global inequalities, while proving themselves capable, as men, of earning money, succeeding in business and building reputations for negotiating transactions in illicit service markets.

The four men's stories depicted how they skilfully negotiated cash-based markets, often using contacts made through legitimate businesses. Local demand for sex, labour, drugs or the laundering of cash were the driving forces for their crimes, those men who were multilingual and who had the contacts needed to marry demand in Western Europe with supplies in poorer parts of the world at a competitive advantage. How they became so enterprising had much to do with their home lives and the disruptions to it, in some cases fostered by geopolitical events, but in all cases in the shadow of upbringings with powerful older men whom they idolized. John, Darius, Idris and Faizel each idolized powerful father figures men who were successful in their own lines of work – the nostalgia for the high esteem in which men they regarded as heroes turned bitter when our participants fell short of it, or others highlighted what they had lost through involvement in crime. High masculine ideals reverberated throughout all four of the men's accounts. These ideals centred around self-sufficiency and the capacity, not only to provide for the family but also to access a high life of luxury, partying or casual intimacy that could verge on the 'mad' or reckless. Aspirations to almost unreachable masculine ideals were evident in John's emulation of his dad, the successful bank robber, who left the family wanting for nothing. They were also evident in the aspiration for privilege Darius, Idris and Faizel all associated with successful father figures they revered, and whose expectations they tried to live up to through the pursuit of illicit enterprises that provided them with the respectability of wealth, travel and relationships with women that were typically constructed in instrumental or primarily sexual terms. It was in these contexts that business was routinely 'mixed with pleasure' in ways that obscured the power imbalances entailed, especially in relation to women who were close to destitution.

The networks that facilitated the illegal and legal activities in which these men were involved were versatile and routinely remade depending on the nature of the task in hand. Drug couriers, document forgers, photographers, border enforcement officers, police officers, drivers, security guards, website technicians and recruiters of sex workers were variously hired on casual bases. How central our interviewees became in the undertaking of illicit work – and it was significant that they regarded their crimes as 'work' – was thus highly contingent on what was being organized and what kind of assistance was required. Illegal travel and the transportation of drugs most typically rely on chains of loosely connected actors who can deliver key services, such as transportation from the home country to another pick-up destination, then a complete package of travel and logistics (Paoli, 2002). Their illicit ventures relied upon subcontracting, not unlike that used in legitimate business and government when margins are tight. As in much seemingly legitimate business, returning a profit can require the avoidance of tax through cash-based transactions, the taking of risks and the cutting of corners. Consequently, the 'success' of much cross-border crime is contingent on: the various people involved; their willingness and availability to work – little of which can be secured on a contractual basis; and their aversion to asking questions so that transactions are organized on an exclusively 'need to know' basis. This perhaps also explains why those who are prosecuted for serious organized crime tend to be older, multilingual and able to travel for long periods. Those involved in organizing trafficking networks are, almost by definition, those who also have international networks established through business or through their parents' professional reputations in government, supply chains or criminal enterprises. If our own interviews are anything to go by, those convicted of such crimes tend also to be those whose self-belief is over-inflated in hypermasculine ways and who are thus largely undeterred by previous histories of criminalization because they remain deluded about their capacities to evade law enforcement and net 'easy money'. It was perhaps no coincidence that two were former police officers.

Many policymakers have followed the footsteps of former Secretary-General to the United Nations, Kofi Annan, in depicting traffickers as barely indistinguishable from terrorists and international drug dealers whose profiteering threatens the very fabric of civil society. Criminologists, conversely, have noted how the criminal careers of those implicated in people smuggling and trafficking tend, by necessity, to be embedded in a network of 'social relations' that provide 'access to suppliers, co-offenders and profitable criminal opportunities' that are not necessarily centrally organized (Kleemans, 2014: 43). This is because the 'most stable illegal enterprises are those relying on pre-existing non-economic ties' (Paoli, 2002: 84), local connections, debts of loyalty and familial relationships. It is, however, also the case that organized crime is not always conceived as ruthlessly profit-driven, much like enterprise within the governmental and business sectors where who you know can matter as much as what you know and making a bit on the side can be justified if all parties can be assumed to have benefitted in some way (Paoli, 2002).

The men whose stories we have presented here often relied on relatives and friends for business opportunities and introductions to people seemingly in need of illicit work or illicit travel. While each had, at times, regarded themselves as Mr Big and each had enabled substantial flow of cash for illicit business, none sustained substantial profits for long. 'Work' and 'business' that came to be defined as trafficking was sometimes little more than a side-line, supplementing income from other legitimate activities or a consequence of working at the margins of the law when things went wrong with sex workers or other desperate people who could not meet the terms of deals struck with numerous others. As each was to learn upon their imprisonment, despite their bravado, John, Darius, Idris and Faizel were replaceable in the illicit enterprises they serviced. In most instances, their acquaintances resumed without them, picking up their work, much as would be the case in any line of businesses, bad or good. What was no less revelatory was how, upon their convictions, the personal lives of each of these men fell apart, evoking new crises of masculinity as they were confronted with aging alone, faltering family relationships, failing health and fewer prospects for succeeding in business again.

5   Sham Marriage

Sham Marriage as Form of Modern Slavery

Followers of the British press could be forgiven for thinking that an epidemic of modern slavery had overtaken the UK during the last decade and for concluding that the epitome of its cruelty was apparent in the phenomenon of 'sham marriage'. The BBC programme *Humans for Sale* (BBC, 2017) reported that 'Eastern European crime gangs are repeatedly forcing trafficked women into sexual exploitation and sham marriages' in Scotland. *The Guardian* has previously reported that in Manchester a 'trafficking ring sold pregnant women into sham marriage' (Press Association, 2014). The *Daily Mail* has drawn attention to those it dubbed 'the Sainsbury's gang who made over £500,000 by arranging sham marriages between Asian immigrants and Eastern European brides' (Riley, 2018), while *The Express* claimed that 'sham marriages have increased by almost 850%' during the 'refugee crisis' as more people turn to 'criminal gangs' that make 'huge profits' by circumventing immigration law (Mowat, 2016). In response, the Director of Public Prosecutions, Alison Saunders, argued for new powers to track 'traffickers and those who assist them' leaving 'a trail of criminal conduct across a number of countries where victims have been exploited or harmed while in transit' before being subject to 'forced labour or domestic servitude, forced criminality, in sexual exploitation or sham marriages' (CPS, 2018a). And the Home Office (2017: 9) issued guidance to practitioners that explained how 'traffickers transport EU national victims to the UK and sell these victims to an exploiter in a one-off transaction' who then 'marry victims to gain immigration advantages and often sexually abuse them'.

This conflation of 'sham marriage' – traditionally an immigration offence between two consenting adults, one of whom might pay the other to gain residency or citizenship – with 'trafficking', 'modern slavery', 'forced marriage' and 'sexual servitude' is more perplexing than this commentary conveys. First, neither the 2014 Modern Slavery Strategy (Home Office, 2014) nor the 2015 Modern Slavery Act referred at all to sham marriages. Their focus was primarily on 'slavery' and 'servitude' in relation to 'forced or compulsory labour', 'sexual exploitation', the 'removal of organs' and the 'securing of services through

DOI: 10.4324/9780429053986-5

threats or deception'. Hence, sham marriage is not a category of modern slavery routinely counted in police and National Referral Mechanism statistical reports. 'Forced marriages' were actually outlawed in separate legislation in 2014 in Scotland and in England under their respective Anti-social Behaviour and Crime and Policing Acts (Home Office/FOCO, 2018). This legislation, mirrored roughly in both jurisdictions, introduced sentences of up to seven years for those who 'forced' others into marriages, while strengthening the provision of protection orders for victims and potential victims (Chantler et al., 2017). Forced marriages, however, were construed then neither as modern slavery nor immigration offending but instead as a form of honour-based violence, involving young people being sent, often by their parents, to countries from which their families originated in order to marry.

Press coverage of a high-profile case of forced marriage in Birmingham in May 2018 was subsequently seized upon by campaigning groups who asked why, four years after the forced marriage legislation had been past, only a couple of cases had been prosecuted, and whether prosecuting forced marriages as modern slavery might deliver better outcomes for victims (Summers, 2018). But such requests came at the tail end of legislative moves that configured tackling modern slavery as an essential component of the hostile environment policy. This began with the sandwiching of the 2015 Modern Slavery Act between the 2014 and 2016 Immigration Acts. In turn, the multi-agency working these new laws fostered led to modern slavery to be conceptualized in practice as a problem of immigration-related offending. Though rarely a focus of policing operations in the year after the Modern Slavery Act was implemented (NPCC, 2016), the Home Office sought subsequently to redefine sham marriage as a modern slavery offence. The *Typology of Modern Slavery*, for example, released by the Home Office in 2017 (Cooper et al., 2017), identified 'sham marriage', 'forced begging', 'child sexual exploitation' and 'county lines' as new forms of modern slavery comparable with sex trafficking and labour exploitation. Yet the inclusion of sham marriage was hard to reconcile within a framework organized around coercion and in the absence of many actual criminal cases. In one part of the typology, the authors suggested that some 'exploiters make no financial gain from the offence' of sham marriage, arguing that the 'motivation may be solely for personal gratification or gaining non-monetary advantage such as immigration status from forced sham marriages' (Cooper et al., 2017: 9). Several pages later, however they explain that 'not all sham marriages are modern slavery' and that only those with an 'element of being forced or deceived' should be conceived as such (p.12). Examples of being forced into a sham marriage then include those attempting to leave sex work who are forced by their pimps into 'other forms of exploitation such as domestic servitude, criminal exploitation or sham marriage, or … raped' (p.31) as well as those who emigrate into the UK with the help of 'traffickers' under the pretence of providing legitimate work and who are then either sold for marriage or married for immigration purposes to repay debts incurred on their journey.

Sham Marriage as an Immigration Offence

Before the advent of modern slavery law, sham marriages were not usually equated with marriages that were 'forced', though there were cases where one partner had deceived the other into believing they were loved. Instead, sham marriages were those 'of convenience', pursued throughout history by people: fleeing persecution because of their 'race' or sexuality; escaping poverty; avoiding marriage to someone they did not wish to live with; and securing property or respectability (Messinger, 2017). These kinds of 'marriages of convenience' between EU and non-EU nationals were criminalized as 'sham marriages' in the UK via Section 24 of the 1999 Immigration and Asylum Act, when the then Labour government began to fear that marriages were being arranged as the principal means by which immigration law was being circumvented (Wray, 2015a). Concern with marriage migration in Britain, however, dates to the days of the British Empire as Wray (2015a) explains. After the Second World War controls were put in place to stop single men from the Commonwealth from entering the UK primarily because dark-skinned unmarried men were regarded, amidst the racism of the time, as sexually predatory and hence a threat to British women. To allay white people's concerns about 'crime' and 'miscegenation', only married men from the Commonwealth were permitted to come with their families to meet labour shortages. As the Windrush commenced, the law incentivized marriage among would-be migrants. Then, as fears were stoked around the possibility of 'floods' of migrants arriving as extended families joined settled workers, the rules were changed again. The 1962 Commonwealth Immigrants Act responded to white racism by redefining as 'second class citizens' those black people who had been welcomed as part of the empire, instigating a train of what now looks like schizophrenic policy-making in relation to marriage migration (Fryer, 1984: 374).

First, the 1962 Act moved to reduce 'the inflow of black people in Britain' by subjecting Commonwealth citizens to entry control and permitting the deportation of those who committed offences within five years of arrival (ibid. p.382). To further restrict immigration, the British banned women from the Commonwealth from bringing non-white husbands with them to the UK, unless a special case could be made (Wray, 2015a). Then in 1974, the 'primary purpose rule' was introduced, requiring non-white migrants to demonstrate that the *primary purpose* of their marriages was *not* to secure entry for their spouse into the UK. This change in law made life more difficult for those families – especially from the Indian subcontinent – who cultivated *arranged marriages* across countries to maintain diaspora ties and who, for cultural and religious reasons, frowned upon marriages entered purely for 'love' (Wray, 2015c). As the question of how to differentiate 'genuine marriages' from 'sham' ones proved increasingly difficult to resolve in practice, politics fixated on the menacing figure of the devious male migrant – 'liable to instrumentalize and manipulate their family ties for their personal advantage' – taunting politicians about their inability to control immigration as promised (Wray, 2015b: 425). Successive British administrations, as Benson and Charsley (2015) note, found themselves stoking moral panics about the vulnerabilities of Britain's borders which they could not then de-escalate. 'Sham marriage' became regarded, they argue, as 'the ultimate deception', offending the state's right to control its borders and an institution idealized, politically, as the cornerstone of family life and hence the nation (p.227). This is why judges summing up or passing sentences on sham marriages describe how such law violations are 'striking at the heart of the immigration system' (Evans, 2013; Williams, 2016) even when no individual victim appears to have been harmed. It is also part of the reason why the UK's purported 'vassalage' to the European Union's commitment to freedom of movement was so castigated by the campaigns that won the Brexit referendum in 2016.

The revoking (in 1997) of the 'primary purpose' rule and the repeal (in 2011) of the Certificate of Approval scheme that came to replace it both occurred because of legal judgements – in the High Court, Court of Appeal and House of Lords (p.223) – which concluded that the UK was in breach of Article 8 of the European Convention on Human Rights. By requiring non-EEA nationals and their EEA partners to get state permission to marry and prove their relationships were genuine, the UK was deemed to be denying its citizens the right to the possibility of a family life. In response, in 2012, the UK's Home Secretary, Theresa May, promised a 'crack down' on sham marriages to 'end' what she regarded as 'the abuse' of Article 8 (Hennessey, 2012; D'Aoust, 2018). While the 2015 Modern Slavery Act became celebrated as her flagship initiative, May's clampdown was achieved through the 2014 Immigration Act and the instructions issued by the Home Office (2021e: 10) that enabled the assessment of marriages against 'intelligence' and 'evidence-based risk profiles'. The new legislation and accompanying practice guidance that supported it extended the powers of the state to investigate marriages and civil partnerships where one party was not a UK national to assess (as chapter 2, para 5: 2 of the 2014 Immigration Act conceptualizes it) whether:

> there is no genuine relationship between the parties to the marriage, and
> … either, or both, of the parties to the marriage enter into the marriage
> for one or more of these purposes: (i) avoiding the effect of one or more
> provisions of United Kingdom immigration law or the immigration rules;
> (ii) enabling a party to the marriage to obtain a right conferred by that law
> or those rules to reside in the United Kingdom.

Foreign nationals found to have entered sham marriages could then be removed, have their leave to remain curtailed or be prosecuted as 'immigration offenders' thus incurring sentences of up to 14 years of imprisonment for assisting unlawful immigration to an EU Member State (Bolt, 2016; CPS, 2018b).

The 2016 Immigration Act further raised the thresholds that non–EU citizens needed to meet in order to enter a marriage that the British government might deem 'genuine'. Sponsors of foreign nationals had to show they had good incomes and steady jobs, or otherwise savings of £62,500. Prospective foreign national spouses had also to prove, as Theresa May insisted, that they had 'a genuine attachment to the UK, be able to speak English, and integrate into our society, and they must not be a burden on the taxpayer' (D'Aoust, 2018: 48). In short, the 'genuineness' of their commitment had to be evidenced towards the state and the economy as much as towards their partners. Registrars had to work with border force to take stock of how well marrying couples knew each other, shared a common language, were of similar age, planned to live together, what they wore at their wedding, the number of guests who attended and how well they were known to the couple, and whether the couple shared a visa compliant history of visiting the UK (Bolt, 2016; D'Aoust, 2013) – the latter increasingly difficult to achieve.

Marriage in the Moral Economy of Suspicion

As the various critiques of this legal reform have underlined, foreign nationals who marry EU citizens now play against high stakes in this 'moral economy of suspicion', especially when their relationships depart from Western 'romantic' norms (D'Aoust, 2018). Indeed, how normative romance is as a basis for marriage among Europeans has been questioned too (Chantler, 2014; Wray, 2015a). Many Western couples who marry for romance, subsequently fall out of love and stay together out of convention or for their children. Many relationships begin with online communication between strangers whose compatibility has been assessed using algorithmic calculations that include location-based and economic factors. And many marriages that are 'arranged' to continue ties of kinship provide a home, 'respectability' and/or a financial union do become loving and romantic. Indeed, such marriages are not only common among some diaspora communities but also among celebrities and monarchy (Wray, 2015a). It is thus grossly unfair when people who consider their relationship to be 'genuine' are prohibited from living in the same country as their partners and children on the basis of the political economy of suspicion that has grown around marriage. It is also deeply problematic that a system designed to reduce illegal immigration has the potential to generate more of the same problem, as those who make the pragmatic decision to marry someone to 'give the relationship a chance' against the hurdles of border controls, and visa restrictions are deemed 'deviant'. Such self-fulfilling tendencies are evident not only in the UK but also in many European states where a 'rescue narrative' predominates, depicting 'poor, deceived women' as victims of calculating men, typically Muslim or African, from whom they must be saved by thankless immigration inspectors (Maskens, 2015: 44; Agustín, 2007).

Case Studies

But what of those who actually do seek to deliberately subvert immigration law through marriage, whose marriages are totally shambolic, based exclusively on a financial exchange to secure residency within the EU? Who are the sham marriage folk devils against which politicians, anti-trafficking tsars, the media and some parts of the NGO sector rile? Are they really and merely exploiters, traffickers and evil-doers as many media commentary claims? In the case studies that follow, we answer some of these questions, presenting a much more complex picture of dependency and indebtedness that reveal the circumstances within which two of our participants were convicted for sham marriage offences. The first is Rasheed a Pakistani national in his late 30s and the second is Estelle, also in her 30s, a Portuguese national whose family were Africans who migrated from the Portuguese colony of Cape Verde before she was born.

Rasheed: Dodging Deportation

Rasheed was serving a lengthy sentence for entering a sham – or as he asserted, 'arranged' – marriage with a younger woman from Eastern Europe who he had purportedly raped and forced into domestic servitude. A man of small build and timid demeanour, his 'heart' was 'broken', tears welling in his eyes many times during the two interviews. These were conducted in English, though quite broken on Rasheed's part, having taught himself the language during his years in custody and not having been at all fluent during his trial. Sometimes out of Islamic respect for the family who was implicated in his crimes, sometimes because he was fearful of insulting the interviewer's home country – Britain – Rasheed's first interview was more guarded than his second and marked by occasional apologies. This was less the case in the second interview, where Rasheed referred to the interviewer as 'brother' (before apologizing), though there were still some words and phrases that were difficult to discern, perhaps because he lapsed into Urdu, the word 'insallah' (God willing), used to preface hopes for the future. Having served five years in prison, and anticipating deportation before the end of his sixth, Rasheed explained he had no reason to 'lie', agreeing to participate in the research because he did not want 'any other Muslim men like' him coming to prison and suffering the 'shame' that was so upsetting for him. Rasheed was struggling with insomnia, loneliness and depression in a prison that had exposed him to 24–72-hour lock ups. In the absence of family visits, under pressure to take and deal drugs, and with his only friend having been suddenly deported, the prison had given him the appearance of 'a 60 year' old. Rasheed's mother, now suffering from heart problems and diabetes, cries when he rings her, while his sister insists that they 'need' him back in Pakistan, even though he has no money to bring with him.

Rasheed was raised in a very rural part of the Khyber Pakhtunkhwa Province (KPK) – the site of militarized conflict between Taliban and US forces post-9/

11 – his family having migrated from Afghanistan a 'long, long time' ago. The region was regarded by the US government to have significant problems with child exploitation, the trafficking out of young men to work in wealthier countries and bonded labour, the latter of which specifically affects men aged 18 who are ineligible for the welfare protections made for children and who put their families at risk of retributive attacks if they report exploitation to the authorities (US Department of State, 2017). In KPK, 'love marriages' are greeted with disapproval and often policed through the threat of violence (EASO, 2015). 'Arranged marriages' to extend and consolidate family ties are the norm (Werbner, 1990), though daughters are still sometimes exchanged to resolve disputes in rural and tribal areas (EASO, 2015).

Rasheed's own parents were farmers – living in a remote area with no main gas supply. They had been taken in by a parliamentarian during the partition of Afghanistan and Pakistan as indentured labourers on his farm. The parliamentarian not only provided the family with shelter, food and clothing but also education for the children in return for their parents' labour. As the oldest son, Rasheed came to occupy a special position on the farm as the 'chicken manager'. The parliamentarian was like a 'father' to him and Rasheed felt deeply indebted to him. When the parliamentarian died, Rasheed, then in his 20s, 'lost everything'. Though in an arranged marriage, with a wife who was pregnant with a daughter he had never seen, Rasheed decided he needed 'to go ... to do something' for his 'family', to seek a 'better life'. An older cousin offered 'sponsorship' so Rasheed could work in the off-licence he owned in Britain. Rasheed wanted to come, knowing Britain to be a 'good country' with 'human rights and healthcare'.

Despite having only secured a tourist visa, Rasheed worked 14–16-hour night shifts – 'like slave' – in the off-license, seven days a week, for just £200, plus bed and food above the shop. This bleak existence proved of concern to at least one of the shop's customers, a man from the mosque who attempted to persuade Rasheed to leave and insisted that selling alcohol was not the 'Islamic way'. Having breached the terms of his tourist visa – which required regular returns to Pakistan – Rasheed was arrested by UK border force two years into his stay. He was then released on a requirement to report back to the police weekly and advised deportation was imminent. Rasheed's cousin offered to help Rasheed resolve his predicament by introducing him to a series of people who charged him money for their advice and services.

In the first instance, Rasheed borrowed money from local Muslims to pay a politician in another city £8,500 for a diplomat's visa which failed to materialize. Then he paid a further £550 to an 'immigration lawyer' – who was probably no more than an unqualified 'advisor' – who suggested he apply for political asylum, Rasheed having a 'real case' because of his engagement in opposition politics in KPK. While this holding response was pursued, the immigration advisor suggested Rasheed pursue another 'arranged' marriage that would secure him citizenship in the UK. The best option, he was advised, was to marry a British Pakistani woman, but as Rasheed could be deported at any time, an alternative 'easy' option was also presented: marriage to an EU national for a fee. Rasheed's cousin then introduced him to an expert 'dealer' who had previously arranged 'fifty' such 'happy' 'arranged marriages'. Rasheed considered taking a second wife to be 'shameful' but the dealer appeased his concerns by explaining that the woman had 'no family' – her father was in prison and her mother was divorced – so she needed a 'hard worker' and would want to live with him 'as wife forever'. In what sounded like a high-pressure sales trick, Rasheed was offered a 75% discount on the dealer's usual £20,000 fee: an 'arranged marriage' for just £5000, £4000 of which was paid to 'a girl from Europe' who he had 'never' seen 'before'. The dealer promised to register the wedding in Scotland where the law was more permissive.

Rasheed thus 'settled' on this exchange: 'She still my wife, including the Islamic way … She's happy and she's agreed'. Immediately after the wedding, however, he realized what a 'big mistake' he had made. The whole problem, he explained, 'start from money': his and her dire need for it. After the wedding, Rasheed's new wife, who, like him, spoke little English, started asking for payment, having been told she would receive a further £5000 from Rasheed. The two of them tried to resolve their dispute via a phone call with the dealer, who told Rasheed the woman was 'crazy' but who also seemed to have encouraged her to keep asking for the extra payment. What happened next is a matter of contention, Rasheed claiming he was set up by his cousin to take the blame and, contrary to what was claimed in court, did not 'rape' the woman or take her 'hostage'. Rasheed's new wife was perturbed by his beard, he explained, asking him to shave it off on their first night, which he was unwilling to do. They did have sexual intercourse, Rasheed admitted, 'but not what she say – not like this … She changed her story' – the charge of rape having compounded his modern slavery conviction. Even she, his sham wife, Rasheed explained, had told the police that Rasheed had said he loved her. He thought that she loved him too and assumed they would be together 'forever': 'I still love her. I still missing her. I have no issue with her'. Asked explicitly if she 'wanted' him to have a 'physical' relationship with her, Rasheed replied, 'She say "no, no"', but when probed he implied that either she or he felt it was necessary to consummate the relationship to meet immigration requirements.

> I don't like this system, but I have no choice … because I need to keep her happy … and she go with me to Scotland and she go with me to the Home Office and immigration. I get visa.

Rasheed was insistent that his new wife was not held hostage by him in the five days they spent together – retaining receipts for basic cosmetics and takeaways they had bought together. He asked how he could 'kidnap' her, given how confined he was to the shop and by border agency's surveillance of him. Meanwhile, in the days that followed the wedding, Rasheed's new wife travelled to five British cities (possibly with the dealer and his partner), mostly staying with friends with whom she felt more 'comfortable'. Rasheed claimed that CCTV footage of their movements had been suppressed at trial and that his wife's claims to have been physically assaulted by him were refuted by a medical examination that concluded her injuries were historic and most likely caused by injecting a 'needle'.

When, seven days after the wedding, they had both been arrested, Rasheed explained, that his new wife was offered an interpreter and he was not, though he really needed one. Rasheed believed that while he was detained in police custody, she was offered the chance to return home if she changed her story to put the blame on him. She was a 'liar' who 'thought up this game', he explained, but she did so because she was also a 'half victim', cheated as much as he was and in a lot of 'trouble' with the law. Rasheed was convicted under the 2015 Modern Slavery Act in part because his defence was prepared by a solicitor who was a life-long friend of his cousin. The cousin had sought to exonerate himself, pleading with Rasheed not to implicate him because he had a disabled child. Rasheed obliged, having been advised he would be deported to Pakistan immediately, only to then see his cousin turn witness against him. Five years on, Rasheed was still desperate to go home, his time in Britain leaving him with 'nothing' but 'fear', 'shame' and 'heart' break: and the religious belief that he should 'try to forget everything and forgive everything'.

Estelle: Indebted Broker

Estelle was serving a four-and-a-half-year custodial sentence for trafficking for the purposes of sham marriage between Portuguese and Nigerian nationals. The interviews were conducted in the mother and baby unit of a prison and in English. Events in her past in the present tense. Estelle's 'life' had 'been hard': a phrase she repeated eight times over the two interviews. Estelle's parents had migrated from Cape Verde (a former Portuguese colony) to Portugal before she was born and although she, unlike her brothers, had never been to Cape Verde she was obligated indirectly to the family there, supporting them through remittances she made to her mother.

Estelle's parents separated when she was eight or younger, and her father died of Hepatitis B a year later. Estelle was treated as an intermediary by her parents when they separated and had suffered enduring grief ever since her father's death. She took a beach job at age 14 'to try to help' her 'mum' before coming to England for the first time, aged 18, in search of work. Failing to find any, she returned to Portugal and did not return to the UK again until five years later. In the intervening years, she had two children with her first husband, an older man who was 'jealous' and 'controlling' and physically violent. Though she felt she had no 'life', Estelle stayed to avoid the stigma a broken relationship would incur from the African community of which she and her mother were a part. In the interim her brother became abusive to her mother, having developed problems with his mental health, drugs, violence and the police. He was subsequently diagnosed with schizophrenia following his release from a prison sentence. Released from her marriage as her husband's infidelity became apparent, Estelle, aged 23, decided to return to the UK fearing her mother and brother would 'die' of starvation if she did not raise an income to support them.

In England, Estelle took various jobs as a cleaner and undertook English language classes. She missed her children, who she had left with her mum, but experienced a sense of liberation from her old life – 'I'm free in this country' – able to send money home to her mum as well as go out clubbing. It was in a nightclub (aged about 25) that Estelle was introduced by friends to a Nigerian man – Mark. Mark arranged for Estelle's children to join her in England, paying for their flights, helping her secure a council house and find schools for them. Mark 'wanted to be more than friends' with Estelle, but she was clear that she did not 'want a relationship' or 'need more babies'. She nevertheless found herself under renewed pressure to send more money back to her mother. Her brother had attacked their mum – now unable to work regularly due to diabetes and cataracts – and had stolen her television and what little money she had. Her mother's new partner, with whom she had another child, started working away from home without sending money back, before he was suddenly killed in a car crash. The money Estelle was earning as a cleaner was simply 'not enough' to support everyone.

It was then that Estelle visited a casino for the first time and won, to her surprise, £36 from a £1 bet. She started visiting casinos more regularly as well as betting shops and gambling online. For a while, she was able to send more money to her mum, pay her bills and buy things for her children. Predictably the gambling got out of control though, causing Estelle to lose '£1,000 one day'. Mark, who knew about the 'situation', suggested – perhaps in a way that was meant to 'intimidate' – that Estelle recruit women to take part in sham marriages to alleviate her financial hardship. At first Estelle 'refused' Mark's request, but when the 'bills' mounted and the implications of her 'mum's disease' became apparent, she agreed.

Estelle's role was 'to convince the girls to do it' – to recruit, persuade and organize travel for women from Portugal in return for £1,000–£2,000 per person while Mark contacted men from Nigeria who would secure a right to remain in the UK through sham marriages. Estelle knew women 'in struggles in Portugal with money for a job' and felt that it was 'easy money, I can do it'. She arranged three sham marriages: two with women from Portugal and men from Nigeria and one with a Nigerian woman, for her cousin, in Portgual, man from Portugal: who had 'problem with money to pay for kids, childcare'. The first woman that Estelle recruited had 'been in a bad life … consumed drugs, drinking and [had a] lot of debt' but spoke little English. Estelle arranged for her travel and introduced the woman to Mark who then bought the travel tickets.

Two years on, having met Brendon, her current husband, Estelle wanted to end her involvement in sham marriages, go back to a 'normal' job and stop gambling. Brendon supported Estelle in this, and she had a child with him a year later. At the same time, the situation with her brother improved as she was able to pay to 'put him in a clinic' costing '600 Euros a month', sparing him the risk of re-imprisonment and her mother the daily threat of violence.

But then Estelle herself was arrested. One of the women whose marriages she had organized had been caught because she 'tried to do it again with another person' because she needed more money. Estelle confessed to her part in the arrangements and went to prison, where she gave birth again. Her cousin and the women who had tried to re-marry were convicted. Mark, however, was never charged as the police had 'no proof' of his involvement, and he did not want to implicate himself: 'he wash his hands of me'. Brendon, Estelle's new husband, was also convicted though he had no knowledge of Estelle having used his credit card to buy a plane ticket. The two of them had, nevertheless, agreed that they would 'start again' upon Estelle's release, Brendon now waiting for her in Portugal having completed his sentence.

Discussion

In this chapter, we have presented the cases of two people convicted for offences involving sham marriage. In neither case was the main 'broker' of the marriages charged. In both cases, the convicted perpetrator was in no sense an organized criminal. They were both better described as destitute and desperate individuals making poor choices against a backcloth of intense pressures that were acutely financial, underscored by a degree of cultural difference and borne out of intergenerational histories of migration in the face of inequalities and insecurities left behind by European colonialism. Rasheed was more a victim of modern slavery than a perpetrator, indentured labour – the only life he had known until he became enslaved working long hours daily for very low pay in a shop in Britain where he lived. He lost what little he had before being duped into purchasing what he regarded as an 'arranged marriage' to avoid deportation, having overstayed on a tourist visa secured initially so he could send money home. As the oldest son in his family at a time when the security offered by indentured labour was being withdrawn amidst the political instability on the border between Pakistan and Afghanistan, he had considered it his duty to seek work abroad, leaving his wife and daughter behind.

Estelle had been under constant financial pressure to provide for her children and her mother, and the extended family she supported when the new crisis of her stepfather's death and the need to fund her brother's mental health treatment came to a head. Her first marriage was abusive and, despite her best efforts to avoid becoming indebted to him, Estelle was cajoled by Mark, after all he had done for her and her children, to enter the sham marriage business as the debts generated by her gambling accumulated. Estelle perceived her role as a 'provider' for her mother and children, a central feature of Cape Verdean communities where 'the mother-child dyad has constituted the backbone of … society' (Drotbohm, 2009: 137). None of the men in her life had provided for her or her mother – not her father, stepfather or first husband. All the men in her life had pursued subsequent relationships that left Estelle responsible for the larger family unit connected to her mother: 'That is the problem with African mans', as she understood it. As with Rasheed, Estelle became responsible for providing for her family from a very young age and without a foundation in education or skills that would generate a substantial income.

To the extent that involvement in sham marriages presented opportunities to overcome these economic pressures, it did so against cultural understandings that neither prohibited polygamous relationship nor anticipated romance as the primary basis for marriage. Although Cape Verdeans cannot be considered a culturally homogenous group (Batalha, 2004), there is a history of male extra-marital relations there which is characterized by fathers/husbands not working, drinking and providing little material, emotional or financial support to the mothers of their children (Åkesson, 2009; Drotbohm, 2009). Marriage in Cape Verde (and in Cape Verdean diasporas) can be regarded as a 'weak institution, unions are unstable and matrifocal households are common' (Åkesson, 2009: 384). This was Estelle's experience too, hence it is hard to imagine that she saw arranging sham marriages as especially immoral, given that there was no discernible victim in the arrangements – all parties receiving remuneration or immigration status – and that her own experience of sexual relationships was one of entrapment and abandonment. Rasheed, by contrast, did find himself caught in a moral dilemma, but this was resolved for him by the broker and his cousin persuading him that he was doing the right thing by providing for the young woman he was 'arranging' to marry and saving her from a terrible home life. 'Love', in the Islamic tradition in which he was raised, came after marriage and was hence not the basis for it. He presumed that sexual consummation would provide evidence to immigration officials of the genuineness of his marriage to a vulnerable woman whom he assumed was knowledgeable about the requirements of immigration law. This presumption motivated the horrific outcome – the rape of an already exploited vulnerable woman whom he barely knew and did not share a common language – cementing his conviction for modern slavery and securing Rasheed a 12-year prison sentence. The case against Rasheed was made in a language he did not understand, in a country he had barely explored given his confinement to a single shop seven days per week, and with legal representation that was serving the best interests of the relative who was exploiting him. The case against Rasheed appeared not to have taken stock of his own entrapment, realized in part by his cousin's ability to exploit his fear of deportation.

What we have shown in these cases is that, faced with prosecution for facilitating illegal immigration under new and old immigration laws, some people submit that they are coerced by the person they married or the people who facilitated sham marriages, despite having sought a union for which they were paid. In this context, modern slavery law re-establishes a false binary between victim and victimizer which repositions the state as vigilante: seeking out hostile foreigners who present an affront to British values and the sanctity of marriage and the family life assumed to underpin it; and whose amorality is underlined by their capacity to commit the heinous crime of exploiting vulnerable European women and girls. What is lost in this framing, as Wray (2015a: 5) argues, is how in 'an unequal world with few opportunities for movement from poor to rich countries, marriage is an important means of procuring global and thus social mobility'. Now marriages procured to secure social mobility among the poorest people in the world are becoming the site for the border policing that the discourse of combatting modern slavery routinely smuggles in. As it became more difficult for non-EU nationals to marry British nationals under UK law, some non-EU nationals sought to regularize their immigration status in the UK by marrying non-British EU citizens before exploiting EU freedom of movement in exchange for payment. By threatening those who facilitate illegal immigration with the prospect of up to 14 years of imprisonment, British immigration law had created unsavoury incentives for EU citizens who had profited – however minimally – from sham marriages to exculpate themselves by presenting as victims of modern slavery and giving evidence against alleged 'perpetrators' they had colluded with.

Hence, one consequence of operationalizing modern slavery law through immigration law, as we have shown, is that some of the world's most destitute people become convicted of modern slavery offences, their crimes presented as involving more coercion and violence than is sometimes claimed. These factors are very rarely considered in the courtroom or in media reports of modern slavery, the absence of access to adequate legal representation for poor foreign national offenders rendering them largely defenceless in court. Post their convictions, there is almost no consideration of their rehabilitation or resettlement needs, since it is assumed they will be deported back to their home countries. The needs of these offenders' own children and parents, who are often dependent on them, rarely feature in such decision-making. While not wishing to deny the horrors experienced by those who are forced into marriages, we conclude that deeper questions need to be asked about why some people pay to enter marriages for immigration purposes or arrange sham marriages and that greater reflection is needed as to whether passing punitive sentences on those desperate enough to do so is genuinely socially just. At present, neither the law nor public debate is sufficiently equipped to deal with the complexities of the lives of the people who become implicated in such cases. The lack of real choices made by 'perpetrators' living at the sharp ends of postcolonial inequalities, international conflicts and unforgiving immigration regulation is rarely, if ever, considered in explanations of why some people become implicated in these crimes.

6   Domestic Servitude

In this chapter we look at the phenomenon of domestic servitude, focussing specifically on a married couple of Nigerian heritage who considered themselves to have been wrongfully convicted of this form of modern slavery. Domestic servitude is technically a subcategory of labour exploitation that happens in the privacy of family homes as opposed to commercial workplaces. Exploiters can be partners, typically husbands and wives, other family members or unrelated employers who have hired a home 'help' to provide cooking, housework or childcare in private residences. Though victims are sometimes physically abused or degraded, their exploitation is fundamentally defined by being unable to leave working conditions that are unbearable in nature or entail labouring for long hours for little or no pay. Entrapment in these kinds of working conditions can be compounded when exploiters withhold the passports of those they are exploiting or threaten violence, but it can also become entrenched for workers whose right to be in the host country is dependent on remaining married to the exploiter or within their employ.

For these reasons, domestic servitude is often depicted as the archetypal form of modern slavery, involving the entrapment of typically young female workers who are socially isolated behind closed doors and afraid to seek the help of law enforcement lest they are deported. Despite this, neither the prevalence nor causes of domestic servitude in the UK are widely understood. Much of the public debate about modern slavery merely lists domestic servitude as an 'exploitation type' that can coincide with sexual exploitation within illicit markets or labour exploitation within commercial workplaces. As with all other forms of modern slavery, figures on the number of offenders holding victims in domestic servitude are hard to come by. As discussed in Chapter 2, relatively few offenders are convicted annually under Modern Slavery Act 2015. No breakdown is currently provided as to how many of those convictions involved domestic servitude as opposed to other forms of slavery and compulsory labour. Official counts of the number of potential victims being considered in the National Referral Mechanism, however, suggest domestic servitude is pervasive in the UK, though less common than most other forms of modern slavery – organ trafficking is the consistent exception. The percentages of cases relating to domestic servitude considered by the NRM varied from 3% to 17% between

DOI: 10.4324/9780429053986-6

2009 and 2018 (ONS, 2020b). During this period, the volume of referrals for domestic servitude rose steadily until 2017.

The majority of victims of domestic servitude considered by the NRM between 2009 and 2018 were women, 361 of the 509 cases considered in 2018 relating to female adults and children. As Table 6.1 illustrates, most were over 18 at the time of their referral. However, as we explain below, many of the adult women who do become trapped in domestic servitude are children or teenagers when they begin providing similar kinds of labour for very low pay.

In 2016, *The Guardian* newspaper reported on the sentencing of Safraz Ahmed, 'the first Briton convicted of forcing their spouse into domestic servitude' (Walker, 2016). Ahmed had 'abused, demeaned and taunted his Pakistani wife, Sumara Iram, over a two-year period'. She had lived like a 'prisoner' who was 'never allowed to step out of the house alone and … was not allowed to make friends': 'I cooked, I cleaned, I washed, I ironed, looked after other people's children and when things were not to the liking of the family I was punished by beatings'. By way of contrast, most journalistic coverage of women who become trapped in providing this kind of domestic labour under exploitative conditions focuses not on spouses but on the cases of nannies, home-helps and carers from overseas who are unable to leave their private homes in which they work, beyond the reach of the regulations and customs that govern most employment, and whose social isolation leaves few clues that might alert the police of a need to investigate. British news reporting has concentrated predominantly on the trafficking of Nigerian girls assumed to be abducted by the militant group known both as Islamic State in West Africa (ISWA) and 'Boko Haram' (Bentham, 2019) – literally translated as 'western education is forbidden' – who demand ransoms for the hundreds of children they have taken hostage in direct raids on schools (UN News, 2021).

The personal tragedies endured by young Nigerian women in Britain hired as domestic helpers are usually relayed anecdotally in the media:

> An unnamed 'Nigerian girl' was 'trafficked aged nine after being sold by a relative for £3,000 and used as a domestic slave … subjected to beatings, sexual harassment and "juju" witchcraft threats and was gang-raped at the age of 13 by a group of boys known to her female enslaver, who forced her to have an abortion after becoming pregnant as a result'.
>
> (Bentham, 2019)

> A 14-year-old called 'Josephine', who 'never knew her parents and spent her childhood working as a servant for relatives in Nigeria' was subjected to physical 'punishments … when she was deemed to be "out of line"' … [A] neighbour … offered her the chance to come to London to work as her housemaid and offered her schooling … But once settled in London, she found herself trapped in the house, spending days and nights alone'.
>
> (Hulland, 2020)

Table 6.1 Number of Referrals to the UK National Referral Mechanism for Domestic Servitude, April 2009–December 2018

	April 2009–Dec 2009	Jan 2010–Dec 2010	Jan 2011–Dec 2011	Jan 2012–Dec 2012	Jan 2013–Dec 2013	Jan 2014–Dec 2014	Jan 2015–Dec 2015	Jan 2016–Dec 2016	Jan 2017–Dec 2017	Jan 2018–Dec 2018
Minors	20	31	42	43	45	73	74	103	118	96
Adults	84	85	119	120	142	238	364	329	363	413
Total	104	116	161	163	187	311	438	432	481	509

Source: Data sourced from Office for National Statistics, 2020, Data Table 3.

Alice who 'woke up at 7 every day. Got the children dressed, gave them their breakfast' and did 'housework all day'. 'During her ... "lost teenage years" ... her mother died of cancer and her family blamed Alice for not sending money back to help treat her ... The husband of the family she was living with then began sexually harassing her'.

(ibid.)

The under-interrogated implication in this reporting is that an international trade in vulnerable children is being orchestrated by organized crime groups that trick the destitute and traffick those captured by Islamic extremists into the homes of people who wish to off-load their domestic responsibilities and who are morally disinterested in the lives of those they pay a pittance to. What is less often reported is how pervasive the exploitation of domestic labour in West Africa actually is and how so many young women become dependent on it for their own or their families' survival. This matters, as we will show, because the legislative frameworks that permit domestic workers to come to the UK not only provide them with few rights as employees but also fail to anticipate the circumstances in which most agree to enter legitimate employment contracts that are exploitative by design. A questionnaire-based study of 1,409 domestic workers in Nigeria conducted for the World Health Organization (2011) in 2007 reported that over half the sample had lost one or both of their parents before the age of 18; nearly half had no formal education or vocational training; and almost 90% had begun working as domestic helps before the age of 15, over two-fifths of whom commenced work before the age of 10. Virtually all disclosed some experience of physical or sexual abuse, though rates were highest among those employed in households headed by non-family members. The WHO attributes this phenomenon to the targeting 'by agents who offer families false promise of fosterage, while instead engaging in trafficking of children for domestic work' (p.1).

The Histories of Child Fosterage and Domestic Help in West Africa

What is fosterage and where has the demand for it come from in West Africa? Though its history has yet to be fully written, the practice of hiring domestic helps in Nigeria cannot be disconnected from the racialized preoccupation with 'dirt' British colonialists brought to Lagos in the 19th century. The 'dirt' became associated with the 'uselessness' and 'idleness' the British ascribed to the 'natives'. Contagion was attributed by colonial administrators to black women's bodies, responsibilizing African women in particular for the health of the empire (Newell, 2020). The Lever brothers marketed soap in Nigeria via an image of a 'jolly' African woman in 1925, capitalizing on the Victorian moral principle that 'cleanliness is next to godliness', while colonial town planners saw it as their mission to instil urbanization that shielded Europeans from the 'filth' associated with 'unsanitary' African bodies and the customs of traditional, rural life (p.4).

> In the Township Ordinance of 1917, Lord Frederick Lugard (1858–1945) established Lagos as a 'First-Class Township', ranked thus not by its infrastructure but by its number of European inhabitants, including the influential white trader community. Through their chambers of commerce in Lagos (est. 1888) and Liverpool (est. 1774), white traders complained continuously to government about what they saw as a proliferation of poor-quality, unplanned, overcrowded, and insanitary dwellings springing up all over town with the potential for the uncontrollable spread of disease and a host of other 'sanitary atrocities'. Many government officials agreed: in the binary racial logic of colonial town planning in the early twentieth century, 'unsanitary native villages block[ed] the way to European expansion on healthy sites'. Even the most ostentatiously wealthy Africans – the 'better class natives' – were regarded as incapable of constructing a 'hygienic home' according to the Eurocentric way of seeing towns.
>
> (Newell, 2020: 17)

While a radical Afrocentric press responded to British racism with requests for home rule, 'educated local elites … in the early twentieth century … were unanimous in their adoption of government public health frameworks' (p.9). While many of the measures the British introduced compounded the problems of the urban poor, 80 years later, many middle-class families in Nigeria had come to internalize some of the colonial administration's norms and values when it came to cleanliness, following the lead of those deemed 'better class natives' (p.17). Hence, by the end of the 20th century, it had become normal among middle-class urban households in Nigeria to hire a domestic help to assist with childcare and maintain a hygienic home (Tade, 2019). The exploitation of these home-helps derives in part from this historical legacy and the interaction of a cultural tradition of child fosterage that was often about overcoming adversities, though not exclusively so. These adversities became acute as the vast inequalities of wealth the legacies of colonialism, cocoa exportation and oil extraction exacerbated armed conflicts in which children were deployed as soldiers, harshened living conditions and accentuated variable access to education among the poor, especially girls (Amzat, 2010).

While westerners tend to assume that children are only sent away to other relatives when their biological parents die or are unfit to care for their children, as the anthropologist Isiugo-Abanihe (1985: 55) reported in the 1980s, child fosterage was, for 20th century West Africans, a means to 'even out hardship'. In Nigeria, 'the sending out of children' was and still is 'practiced by both stable and unstable families, married and single mothers, healthy and handicapped [sic] parents, rural and urban homes, and wealthy and poor parents' (p.56). The meaning and the necessity of child fosterage varied from place to place and family to family providing a solution to a multiplicity of social problems and economic challenges. Child fosterage was sometimes used to avoid the stigma of a child being born out of wedlock, but it could also be used to confer a sense of 'blessing' on an older woman whose prestige was measured by the number of grandchildren and great-grandchildren she had; 'the occasional visits and gifts of money, foodstuff, and clothing by parents to grandparents' forming 'an important part of their resource accumulation' that goes with child fosterage (p.56). Child fosterage is also used to form alliances between families, especially when children are sent away to learn a trade or receive an education that ensures their social mobility. Some Nigerian parents assumed that a 'surrogate parent' is 'in a better position to inculcate acceptable forms of social behavior', 'to spank' or 'discipline' 'a child', or inflict other punishment, until the child learns to perform useful functions (p.57). And in many households 'children' are still regarded as 'an important part of the domestic labor force ... needed to perform various household tasks and small services ... Female children particularly are sent to experienced women to learn the domestic roles they will perform in their future homes' (pp.57–58).

In the 21st century, it has become increasingly common for Nigerian middle-class families to hire non-relatives instead of fostering relatives. The reasons for this have little to do with trafficking and Islamic extremism. Instead, they reflect the merging of the tradition of child fosterage, whereby some (typically poorer or rurally based) parents seek to send their children away to other families to receive education, and the shifting aspirations of middle-class women in a society that remains organized along patriarchal lines and in which the cost of living has risen faster than professional salaries. As Tade and Aderinto's (2012: 521) in-depth interview study uncovered: 'role dualism, workload and the need for companionship' lie behind many urban middle-class women's decisions to hire domestic helps in contemporary Nigeria. Across professional patrilineal families in which most women pursue careers that are considered secondary to their husbands, women still have to ensure domestic duties are complete. Many are now more reluctant to hire a relative, feeling that a stranger secures more privacy from extended family, where a relative might share a couple's problems with older kin. Some also welcome the extra power contracted employment confers, and while few consider themselves 'cruel', there remains some cultural acceptance that employers can 'mete out punishment to an employee that wouldn't be tolerated by a family member' (Tade, 2019). The striving for professional careers among women still constrained by patriarchal norms thus creates the situation in which many middle-class families come to regard hiring a home-help as a necessity.

> Cognisant of the cultural and social expectations and the need to accomplish observable social regularity and order in the domestic sphere, women negotiate with their husbands to reduce the 'burden of roles' by outsourcing some tasks.
>
> (Tade and Aderinto, 2012: 523)

The situation can easily become self-perpetuating with some husbands requiring their wives to work in order to meet the costs of domestic help that have increased as a proportion of household expenditure in recent years. Likewise, some young middle-class women hire domestic helps in the hope of maintaining strong emotional relationships with husbands when faced with the demands of sustaining their own careers, pregnancy, housework and childcare. Meanwhile:

> Older women cited the need for companionship rather than perform-ance of domestic chores … Women complained of boredom when their husbands were away at work stations outside the state. Another critical factor was the number of children in a household, and their ages. The domestic tasks increase with the number of children; their age determines the attention they require.
>
> (Tade, 2019: unpaginated)

Most tellingly of all, 'households where husbands assist in performing domestic duties, though not common, often didn't see the need for a domestic servant' (ibid.).

Overseas Worker Visas in the UK

British modern slavery policies have only engaged at the most superficial levels with the historical, cultural and economic complexities facing West Africa, the exploitation of Nigerian domestic workers often constructed primarily as a problem of 'serious and organised crime' that can be solved through police investigations if more Nigerians and local communities are prepared to 'spot the signs' (HM Government, 2018: 41). The charity, Kalayaan (2019), has campaigned to expose how the UK's immigration laws render migrant workers vulnerable to exploitation in spite of the modern slavery agenda. Before 1998 foreign national domestic workers employed in private residences in the UK had no rights as workers and entered predominantly as 'visitors'. The advent of the Overseas Domestic Worker Visa conferred on domestic workers the right to change employer, instilling a minimal protection from exploitation. Those who came between 1998 and April 2012 were also able to apply to extend their stay every 12 months; apply to settle permanently in the UK after five years; bring a partner and children under the age of 18 with them; and access public funds when experiencing hardship or seeking legal aid.[1]

This changed in 2013 when a 'tied visa' system was introduced. The tied visa system exposed those on domestic worker visas – around 16,000 of which were being issued each year – to the risk of forfeiting their right to live and work in the UK should they or their employer terminate their employment. The tied visa system thus inadvertently provided unscrupulous employers with more power to treat domestic workers badly with considerable impunity. In 2013, the government also rescinded the right for overseas workers to apply to extend their stays after six months, further compounding the power imbalance. The 2015 Modern Slavery Act proved a missed opportunity to reduce the vulnerabilities to exploitation these immigration policies engendered. Instead, Theresa May commissioned an independent review of the overseas domestic workers visa policy that only reported after the legislation received royal assent (Kenway, 2021). This review concluded by emphasizing what those representing the rights of migrants had explained to parliamentarians years prior, namely: that 'the existence of a tie to a specific employer and the absence of a universal right to change employer and apply for extensions of the visa are incompatible with the reasonable protection of overseas domestic workers while in the UK' (Ewins, 2015: 5). In other words, the UK's immigration policies exposed overseas domestic workers to the threat of modern slavery. The review recommended untying the visa and extending the period overseas workers could work in private households to 30 months, so that those unhappy with their terms of work had a reasonable chance of finding alternative employment.

The 2016 Immigration Act duly untied the visa enabling domestic workers to change employers, but it did not enable renewal beyond six months because the British government was keen to close routes to permanent settled status for all those it deemed 'unskilled workers', aside from domestic workers in 'diplomatic households' for whom extensions of up to five years remained permissible. This left overseas domestic workers who were being exploited in an impossible position, since few parents would hire an unemployed stranger from overseas, who is destitute and at risk of imminent deportation to care for their children (Kenway, 2021). Having dismissed the enquiry's proposition that, in these circumstances, it would be 'both impractical and invidious to discriminate between seriously abused, mildly abused and non-abused workers', the government tightened up the eligibility requirements for becoming an overseas domestic worker while conceding that those found to be victims of modern slavery could apply for temporary leave to remain in the UK (Gower, 2016: 19). This extension of the modern slavery provisions offered only a safeguard of last resort to workers who had to meet an ever-growing list of conditions that otherwise legitimized their entrapment in highly exploitative working conditions.

By 2021, in order to become a cook, cleaner, chauffeur, carer or nanny, in a private UK household those from overseas needed to: have worked for their employer 'for at least one year'; be '19 or older'; 'work in the same household as' the 'employer or one they use regularly', 'plan to travel to the UK with' the 'employer, their partner or children'; 'intend to work as a full-time domestic worker in a UK household' the 'employer will live in'; 'plan to leave the UK at the end of six months or at the same time as [their] employer, whichever is sooner'; and be 'able to support' themselves 'in the UK without the need for public funds'.[2] The employer had to be either 'a British citizen who usually lives outside the UK and who does not intend to remain in the UK for more than six months' or a 'foreign citizen who is coming to the UK on a visit and who does not intend to remain for more than six months'. Given that most who enter this form of domestic work are, as a parliamentary briefing described them, in 'relative desperation' – 'being unable to find adequate (or any) work in their own community/country, they have left that country to find other work abroad in order to make remittances back home, sometimes as little as £25 per week, for the general living, health and education costs of their relatives' – the requirement to be able to 'support oneself without the need for public funds' placed virtually all domestic workers at the mercy of their employers. These employers were only obliged to pay 'minimum wages', from which a deduction of £49 per month could be made for accommodation and subsistence. The employee had also, ultimately, to recover the costs of their health insurance and the £516 it costs to make a visa application from this meagre wage.[3]

Remember these are the *legitimate terms* under which domestic workers are employed in the UK. Only those who find themselves being exploited in ways that are worse – whether because of non- or under-payment, physical and sexual abuse, or because of breaches of employment and health safety law – have a case for officially claiming they have been subject to modern slavery. When those exploited to this degree seek to enter the National Referral Mechanism, they effectively opt to live precariously in a country in which they have few rights and no income until their case is resolved. And even then, resolution guarantees few benefits. Those overseas domestic workers who secure a positive conclusive grounds decision that validates their claim to be a victim of modern slavery have then to meet at least one of three conditions before Discretionary Leave to Remain in the UK can be pursued. They must:

1   Have 'compelling personal circumstances', such as a severe medical condition that requires treatment.
2   Make a 'claim for compensation against their traffickers' or 'modern slavery facilitators' that cannot be reasonably pursued from overseas; or
3   Have 'agreed to cooperate with police enquiries and the investigating police force has requested a grant of Discretionary Leave' (Gower, 2016: 14).

While this highly restrictive framework makes a mockery of any political claim to be redressing the drivers of modern slavery, it has – we argue in the rest of this chapter – the potential to generate and legitimize new forms of exploitation and the perception of a new wave of potentially fictitious claimants (ab)using the National Referral Mechanism to prolong their stays. In short, in order to stay beyond the termination or expiry of their contracts, overseas domestic workers have: to be exploited to a degree beyond which the least protective of employment laws allows; to have received a positive conclusive grounds decision from the NRM; be able to illustrate they are severely unwell; or have secured the support of a police force that needs their help to prosecute a suspected trafficker, who ideally has profited in a way that can be made good through reclaiming the proceeds of crime. Within this complex legal framework it is easy to see how many overseas domestic workers become exploited, while their employers consider themselves to have acted fairly and legitimately.

To illustrate this point we present a case study of a married couple who were convicted of exploiting a Nigerian domestic worker.

Case Study: Ademola and Tambara

Raised in Nigeria

Tambara and Ademola were a married couple with four children, who had both been convicted for trafficking for the purposes of domestic servitude a Nigerian woman, called Julia, they had hired as a live-in 'domestic help'. Though born in the UK, Ademola was raised in Nigeria by a family headed by his father – a very 'decent man', a vicar and the principal of the local secondary school – and his mother – a primary school teacher at the school Ademola attended – along with various domestic workers. Ademola remembered there were two domestic workers, in particular, both 16-year-old women, who helped take his younger siblings to school when he was about 10 or 11 years old. The domestics did 'everything' for the children, including the cooking, but were also regarded as part of the family – the domestic helps 'did everything. We did everything together, basically' – back then and to this day.

> They grew up in our household, got married in our household, they still – up till today they still go back to my dad's house. They might bring their children to visit … I'm still in contact with them. They are on my Facebook and my – we, we chat at times, you know, they, they – we're still very, very close.

Ademola's wife, Tambara, also grew up in Nigeria and was raised by two 'very well-educated' professional parents alongside four siblings, all of whom have successful professional careers. Tambara recalled that they were a 'happy family' who 'had the things they needed', the children looked after by 'house helps' whom their parents regarded as family, and 'considered as their children as well'. The helps fulfilled parental roles in the household while the parents worked – taking the children to school and doing homework with them – as was 'extremely common' in Nigerian households where 'both parents work'. The helps were typically 'house girls', unless all the children who needed caring for were boys. Tambara explained that Nigerian law requires the 'house girls' to be 18, though often they had 'just finished secondary school or' were 'waiting to go to university'.

Marriage, Children and Childcare

After he completed his degree and a year of civic service in Nigeria, Ademola came to the UK for a holiday. It was there he met Tambara, who was a student on vacation. The couple returned to Nigeria for traditional marriage but decided to settle in the UK, Tambara securing a spousal visa enabling her to join Ademola and work as she concluded her studies. As he too worked full time, the couple had to juggle their shifts to cover their childcare after their first three children were born. This became too demanding for Tambara during her fourth pregnancy, but as Ademola explained, neither he nor she could afford to reduce their working hours. They had enrolled their older children in fee-paying schools and there was pressure to send money back to each of their parents, even though the parents had their own pensions: 'our custom … is such that one has to look after your parents. In … the African culture … you send what you can afford'.

In order to 'juggle work, childcare and all of that' the couple hired 'three or four' au pairs, in succession. Most of the au pairs left at short notice, but one – a Hungarian lady, who Tambara remembered as 'very, very lovely' – stayed long enough to go on several holidays with the family. The couple usually paid the au pairs 'cash', 'every Saturday', '£60' and 'never owed them a penny'. These were terms the au pairs had generally been happy with, the Hungarian one even offering to testify in favour of the couple when they were subsequently charged under the 2015 Modern Slavery Act with keeping two domestic workers in servitude. It was after the Hungarian au pair had given notice that she needed to return home to look after her own family that Ademola and Tambara decided that 'engaging somebody from Nigeria' would be more stable (as Tambara recalled it) and that it would be preferable to hire someone 'of the same background as us that would be able to cook native – because we just wanted the kids to grow up, you know, with … someone who's from that background' (as Ademola recalled it). The solution to balancing the pressures of being dual earners in full-time work and the need to raise a family was thus resolved by importing Nigerian domestic workers whom they would hire 'by the books' by seeking the relevant permit from the Home Office.

Domestic Helps

Ademola explained that, at first, they 'took on' a Nigerian 'homeless' woman called Wendy. The couple 'tried to help' Wendy, employing her to 'do exactly the same things' as the Hungarian au pair, who stayed on for a week to ease the handover. Wendy had worked for Ademola's father previously. Having found her 'quite good' Tambara thought Wendy would be 'perfect' to look after the children. Wendy – who must have been in her early 20s at most – was with the family for 14 months, during which time she was paid £350 a month in cash, plus food and lodgings while additional money was sent to her parents. Ademola said that neither he nor his wife had any 'inkling' until then that Wendy was 'unhappy' and had no understanding of why she left their employment sud-denly, leaving all her belongings in the house. Tambara, however, explained that Wendy had left because of 'shame', having 'met somebody and got pregnant' just before she was due to start college. Wendy's family had 'begged' Tambara to be understanding, but Tambara, nevertheless, had to inform the police – as the domestic worker visa that permitted Wendy to work in the UK required her to inform the authorities if she was 'not in our custody anymore'. Wendy married the father of her baby and stayed in the UK, as Tambara explained: 'they never go back, that's part of the ... they never go back'.

After Wendy left, the couple approached Ademola's father to see if it was possible to hire another domestic worker. Tambara visited Ademola's 'father's house' and contracted an 18-year-old woman to come and work for them in the UK. The new help, Julia, had lived with Ademola's father since she was 12, he having 'enrolled her in a school' after her mother died of 'an ectopic pregnancy'. Julia's father had been struggling to care for his three other children since then. He told Tambara that she would be doing his family 'a huge favour' by taking Julia to the UK and looking 'after her health'. Tambara recalled that Julia had 'marasmus' – she was severely 'malnourished'. Ademola emphasized that Julia was 'not coerced in any way' to come to the UK and that her father's consent was formally sought – he swearing 'onto an affidavit' – as is 'the custom'. Julia's father was apparently happy to give his consent without payment, given that Julia would be 'better off' and the 'load' of having to provide for her would be taken off him, though Tambara declined this offer.

Tambara paid for Julia's flight, and she and Ademola celebrated her arrival with a party to celebrate her 19th birthday, Tamabara gifting 'her clothes' and buying 'her everything that she could have'. Ademola and Tambara said they wanted Julia to feel 'as if she was' their 'own daughter'. They could not adopt her, as she was already an adult, but Julia took their surname and, from their perspective, became part of their family in its everyday activities; another 'child' and daughter they 'treated as' their 'own'. Julia, they explained, 'would stay and watch videos or go out with us to the park or do stuff with us', had her hair braided just like the couple's oldest daughter; and referred to Ademola and Tambara as 'daddy' and 'mummy' 'because she grew up' with Ademola's 'folks back home'. The couple even tried, twice, to take Julia abroad on holiday with them, only to be thwarted by the overseas visa regime.

Conflict and Counterclaims

There were, though, key differences between how Julia was treated and how the couple cared for their own children. First, Julia was not enrolled in private schooling, like Ademola and Tambara's own children, though they did pay the deposit for Julia to enrol in college, hoping she would 'make a life' for herself. Second, while Julia was 'meant to take time off whenever she wanted', she 'had to work every day'. From Ademola's perspective, it 'wasn't an employer/ employee relationship'. Julia's duties were 'light': taking the children to school and nursery, cooking their meals and after school 'finger food' – but not his or his wife's as he only ate his wife's cooking – 'washing up after them' and doing their laundry. Once the children were out, Julia 'would do whatever she wanted to do'. She could still live with us and continue doing whatever she wanted, or she could move out, depending on whatever she wanted to do', Ademola explained. So while there were not 'any strict rules' and Julia could go out when he was home, she did have responsibilities, unlike their own daughter, and did not stay out overnight, aside from when the family went on holiday without her. Finally, Julia had duties in relation to the other children, which they did not have in respect to her, and she could be reprimanded if she did not do these, Tambara having 'snapped at her' if she 'didn't do what I wanted her to do'.

In other words, while Ademola and Tambara regarded Julia as their child, Julia was also contracted into a financial arrangement that came with expectations that, when breached, confirmed her position on the margins of the family. The couple's accounts of the financial arrangements with Julia were also a little inconsistent. While Tambara was clear that 'you cannot bring somebody in and not pay them' she appeared to have committed to sending money principally to Julia's father regularly, 'so that he could look after' Julia's siblings: 'he said instead of giving Julia the money, please just send the money to us'. Ademola suggested that the payment was split, however. Julia's father was to be paid £100 a month directly on top of the £350 Julia received: the latter rate consistent with what they had paid both Wendy and the Hungarian au pair. And the expectations the couple had of Julia were not confined to doing domestic work. Hence, while the couple was sometimes critical of how little Julia appeared to have done in the day, they seemed most disappointed that she had failed to take up the college education they had enrolled her in. They 'instilled in her that she had to get education, because she had no qualifications in Nigeria', but Julia attended college infrequently. Instead, she spent her spare time with a 'boyfriend' she met at college and her own friends in the church choir.

As with Wendy, the couple had 'no inkling'. Julia was unhappy. It thus came as a shock to them when two years into a five-year contract that they believed would have enabled her to apply for indefinite leave to remain, Julia failed to collect their children from school. Tambara came home from work and 'found' Julia's 'keys on the staircase' and her room 'ransacked'. Julia had apparently been looking for her passport which was kept with those of other family members. Unable to contact Julia because her phone was switched off, the couple phoned her 'uncle' – actually a friend of Julia's father who lived in the vicinity – who explained that she was 'old enough to look after herself and wouldn't be coming back'. Suspecting the uncle of having advised Julia she could 'get better some-where else', Ademola left Julia's passport with a 'pastor' at their church and reported her disappearance to the police. They were unsympathetic when Julia returned six months later having had a 'terrible' time and started to 'beg' for her job back: 'mummy' – 'mummy, I'm really sorry … I want to come back home, it was a mistake'. Tambara 'wouldn't allow her back in' the family home and threatened to call the police if Julia did not stop loitering outside.

Arrest and Prosecution

It was not until several years later that the police came at six in the morning and arrested Ademola and Tambara for keeping Julia and Wendy in domestic servitude. Initially, Tambara 'did not think anything of it' because 'we were absolutely good to this girl', having evidence that they had included her in family parties, holidays and giving her 'a TV … a computer … a phone' and a front door 'key'. Wendy alleged that Tambara would 'slap her, that, you know, she was all – she was rude to her, she, she treat her so badly', but a medical examination was to show that her scars were from self-inflicted injuries. The case nevertheless went to trial, where both Ademola and Tambara said events were grossly misrepresented. It was alleged that Julia was never paid because there were no bank transactions evidencing payment, but the couple explained that Julia had repeatedly been refused a bank account – even though the couple offered to act as her guarantors – because she was not on the electoral register. Julia only managed to open a bank account in the last few months of her employment. Tambara became tearful explaining that 'evidence' of how they had looked after Julia, such as her birthday parties, was dismissed in court as a charade – 'to let people think that I loved her'. It was also alleged that Julia would be woken from her sleep at night to cook for the couple – contrary to their assertion that Ademola only ate food cooked by Tambara – and further that after Tambara had eaten, Julia had to 'kneel down and hold the bowl of water … to wash her hands'. 'That was, that was a blatant … lie', Ademola asserted.

The couple was acquitted of exploiting Wendy, because 'unfortunately for her, there were bank statements to say that she was paid' and 'lots and lots of pictures', but they were convicted of exploiting Julia, the court calculating that the money paid into her bank account amounted to just one pound per week. Tambara was sentenced to a longer prison term than Ademola because she managed the domestic helps – 'it's the woman of the house that deals with the domestic' to 'protect your husband' from allegations of abuse. '[T]hat's why things are this way', she explained. Tambara felt deeply betrayed by Julia – 'for such a person to turn completely against you is just unbelievable' – while Ademola felt they had been unjustly stigmatized as 'African' 'monsters'.

> We brought this person into this country not to exploit, but to give them a chance … they've turned the whole thing around and it's, it's taken our own chance away from us, yeah … I mean, she had the keys to the house. If someone says, well, you, you have kept this person as a slave. A slave, as far as I, I understand has no right to go out on her own, is locked in. Slaves don't have mobile phones … access to computers, you know. She was free to go anywhere.

Ademola and Tambara learned that in the intervening years, Julia had made three asylum attempts, all of which had been refused, before she claimed to be a victim of modern slavery. Ademola speculated that she had been 'coached' by an NGO to make the case against them in order to avoid deportation but had not 'expected it to go this far'. Since their own families were obligated to Ademola's father, Ademola suggested both Wendy and Julia had been hesitant to incriminate him and instead fabricated complaints that depicted Tambara as the 'bad one'. Julia had even pled with Ademola's father 'so that her life would not be miserable' after the trial. The couple was unforgiving though. Ademola and Tambara lost their jobs. Prison proved to be a frightening experience, and the children developed problems of their own while their parents were in custody. They had to leave their fee-paying schools. Their daughter began self-harming; the older son developed a 'phobia' of the police and 'anger issues'; and the family's youngest son was 'excluded' from school for disruptive behaviour. The couple has since joined a support group for Nigerians who have been maliciously accused of trafficking domestic workers. They maintain their innocence.

Discussion

In the absence of testimonies from Julia, Wendy and other witnesses to what went on in the family home we can neither verify nor repudiate Ademola and Tambara's claims of innocence. From their perspectives, they were wrongfully convicted. They hired two domestic workers, complying with both 'the custom' in Nigeria and the law in the UK. They did so in order to maintain two professional careers, while ensuring that their children were looked after and could receive private education, and so they could continue to send money home to their own parents. They provided two women with better lives (for a short time) than they might have had before, extending the opportunities provided by Ademola's father. And they went beyond the requirements of the Overseas Domestic Worker Visa, welcoming the women into their families and helping to secure them a college education.

From Wendy and Julia's perspectives, however, one can also appreciate how this arrangement was not as generous as Ademola and Tambara presented it. Both domestic helps had effectively been introduced as children into Ademola's father's house. How well they were cared for there is not entirely clear: Wendy was ultimately left homeless; Julia remained malnourished to her late teens. It was from there that they were given the option, though one largely determined by their own fathers, to come to the UK. Once in the UK, they were not free to live as other teenagers. They had domestic duties that Ademola and Tambara's own children did not have. The domestic helps were estranged from both their own families and the second families that had claimed them as their own in Nigeria. Their wages were – at best – low and split with their fathers back home – and at worst not always received into their bank accounts or potentially received at all. They could not seek alternative employment. But they were under pressure to better themselves through education at college in a community where they were strangers and from a household where the other children did not work and instead received a private education. They faced the stigma of taking those children to school and, despite claims to the contrary, were not loved as they were, but regarded as domestic helps who were imminently replaceable.

In some respects, whether or not the domestic helps were victims of modern slavery as defined by UK legislation is beside the point, for even the *legitimate terms* under which the two women were hired were highly exploitative. These legitimate terms also reaffirmed culturally normal fosterage practices that have evolved postcolonialism in Nigeria to enable professional dual-career couples to keep working full-time despite the persistence of patriarchal family relations that place the burdens of housework and childcare predominantly on the shoulders of women, whatever their occupations. Tellingly, neither Wendy nor Julia cooked for Ademola, despite him seeking domestic helps who could 'cook native', because he preferred Tambara's cooking. Tambara ultimately served the longer sentence because a British court also deemed the domestic work and the management of the labour to complete it to be primarily her responsibility.

Moreover, recognizing what motivated the couple to hire domestic helps on exploitive terms – whether legitimate or not – need not negate the possibility that Wendy and Julia were persuaded to overstate claims about modern slavery. Given their precarious positions in the UK they had good reasons to make such claims. Once they had left the employ of the family neither Wendy nor Julia would have had a legal right to remain in the UK. Julia appeared to have realized this when she 'begged' for her job, much as Wendy's family did when she became pregnant and forfeited hers. These acts of desperation – begging – would have surely underlined to both women that they were not necessarily part of the family in the same sense that Ademola and Tambara's own children were and forced them to consider their options if they were to avoid deportation. Presenting as victims of modern slavery would have probably been their only recourse to law in these circumstances, and one with some foundation given that neither was technically employed by a visiting Nigerian national. Maybe the claims about physical violence were unnecessarily embellished to establish a prima facia case that ultimately succeeded through the happenstance that Julia could not – because of the requirements of UK immigration law – easily secure a bank account and appeared to have been substantially underpaid? Both things could be true. The women were exploited. The couple that hired them operated largely within the law and did not physically abuse them.

Perhaps, the more profound lesson to extrapolate from this case is that modern slavery law is ultimately a blunt instrument for redressing problems of labour exploitation that have roots in the harsh inequalities and high aspirations colonialism itself produced, and which now return to the UK in more complex forms as globalization reconfigures relationships across continents between upwardly mobile migrants, their families back home, and the poor who service them. Those hired as domestic helps are products of the many social, interfamilial and economic challenges the West African system of fosterage has been used to redress. But the demand for their poorly paid labour is also mediated by immigration regimes, patriarchal cultures, long working hours and presumptions about what counts as a good life for oneself, one's children and one's parents, by people living and working as professionals in the West who seek to secure their own prosperity by capitalizing on the precarity of others who can be persuaded to migrate in order to better care for their own families. These processes are themselves globally pervasive ones that rely on divisions of labour that span generations and continents. The problem of domestic servitude typically owes much more to the absence of rights conferred on those who have little choice but to migrate or live in destitution or see their siblings go without food or education than it does to the 'evil' intentions of traffickers, organized criminals or militant extremists.

Notes

1 www.gov.uk/domestic-workers-in-a-private-household-visa/domestic-workers-who-applied-before-5-april-2012
2 www.gov.uk/domestic-workers-in-a-private-household-visa
3 https://assets.publishing.service.gov.uk/government/uploads/system/uploads/atta chment_data/file/730783/Overseas_Domestic_Worker_applicant_leaflet_2018_V2.1.pdf

7   Labour Exploitation

During 2020, as public attention was drawn to where outbreaks of Covid-19 were proliferating, labour exploitation in the UK became more newsworthy. Rapidly rising rates of coronavirus in the city of Leicester were attributed to working conditions in factories supplying fast-fashion retailers, including Boohoo (Inman, 2020), exposing the government's failure to tackle labour exploitation the House of Commons' report *Fixing Fashion* had exposed the year prior (House of Commons, 2019). Similar cases involving the exploitation of overseas workers supplying clothes to H&M (Guilbert, 2018), Christmas cards to Tesco (Siddique, 2019) and farm food to Aldi (Smithers, 2019) featured in the news during the 2010s, while the high street retailer SportsDirect (Lawrence, 2017) was criticized for underpaying workers and denying them breaks in its UK shops and warehouses. As the world became dependent upon online deliveries, so exploitation that had long been regarded as endemic for employees of Amazon (Bowden, 2016) appeared to proliferate in the 'gig' economy (Nair, 2017).

While labour exploitation became the most commonly reported form of modern slavery in the UK in the mid-2000s, offenders were rarely prosecuted. Where they were, they were hardly ever the directors of large corporations and tend to be, instead, the owners of small- and medium-sized businesses, or companies working at the lower levels of supply chains. By 2021, the UK had yet to build any criminal cases, let alone prosecute the CEOs of any global corporations. Indeed, while labour rights organizations and official agencies highlighted the endemic exploitation within agricultural (GLAA, 2019), fishing (International Labour Rights Forum, 2018), food processing (JRF, 2012), construction (FLEX, 2018), information technology production (World Vision, 2012), clothing (Anti-Slavery International, 2018) and jewellery sectors (Human Rights Watch, 2018), official modern slavery awareness-raising campaigns in the UK concentrated on unregulated, cash-based businesses, such as car washes and nail bars (Salvation Army, n.d.). The Transparency in the Supply Chain (TISC) provisions of the 2015 Modern Slavery Act were designed around the presumption that the state need only require very large corporations to invest in self-regulation and the development of modern slavery statements that would enable consumers to make ethically informed choices as to whether

DOI: 10.4324/9780429053986-7

to buy from them. Consequently, as we argue in this chapter, the focus of law enforcement and regulation in the UK remains largely addressed to small- and medium-sized businesses, leaving bigger employers who dominate the market and global supply chains to persist with the kinds of exploitation and unsafe working conditions criticized by Box (1983) 40 years ago. Today, of course, the workforces exposed to these conditions tend to be more mobile – international migration having become much more commonplace – but no less precarious in terms of their job security and rights as employees.

In this chapter our focus is on crimes of exploitation committed in the interests of ostensibly legitimate business activity. Hence we have excluded those cases where businesses were defrauded by those seeking illegal entry into the UK and cases involving predominantly criminal enterprises, which are discussed in Chapter 4. The case studies presented in this chapter describe the lives of three individuals who were convicted for exploitation of workers within the food processing, garment and catering sectors. As with those depicted in Box's classic analysis of white-collar crime, the offences we depict here also involved omissions with regard to employers' obligations – failures to act to ensure the fair and safe working conditions employees are entitled to – typically in businesses that were operating with very tight margins. Our case examples included a local takeaway, a garment manufacturer employing Pakistani workers to make clothes in the UK and a global logistics and labour force supplier, demonstrating how modern slavery can be facilitated within businesses that are small, medium and large scale.

The Policy Context

Prior to the implementation of the Modern Slavery Act 2015, the UK had almost no formal law enforcement response to labour exploitation, which was regarded as a matter of civil law unless the exploitation was enforced by physical violence, the threat of it, or false imprisonment. Prior to 2015, business practices causing harm within the context of employment would typically be dealt with by recourse to health and safety frameworks or as a matter of corporate liability when people became sick as a consequence of their working conditions or were injured or killed at work. Following the Palermo Protocol, an offence of trafficking which could be applied to labour exploitation was introduced into the 2004 Asylum and Immigration Act. The Act was limited in its scope with regard to labour exploitation, however. If the trafficking element could not be proven, the forced labour element of the offence could not be prosecuted.

Following campaigns by NGOs, Section 71 of the Coroners and Justice Act 2009 introduced a new offence of 'slavery, servitude and forced labour'. The establishment of this new offence was in part a response to the circumstances within which 23 Chinese cockle pickers died in Morecambe Bay in February 2004. In response to the tragedy, the Gangmasters Licensing Authority (GLA) was established in 2005 to increase the regulation of labour, initially within the agriculture, fisheries and food production sectors. Its remit expanded to include labour abuses in every sector of employment in 2017 when it was renamed the Gangmasters and Labour Abuse Authority (GLAA). Despite this, concerns remained regarding its effectiveness and capabilities, the GLAA's total staff size numbering just 126 in 2018/2019 (HM Government, 2019: 40). Prosecutions via the GLAA remained rare, numbering just 13 in 2019–2020 and 10 in 2020–2021 (GLAA, 2021). Questions have therefore been raised about the GLAA's effectiveness, particularly in relation to intelligence gathering and data sharing provisions with other statutory agencies. Arguably, the GLAA's limited resources have left it reliant on the police, immigration enforcement and border force to bring prosecutions, compromising its independence and rendering it an unlikely choice of support for irregular migrants needing assistance (HM Government, 2019; Guild and Barylska, 2021).

In this respect, Box's observation, made in 1983, that the 'resources' the state-driven labour regulation sector has at its disposal are 'no match for national and transnational corporations' remains just as true today (p.45). The policy framework that has developed in the UK to counter labour exploitation is unable to compete with the power of multi-national corporations that routinely deploy their global reach to drive down the costs of production and labour. While the British government's rhetoric with regard to modern slavery has been uncompromising, its strategy in relation to labour exploitation has been quite the reverse. It seeks instead to 'work with regulators and the private sector' (HM Government, 2014: 12) to develop a non-binding 'framework' that engages with 'businesses on a voluntary basis' (Home Office, 2013: 18). It is able to pursue this light-touch approach because the Transparency in Supply Chain (TISC) provisions in the 2015 Modern Slavery Act were 'extremely lightweight legislation' (Kenway, 2021: 106) that never 'meaningfully bolstered public labour standards' (LeBaron and Rühmkorf, 2019: 710). Fair trade was thus cast as an optional extra by businesses whose margins relied on free, unregulated competition to drive wage levels down. Despite the much-heralded introduction of the TISC provisions as mechanisms for corporate accountability, few consequences have followed for British businesses that exploit their workers. Corruption and bribery, though also rarely prosecuted successfully, are regarded as more serious forms of corporate crime in UK criminal law (Lord and Broad, 2018).

Indeed, while many governments across the world have promised to strengthen the regulatory structures that govern business practices, in most countries, developments have been little more than piecemeal (LeBaron and Rühmkorf, 2019). As Balch argues, the problems with modern slavery legislation relating to labour exploitation can be attributed to 'an aversion towards understanding forced labour as either an issue for businesses to address … or a question of more rigorous enforcement of workplace rights' among many governments wishing to appear 'business-friendly' (Balch, 2015: 90; 94). Consequently, the framing of human trafficking – and subsequently modern slavery – as essentially a problem of crime transcending international borders has meant that in many places 'some indices of forced labour' have been 'overlooked by enforcement agencies because of the emphasis within anti-trafficking policies on sexual exploitation and immigration', despite 'overwhelming evidence that cases of forced labour can occur without a trafficking' element (Balch, 2015: 90). In turn, corporate governance responses to labour exploitation framed in terms of crime, immigration and border security generally failed to deal with the structural inequalities embedded in supply chains and labour markets which generate conditions conducive to exploitation. Because criminal law mainly focuses on exploitation at the severe end of the spectrum, those workers who experience less severe exploitation have limited avenues for redress (Davies, 2020). This is especially the case for many migrant workers, whose rights under the hostile environment policy are minimal, whose access to welfare benefits in the event of redundancy is marginal, and whose recourse to legal assistance in the event of mistreatment or underpayment is highly restricted. The New Plan for Immigration, announced in 2021, sought to further limit the access of irregular migrants to employment. This will further deter potential victims of modern slavery from reporting exploitation, as to do so will place many in absolute destitution, as well as at risk of criminalization and prospective deportation as 'illegal' migrants (Anti-Slavery International, 2021).

Misinformation and Mystification

Internationally, there have been many developments to increase the accountability of corporations for human rights abuses and exploitation in their supply chains, brought about partially through the rise of the business and human rights and corporate social responsibility agendas bolstered, most notably, by the 2011 United Nations Guiding Principles on Business and Human Rights (UNGPs). However, much like the TISC provisions of the 2015 Modern Slavery Act, the UNGP does not mandate compliance (Sarfaty, 2015) or speak to the wider inequalities that leave many workers little choice but to accept arduous working conditions in return for long hours and low pay that entrap them in acute poverty (Kenway, 2021; New, 2015; Philips, 2015; Bernstein, 2007). Just as the problem of crime continues to be politically mystified in public debates as one caused exclusively by amoral street criminals, many of those who work in business suites remain oblivious as to how their practices contribute to exploitation (Box, 1983: 16). In turn, many businesses operate with insufficient understanding of how 'indifference rather than intent' can be 'the greater cause of avoidable human suffering' or that 'omissions' to act responsibly on behalf of employees [are] as problematic as deliberate efforts to exploit (Box, 1983: 21). 'Strivings to realise organisational goals' in 'an uncertain and unpredictable environment', marked by 'competition under conditions of scarce or diminishing resources and markets' (p.22) are the contexts in which businesses seeking to remain competitive innovate, cut corners, or turn a blind eye to prospective harms to employees and consumers 'for the good of the company' (Box, 1983: 55). And because keeping the company afloat also keeps the workers in work, it can be harder to appreciate that there is any 'real criminal victim' (p.56) when a worker is underpaid, especially if that same worker is of the view that their conditions of employment are better than they were in another country they have worked in, especially if they are also reliant upon state benefits or working illegally to survive.

To meet the situational demands of competitive markets, a 'subculture of structured immoralities' celebrates free enterprise as a virtue and castigates human rights as a bureaucratic inconvenience (Box, 1983: 64). Hence, when exploitation is exposed, the temptation in many organizations is, as Box (1983:57, adapting Sykes and Matza, 1957) observed, to evoke these structured immoralities to induce similar 'techniques of neutralization' to the ones street criminals use to exculpate themselves: to deny responsibility by blaming someone else; to deny injury by suggesting no-one was really harmed; to deny the victim by suggesting those who were harmed deserved what they got; to 'condemn the condemners' by suggesting that they are no better or that their rules or 'red tape' caused the problem; or to reach for higher loyalties, by explaining that what they did was for a greater good, in the case of white-collar criminals, typically to ensure the long-term survival of the company.

These insights were further expanded upon by Cohen (2001) in his analysis of states of denial that explains how it is that individuals, businesses and governments collude in modes of thinking that protect them from the 'troubling recognition' that what they are doing is unjust, harmful or even life threatening. Cohen suggested that these denials articulated themselves in three modes: literal denial – an absolute refusal to accept the evidence that something wrong was done, akin to a 'twilight state of self-deception where some of the truth is hidden from yourself' (p.9); interpretive denial – the assertion that while the act looked like wrong-doing it was actually something more benign or commonplace, often informed by an 'inability to grasp what the facts mean to others' or a 'cynical renaming to avoid moral censure or legal accountability'; and implicatory denial – the acceptance of the facts of what happened, but not their 'significance or implications', disasters redefined as aberrations and not evidence of an endemic problem that should arouse wider concern (p.8).

What Do We Know about Labour Traffickers?

As discussed in Chapter 2 binaries evoked within stereotypical constructions of traffickers and slaveholders tend to proliferate across the media, policy documents and the fund-raising activities of NGOs in the absence of primary research studies of modern slavery offenders. The few primary studies of traffickers have mostly involved speaking to those engaged in sexual exploitation (as discussed in Chapter 8 and see also Albanese et al., 2022; Choi-Fitzpatrick, 2016). Consequently, as Cockbain et al.'s (2018: 321) review of the European evidence base on trafficking for labour exploitation concluded, there remain 'major knowledge gaps' on the subject because no empirical research that captures the first-hand accounts of perpetrators has been conducted. Choi-Fitzpatrick's (2017) interviews with farmers and landlords who benefitted from the enslavement of indentured labourers in rural India reveal how many 'appear to have been blinded by their own rationalization of these relationships, having convinced themselves that they were helping the laborers in some way' (pp.12–13). Indian 'slaveholders' depicted the work and credit they provided as a gift of help offered to indentured labourers in paternalistic terms; a gift they could barely afford to offer in what was increasingly strained times but gave nonetheless because it was in the best interests of the workers. In this way slaveholders presented themselves as respected and respectable, distancing themselves from the self-interested and abusive practices they assumed their 'exploitative neighbours' were perpetrating (p.14). Much like Box's corporate criminals who justified their offending as a response to the bureaucracy that was stifling their competitiveness, the rural landlords Choi-Fitzpatrick interviewed, 'made clear, that at some level the government and its policies were responsible for the problems' (p.72) they had with workers who had been empowered by being apprised of their rights and who had started to complain about conditions that had hitherto been regarded as just, generous or part of the natural order of things. Similarly, as discussed in Chapter 2, Howard's (2017; 2019) ethnographic research with workers, employers and intermediaries in West Africa and Italy highlighted the essential role played by those scapegoated as 'traffickers' in brokering labour in industries where indigenous workers are unwilling to accept declining rates of pay. For Howard (2019: 16), the 'mainstream discourses around trafficking obscure far more than they reveal … they reduce complex lives and their gendered and generational trajectories as well as the interrelationship between these and political-economic structures, to a flattening and simplified binary'. Within fiercely competitive global markets, intermediaries make small margins by introducing migrant labourers from their home countries to farmers and construction workers from host countries who are struggling to break even or recruit local workers.

Much the same logic is articulated in the three UK-based case studies presented in this chapter. Each illustrates how individuals working in legitimate businesses negotiated regulatory and legal frameworks, before breaking the law as they attempted to balance the need to remain competitive against varying degrees of concern about those in their employ. As regulatory and legal requirements tightened, along with their profit margins, our participants neglected to probe doubts they had about whether those supplying workers on a casual basis were licensed to do so (Charles), reminded employees that they could be deported if their services were no longer required (Hina) and paid destitute employees in food, 'favours', drugs and alcohol in exchange for their labour (Sammy). All three employers were to some extent mystified about how their actions became construed as criminal abuses of power, without denying that they could have ensured their workers' interests were better protected. All were invested in states of denial that protected them from the troubling recognition that their own business practices had perpetuated modern slavery, denying that it was anything of the sort (Sammy); suggesting it was unfortunate but a morally acceptable business practice (Hina); or accepting that while it was wrong, the consequences were comparatively trifling, and not evidence of endemic exploitation in global supply chains (Charles). The question their cases raise is what should be done to change the culture of business practices to make these states of denial harder to sustain and defend in industries where poorly paid and destitute people are at daily risk of exploitation.

Case Studies

Sammy: Literal Denial – Labour Exploitation as 'Tough Love'

Sammy was a 47-year-old British Asian, a father of one, and a Sikh, born in Singapore to a military family who was stationed there. At the time of the interview, he was serving seven years for 'compulsory labour' exploitation, prosecuted under the Modern Slavery Act, as well as 18 months for supplying drugs, available through prescription to aid sleeping, to at least one of the four male complainants who had worked for little or no pay in the takeaway he owned. Sammy insisted he 'was 100% not guilty of' these crimes, insisting that he was a victim of two decades of police harassment and that the judge had pressurized the jury into convicting him. This, however, was not anywhere near the whole story, the 'tough love' Sammy imparted to his tenants involving at least tacit intimidation of destitute, substance-dependent and hungry people at risk of homelessness, whose labour he exploited to shore up a business that was at risk of bankruptcy as a product of his own mismanagement.

Sammy described himself as a 'businessman' who ran a takeaway and a house of multiple occupation (HMO) – temporary property rentals – where tenants, most of whom in this case had been previously homeless, shared toilet, bathroom or kitchen facilities. The tenants' housing benefits were paid directly to Sammy. Sammy admitted he had a 'criminal record' prior to the modern slavery charges and was 'no angel' but insisted he would 'never hurt innocent people' or 'pick on the vulnerable'. Rather he insisted, as a 'good Sikh', 'money was never [an] interest', and he would 'go out of his way for anybody'. His approach to helping others, however, was one of 'tough love' which sometimes meant coercing people to do what he saw as the right thing even when they disagreed. A compelling example of this was a time when he lifted a male tenant into a bath against his will: 'really nice bloke, but he didn't like having a bath … Cause I give a shit about these people'. Sammy was proud of the fact that he, unlike 'these people' who benefitted from his 'tough love', had never been 'on the dole' or a recipient of 'housing benefit'. Though as a landlord he profited from other people's dependence on benefits, it seemed important to Sammy to highlight how generous and hospitable he was to his tenants whom he said he 'always' invited to his barbeques along with other businesspeople and his 'rich friends'.

During his late teens, Sammy and his two older brothers had become 'well-known' in their town as people who 'hate bullies', 'don't tolerate any crap' ('there was a lot of racism so we had to defend ourselves') and were regarded as men who could 'sort out' a 'problem' if someone came to them with it, a life philosophy he equated with being a Sikh. An example of righting these kinds of wrongs happened when Sammy was 18 and intervened when a white, female neighbour called him and his brothers over because she was being beaten up by her husband. The husband called Sammy a 'Paki', so Sammy 'had a word with the guy'. The guy hit Sammy but 'got a broken jaw and … had his ribs broken' in response. The courts let Sammy get 'away with it': 'just common sense … the wife went on our side'. Later Sammy was to become involved in buying stolen goods, possibly through an off-license he ran with his brothers. The goods were typically electrical items bought from people he went to the gym with, 'insurance jobs' done on 'factories' or 'five bottles of spirits' that had been 'pinched', but Sammy did not take them if they were 'personal things' stolen from victims of burglary. Sometimes the goods were simply 'fakes', Sammy was convicted for selling counterfeit designer clothing in his early 30s.

It was in these contexts of racism and involvement in business crime – together with driving under the influence of alcohol – that Sammy said he was 'hounded' by the police, for a period of three decades. In his 40s, Sammy conceded that he had fallen into a 'rut' and developed 'a drinking problem', rationalized as a response to industriousness – 'work hard, play hard' – but compounded by the deaths of his father and mother, and a divorce. His business began to fail for which Sammy blamed the police, whom he claimed, implausibly, harassed him for a failure to pay his tax returns over five years and the mortgage on his properties over three. Sammy admitted that during this period he had become 'depressed' and lost a sense of 'purpose in life', buying tranquilizers 'off the street' because his own doctor had repeatedly refused to prescribe the medication to aid his sleep.

It was around this time, with his own mental health and business faltering, that Sammy asked his tenants to 'wash dishes and stuff' in his shop, for no or little pay, and was alleged to have supplied them with drugs to facilitate their compliance. This latter allegation, Sammy said, was untrue. Rather the people in question, he said, were 'alkies', 'homeless kind of people' who were 'not capable of working at all'. They were 'vulnerable', had a 'bad habit' with 'drink' and 'drugs', were on 'script', on probation and known to the police. Sammy claimed he 'used to tell them to stop shoplifting' and explained how he had given 'them' 'food' from his 'shop' to do them 'a favour'.

> I used to give them food every night from the – this is free of charge food, leftover food. I didn't have to and I've been doing it for 15, 20 years. Nobody does that. I'd give it away to anybody instead of throwing it away … Every time I had a barbecue or a party, they were always invited … I never treat them … below me or beneath me or as a worker. It was a case of just trying to put them out of their rut.

The accusation that he was 'bullying' the tenants to get them to work' in his takeaway shop was a 'pure joke', Sammy insisted, though he had told his HMO tenants that 'they gotta behave themselves when they were drinking and they were fighting … acting bad … when the neighbours were complaining'. From his perspective, Sammy had given 'them tough love', a structured second chance, explaining, 'If you don't pack it in, I'm gonna kick you out'. Sammy did not recognize that these tenants-turned casual-workers were so destitute that they had little option but to comply or that his own reputation as someone who would 'defend' himself might have intimated them into compliance. Rather, he simply assumed that he knew best how to help untrustworthy people without infringing their freedom:

> Sir, these people, these people, right, had long – long criminal records …
> So if these guys were scared of me or I used to persuade them, I used to force them … They all had keys for the properties …
>
> These people are full-blown al – alcohols. That means they cannot wake up without a drink. They smell, they don't have a bath, you know what I mean? They've got a habit. Their only thing about – if they've got £2, they will not buy food, they'll buy – buy drink. And so these are the kind of people that the police are saying that were working in my shop who were doing 10, 12 hours a day.

Whether or not any of these drink-dependent men worked full shifts, Sammy did let slip that they were barely or rarely paid, except in kind or with gifts or loans they had ultimately to repay. The man who was most well paid was described by Sammy as a 'Polish kid' (actually in his 30s) called Mirek, who cooked the kebabs and pizzas for '20, 30 quid every night'. Sammy had 'lent Mirek a couple of hundred pound before he even started working to help him to get some clothes' because he 'wanted to change his life'. Nevertheless, at least 'some' of Mirek's wages were also deducted from his 'rent'. Mirek's employment ended abruptly after eight shifts when Sammy 'fell out with him', having warned him twice previously about using 'drugs' and Mirek responding in a 'rude' way when Sammy forbade him from hanging out with a drug-using guy who had been released from a 'mental hospital'. In addition to Mirek, Sammy also employed 'Fred' (in his late forties) – a homeless man – who worked 'for one or two weeks because he wanted to come off the drink' or 'for a good three or four weeks', and in another version for 'six weeks':

> I'm not gonna lie to you. He did have one [a drink] because he wanted to change his lifestyle but mind you I – I lent him money for – because his son's funeral, I lent him money [£150] for – I helped him out as well. …
> I helped him out. I helped him out financially and bought him a suit and stuff like that, you know, so he helped me out and I helped him out for about two or three weeks it was, that was it.

While he appeared not to have paid Fred, Sammy repeatedly insisted that he had nevertheless helped him at a time of dire need, Fred apparently like many of 'these people' having 'cried' on Sammy's 'shoulders' and benefitted from being able to 'stay off the drink' while he moved boxes in the shop.

Sammy had also 'helped' a 'shoplifter' called Wayne – another man in need of a bath – by encouraging him to take food from the takeaway rather than go thieving. Upon arrival, however, Sammy decided to confiscate Wayne's shoes. Sammy claimed he did this to stop Wayne from shoplifting, but in so doing he effectively confined Wayne to the takeaway. This act of 'tough love', Sammy considered to have been blown 'out of proportion' by Wayne's probation officer, and by Wayne himself who could be 'nasty' when drunk. Two other complainants were depicted as both unclean and untrustworthy by Sammy, namely: Martin, who alleged he had been 'working all the time' in the takeaway for 'five years', while Sammy claimed only to have 'met' him 'three or four times'; and Peter, one of Sammy's HMO tenants who was 'a heroin addict' who 'used to cry wolf all the time' and 'feel sorry for himself'. Again, Sammy claimed to be looking after this destitute man: he would come to the takeaway shop to 'borrow ten pound … to get phone credits' or hide 'from drug dealers' to whom he owed money. What Sammy could not concede was that he needed these destitute workers to keep a business he had failed to maintain afloat, nor that in doing them 'favours' – lending them money and giving them food – he was essentially entrapping people who were either homeless or tenants of his HMO in a state of servitude.

Hina: Interpretive Denial – Doing What's Needed in a Hostile Business Environment

Hina was a British Muslim mother of three in her 30s, serving a custodial sentence of over four years for an offence of trafficking for labour exploitation that involved underpaying a team of 12 tailors who worked in a UK-based garment factory she owned. She admitted the underpayments and making deductions from her workers' pay but denied that what she had done amounted to exploitation or criminality, interpreting what happened as a labour dispute in which 'greedy' workers would not shoulder the costs of a business dependent on migrant workers.

Hina's parents were Pakistanis who came to the UK in the 1970s when the British government 'wanted labourers'. Both parents had high aspirations for their six children in terms of securing a good education and professional jobs. Hina's dad, however, was violent and abusive to her mum. All the siblings heard their 'mum screaming in the other room', but the couple stayed together because of their 'culture' and 'tradition'.

At 18, Hina's parents 'shipped' Hina and her sisters off to Pakistan and 'forced' them 'to get married', having discovered Hina had a boyfriend – Fawad – in the UK. On her return to the UK, Hina resumed her relationship with Fawad to whom she became pregnant. Afraid her father might 'kill' her, Hina returned to Pakistan during her pregnancy in an attempt to deceive the cousin she had been forced to marry into thinking the baby was his. Her plans changed on the journey over, however, when she almost lost the baby. After she confessed that the baby was Fawad's, Hina's father stopped speaking to her. Hina then married

Fawad, only to discover that he had 'women galore', was dependent on illicit drugs, and would be violent towards her in the presence of their son.

Hina did what she could to become financially independent of both her father and Fawad. Troubled by her own experiences of being 'trekked abroad' and forced into marriage, Hina undertook a legal executive course, specializing in immigration law, before opening her own immigration practice with a friend – despite neither being qualified solicitors. The two women secured some charitable funding and 'slowly but surely ... started building clientele'. Hina was passionate about her work and helping people, especially women who had suffered brutal injustices.

> I had real cases where I was fighting for real people who'd been raped ten times over, gang raped, who'd had FGM, still happening, who'd had families shot in front of their face, their husband or their parents, or their siblings. They'd been injured, bombs and shells had actually blown up their hands or their feet as well. I was trying to fight for their leave to remain. There was solid genuine evidence, and the Home Office, the immigration officers would not have it.

After Fawad's behaviour worsened, the 'penny dropped' and Hina 'called the police' on him. The couple divorced, and Hina became a single parent of two, inheriting a debt of £200,000 generated by her ex-husband's drug use and failed costs of treatment. Hina registered for insolvency to clear the debt and then remortgaged some properties she owned to establish a tailoring business, her interest in fashion stemming from her mum sewing 'clothes for factories' and a fashion course she had taken in college.

Aware that many people travel to Pakistan and India to buy eastern clothing, Hina spotted the opportunity to manufacture clothing within the UK. Her brother-in-law, Yusuf, and sister, Sadia, entered the business with her, though Yusuf only took a 'minimum wage', while Sadia was a 'trustee basically' who took charge of the banking and (subsequently) running of the shop. Hina's role was to travel to Pakistan, where she 'selected' 'qualified' 'tailors, the best of the best, via word of mouth, advertising', some of whom she had known for years 'via family' or friends. As an (unqualified) immigration 'lawyer', Hina arranged travel and work permits for the tailors – even going to tribunals to appeal their cases when the Home Office refused some of them visas. The process of bringing the tailors over was nevertheless time-consuming, complicated and expensive. Hina applied through the Home Office and the British High Commission in Pakistan and 'had to stringently vet every single tailor ... to stop bogus migrants coming from abroad'. Fifteen tailors were granted their applications and '12 worked for' her. As the tailors' employer, Hina guaranteed their work. Unlike less scrupulous employers who 'abuse them and bring them here', Hina felt she offered the tailors 'a good wage' of between £10,000 and £15,000 per year.

While her business was soon 'booming', problems began to arise as the tailors became unhappy with their pay. At least initially, Hina had been 'flexible' about when the tailors repaid her the immigration charges she had paid on their behalves, allowing them to pay as they earned, and not charging them the full cost of her legal advice: 'I even said, you don't even have to pay all the fees, as long as you pay me something … I was a little bit slack with them, and a bit flexible with them'. But conflicts arose as the tailors discovered how the profits of their labour were split. Although they would have been paid only '£60, £70 a month' in Pakistan, when they realized that Hina was profiting '£400, £500 a week' the tailors tried to renegotiate a better split of the profits. Hina advised them that if they did not work for her, they would need to find another employer to sponsor their visas or go home. She knew few would want to risk this as their 'kids were going to school' in the UK and some were 'getting their medical treatment'. But the government was also introducing changes to immigration and employment laws she could not afford to implement. In 2012, the Home Office raised the cost of applying for work permits to £1,200 and introduced a points system which meant that employers had to pay migrants a minimum of £20,000. Hina was incredulous, explaining that she, like many employers, was 'screwed up by it'. The clothing company's annual profits were only £5,000 to £10,000 per year. Hina 'didn't want to lose' the tailors – 'they were good … they were making me money and I thought they were – they were happy, but no, their greed kicked in'. Unable to get away with paying the tailors 'cash in hand', as she had previously, Hina passed on the new cost of visa applications to the tailors who presumed she was 'stealing and paying off tax and NI' out of their pay when she was paying it out of her 'own damn pocket'.

In turn, some of the tailors began supplementing their incomes by making clothes directly for customers, taking the business away from Hina. Feeling betrayed, Hina sacked those tailors to make an example of them to the others, explaining that they had breached the immigration rules and would be 'put back on a plane'. At this point, one worker went on long-term sick leave for two years, presumably to avoid dismissal. Others played 'naïve', claiming they 'didn't understand' and were 'not that educated'. A subgroup made asylum applications because 'they needed to secure their leave to remain in the UK'. Their claims were rejected, but the tailors – Hina argued with no hint of self-awareness – sought legal advice from a 'dodgy immigration lawyer' who said they were in 'slave labour', opening the criminal proceedings that secured her conviction.

Though she had stepped down as company director a couple of years prior to her arrest, Hina's home was 'raided' by 33 police officers: 'They took absolutely everything' – 'flipping houses with kids and wives' – but found 'fuck all'. The police, she claimed, 'needed a conviction' to 'justify the £1.5 million' they had spent on the case, while the jury were – according to her – 'manipulated'. Advised that she could receive a nine-year prison sentence, Hina fled to Pakistan, but returned when she discovered that she was pregnant to serve her sentence with her third baby in prison. She remains of the view that she was wrongfully convicted, believing the evidence against her was secured through a combination of police corruption and coached victim testimonies from 'migrants who

… just desperately wanted to live in this country'. Hina said she had done 'everything' for her employees and 'everything by the book', but the workers exploited her 'weaknesses': 'They knew I was in debt. They knew everything about me because my life was an open book because of my crackhead of a fucking husband'. 'How can somebody be trafficked on a work permit and who came to the UK voluntarily?' Hina asked rhetorically. She denied the tailors had been kept as 'slaves' by her company – as had been argued in court – explaining that she only kept the tailors' passports when she needed them for Home Office applications and maintaining that the migrant workers were free to collect them whenever they wished.

Charles: Implicatory Denial – Administrative Omissions in a Global Supply Chain

Charles, mid-40s, was a white British man, serving a community sentence for breach of a gangmaster's licence during his employment as an operations manager for a company that supplied industrial labour in the meat-processing sector. He was the only participant in our study who had not received a custodial sentence. He considered his conviction to have placed a considerable stress on his family and that his sentence had been an 'inconvenience'. He did not deny that the law had been broken and that ensuring compliance with it had been his responsibility, but he regarded the exploitation of 30 Romanian workers, whose wages were being deducted by an unlicensed intermediary who supplied labour to a company with a multi-million-pound turnover, as an administrative 'mistake'.

Charles' childhood had been happy, and he had no prior history of criminal involvement. Charles had entered banking in his 30s, becoming the accounts manager for a global workforce management consultancy. Having proved successful at managing 'compliance and service delivery' and leveraging 'really good financial deals' on the back of 'strong relationships' with the company's clients, Charles was tempted by a job offer from one of the firm's clients: a company with an annual turnover of around half a billion pounds, located near where he lived. Charles took a position as operations manager at the agency for better pay and a better work-life balance that enabled him to be at home in time for evening meals with his family. Charles and the managing director were the holders of the gangmaster's licence at the company.

The company managed a significant portfolio organized across different 'desks' that dealt with different industrial sectors to whom it supplied casual labour and logistical support: waste management and recycling, social housing maintenance, warehousing and food processing. Across all sectors, Eastern Europeans were a 'huge source' of 'temp labour'. Food processing – the area in which the breach of the corporation's gangmaster's licence occurred – was the company's least profitable sector: 'a really poor earning account' that Charles had advised the company's director to 'dump' because it was such a 'hassle' to manage and took his time away from other more profitable sectors. Charles

explained that this was partly because most workers preferred waste management to meat-processing, but also because the general manager at the meat
factory 'was very blunt' and 'rude' to the regular workforce there – who were
becoming unreliable – as were the casual staff the agency sent. Food processing
was not Charles' 'strength' or 'remit', meaning that while he was responsible for
supplying labour there, it was one of the sectors in which he had few contacts
and limited experience (unlike the company's managing director who would
have 'spotted' the problems that later materialized had he not delegated responsibility to Charles).

The first sign of apparent problems in the food processing plant was when
three workers complained they had not received their holiday pay. Charles
discovered that the money had been stolen by the firm's recruitment consultant – a 'young lad' who it materialized had a 'gambling problem'. Not
wanting to 'ruin' this young man's 'life over a mistake', Charles asked the consultant to resign and the company made good to the workers, reissuing their
holiday pay. This, however, was not the end of the problems, as Charles received
a complaint from the general manager at the factory that unregistered substi-
tute workers were turning up alongside the agency workers, giving the names
of registered workers, under the direction of another man who it materialized
had acted as a Romanian interpreter to the agency.

The interpreter had not only worked with the recruitment consultant who
resigned but also with his successors, helping to interview and secure employment for workers who were not fluent in English. When the complaint was
made by the meat factory general manager, the interpreter proved elusive to
Charles' team, so Charles decided to 'chase' him up directly and asked the man
to clarify why he was doing so much interpreting at no charge to the agency.
Charles learned that the interpreter was also a 'landlord' to the workers who
lived in 'houses of multiple occupation' he rented to them. Charles met with the
interpreter and visited three terraced houses, keen to avoid any 'horror stories
of fifty people crammed in a room'. While they were not 'amazing homes',
Charles noted that there was a bed and a television in each room and storage
for clothes. Though assured that the workers were not 'living in total squalor',
the visit also revealed that the interpreter was also hiring cars for the workers
and charging them for insurance.

> I suppose what I could have done is looked at it the other way around
> and said, you know, all right, this guy is actually getting rent off these guys,
> he's got a lot of involvement with them, he's even going to the trouble of
> sorting cars out and stuff, what – you know, there, there should be more
> to it. They were the alarms, they were the alarms sort of thing that actually
> I should have noticed.

Charles knew then that it tended to be people with 'poor English' and hence
the 'least employable' who ended up working in the food processing plants
on the labour agency's accounts. He thus regretted his own 'naivety' in not

recognizing the 'opportunity to control' the Romanian workers' interpreter had cultivated for himself. He did, nevertheless, raise his concerns with the GLAA. They advised him not to do anything as their investigation was already 'ongoing'. Charles contacted the GLAA again subsequently when a Romanian woman in his own office alerted him that the workers were complaining about the interpreter being 'controlling', saying he would 'not let them out' or was 'locking them up'. However, Charles concluded that the meaning of these claims had been distorted in translation, the interpreter – then acting as an unlicensed gangmaster – probably 'dictating' who could work at which of the employment sites he was operating on rather than forcing anyone. In response to his report, the GLAA interviewed Charles again, but he heard no more from them until after he had left the company to set up his own labour agency.

Charles then received an SMS from the GLAA asking him to confirm his address. This was followed by written notification from the police, advising that he was being charged with breach of a gangmaster's licence. In court, Charles pled guilty to the charge, expecting it to relate primarily to the recruitment manager's theft of the holiday pay, his solicitor receiving no details of the case from the CPS until the second hearing. When the case was heard it became apparent that the interpreter's fraud was more extensive. The interpreter had secured access to the prepaid debit cards to which the agency was paying wages and was making his own deductions – 'of fifty to one hundred pounds a week' from the £300 the workers would earn. The interpreter committed this fraud with the help of his wife who helped the workers get 'settled' and the unwitting assistance of two women in the agency's accounts office who had copied him into emails that contained the workers' bank details.

> I'd no idea how much, and how reliant some of the girls were on the desk in, in helping them to sort of run it, if you like … To … make sure people were coming in and stuff.

Only in hindsight did Charles realize that the judge had assumed he was somehow in on the fraud – which amounted to a total of £30,000 taken from approximately 30 workers – for which the company's recruitment consultant together with the Romanian interpreter-turned-unlicensed-gangmaster and his wife all received custodial sentences. From Charles' perspective, however, the blame really fell across several 'desks' that were not his own. He accepted that he was 'responsible as the ops director for … anybody working within' the company and that it was 'a serious issue', which as the person 'named' on the GLAA licence, he was 'culpable for'. But he did not regard this kind of labour abuse as endemic in his company. Not having met any of the victims or profited from them, Charles did not see his offence as equivalent to that of the interpreter who had defrauded the workers directly. His was merely a 'mistake' with no malice intended from which he made no profit personally. Having to leave that line of work was a more severe consequence for Charles than the community penalty he was sentenced to: 'I just look at it and think, you know, it is what it is, I made those mistakes so I have … to live with those mistakes at the end of the day'.

Discussion

In this chapter, we have looked at examples of labour exploitation in large, medium and small business enterprises. Each was quite different in character, with Charles never meeting the Romanian workers who were being exploited within global supply chains; Hina utilizing family contacts to bring workers and their families over from Pakistan; and Sammy, assuming his tenants were also his friends, inviting them to socialize with other local business people while also expecting them to work in his shop for little or no pay as they became indebted to him in the most dire of circumstances. All regarded themselves as doing the right thing, by and large, for the people in their employ.

Those employed by Sammy, Hina and Charles worked in jobs at the periphery of the labour market with very few prospects in sectors in which employers struggle to attract UK workers (Nye, 2017). Filling labour shortages in the garment sector, in food processing and in takeaways has become increasingly difficult for employers as immigration restrictions increase. It is those whose lives and rights are most precarious who take these jobs in the absence of better options. And hence it is those whose lives are precarious who most easily become dependent on employers who underpay them or make deductions from their wages as they cannot find alternative work. As we have seen in the examples above, some of those migrant workers who challenge such conditions can risk losing their homes, right to live in the UK and access to medical care or schooling for their children. This is then a problem of the labour market, of inequalities in access to decent work both in countries of origin and in the UK and of market subcultures of structured immoralities that demand innovations that keep labour costs as low as possible in order to keep businesses viable and the costs of goods and services competitive. It is an acute problem embedded within the wider structures of labour markets that are under-regulated and which rely on 'free' market enterprise to establish a profit margin to the detriment of fair pay. And it is a problem that is not readily resolved through criminal justice interventions that rely on harnessing the testimonies of victims and witnesses whose credibility is easily undermined by virtue of being 'illegal' immigrants or petty offenders whose crimes are derivative of destitution (Cockbain and Brayley-Morris, 2018).

In sum, the stories of labour exploitation relayed in this chapter are better conceived of as deviations from ordinary business practices rather than a total departure from the conventions practiced every day in corporate supply chains and on our high streets. This is why neither Sammy, Hina and Charles considered themselves to be traffickers or to have held people in slavery. Doubtless these three individuals, and many like them who are in the criminal justice system for labour exploitation, had profited from the exploitation of other people, whether because they knew they were being underpaid, made deductions from their pay, or because they failed to explore or acknowledge the conditions that limited their capacities to enter and leave employment freely. In all three cases, the direct profits accumulated by the individuals convicted were comparatively small and reflective of unviable business models: in Charles' case in the mainstream meat-processing sector; in Hina's case in the hiring of migrant workers to make garments at prices that could compete with cheap labour in foreign markets; and in Sammy's case in a takeaway business that he was not capable of running proficiently. And while these profits were small for those hiring the labour, the money accumulated, loans offered, payments in food or deductions for visa and accommodation were the bare basics of what their employees needed to live.

Box (1983: 80) identifies 'moments of history when the state does create laws apparently against the interests of business'. Legislation brought to hold corporations responsible for exploitation in their supply chains had the potential to be such a moment in history. Some of the activities that take place within corporations and lead to the exploitation of workers were previously regulated outside the criminal law. The 2015 Modern Slavery Act and the licensing processes of the GLAA have brought some of these activities within UK criminal law – but these have only held a small number of individuals responsible for the exploitation of workers under their management, rather than businesses and corporations. The problem remains then that instances of exploitation are viewed as aberrations of the labour market rather than relatively normal practices in deregulated sectors in which competition is fierce and margins are tight (Kenway, 2021). When it happens, employers, as those depicted in this chapter reveal, retort that they were really trying to help their workers, that what happened was not really exploitation but a misunderstanding, that in highly competitive industries 'mistakes' get made and that the law itself generates more problems than it solves, especially when it is constantly changing and its enforcers are slow to respond and unavailable to advise and assist. One might read these as the literal, interpretive and implicatory denials of comparatively privileged people who are troubled by the recognition that their success derives from the exploitation of others. However, these responses must also be set in social and legal contexts. In the UK, this context is one in which redressing exploitation in supply chains has been defined by the government primarily as a voluntary, benevolent act by businesses that wish to promote themselves as ethical to consumers and shareholders, rather than as a legal obligation to ensure safe and fair working conditions for employees.

While campaigns to combat modern slavery typically seek to arrest, prosecute and deport foreign national offenders who have forced or coerced Eastern European workers into low-paid farm and factory work, when it comes to transparency in the supply chains of business the British government's approach has been much more conciliatory, seeking to 'work with' the private sector rather than developing and enforcing frameworks that would tackle the practices that allow exploitation to occur. Redressing cultures of employment where employers are convinced that providing work, however precarious and poorly paid, is in the best interests of their employees, has surely to be the starting point for tackling labour exploitation and stopping the kinds of modern slavery that take place within largely legitimate enterprises. Providing rights to guaranteed minimum rates of pay and secure accommodation for all those who live in the UK must surely be the most fundamental starting point for ending labour exploitation.

8 Adult Sex Trafficking

In this chapter we explore the lives of three people convicted of sex trafficking adults in the UK, noting the cultural frameworks – 'normal' family life, an escape from exploitation, a comparatively harmless business proposition – through which they justified their crimes as well as the extent to which they profited from the sex work of economically and legally precarious migrant women. In revealing how collaborations with sex workers are normalized in the lives of those convicted of modern slavery, the chapter challenges the stereotype of the 'evil trafficker' enslaving 'innocent' women and instead notes how the modern slavery agenda imposes a binary distinction on a diffuse industry that is reconstituted hourly, online and in person, via unregulated financial exchanges and profiteering that take place in the context of largely unpoliced illegality. The chapter concludes that, if the objective of state intervention is to limit the degree of exploitation within the sex industry, it would be better to replace prohibitions against running brothels with clarity regarding the terms around which third parties can provide security, premises, transportation and advertising to sex workers.

While the literature on sex trafficking is vast, there are few credible primary research studies of 'sex traffickers' per se. One could be forgiven for thinking that this is simply because sex traffickers are elusive and unwilling to speak to curious researchers about crimes that are universally regarded as abhorrent. But, as we explain in this chapter, the issue is more complex. While 'trafficking for the purposes of sexual exploitation' is an abuse that is exceptionally damaging to many victims, responsibility for it is not easily attributed to individual traffickers operating beyond both social conventions and the law. Rather, it is better to conceive of what gets labelled 'sex trafficking' as profiteering from the efforts of poor, predominantly migrant women, to overcome their own dire straits through engagement in illicit sex work. These women are often compelled to turn to 'third parties' – who are enterprising or internationally mobile men and women with backgrounds similar to their own – to surmount vulnerabilities that have been accentuated by multiple crises in their personal and family lives, intersecting layers of sexist and racist discrimination in domestic labour markets, and complex legal regimes that deny them basic financial and physical security.

DOI: 10.4324/9780429053986-8

One reason why sex traffickers tend to be presented in both media reports and anti-slavery campaigning materials as unscrupulous organized criminals with illiberal values is that this provides a simple explanation for the acute harms and hurts with which women who have been trafficked into prostitution present (Doezema, 2010). These harms and hurts include a heightened risk of being murdered, serially raped and seriously injured (Walby et al., 2016). They also include substance dependence, serious mental health conditions – including obsessive-compulsive and post-traumatic stress disorders – exposure to sexually transmitted diseases, serial pregnancies and abortions and, for those who try to escape without paying debts, abduction, threats to their families, coercion to marry, shame of exposure, destitution and homelessness (ibid). Once it is considered how gendered sexual exploitation is – 96% of the 34,000 sex trafficking victims officially detected within the European Union between 2012 and 2014 were female, while 75% of convicted traffickers were male – the stereotype of evil men victimizing vulnerable women gains greater currency (European Parliament, 2017). But what is rarely explained in public debate is that being trafficked into prostitution in Western countries is hardly ever a singular event in which a woman is deceived, abducted and repeatedly raped. Such scenarios provide compelling plot lines for movies (such as the *Taken* films, *Room*, *Lilja-4-Ever* and *Trafficked*) that enable easy identification with victims through the drama of escape and rescue from depraved psychopaths and foreign mafias. However, the reality of sexual exploitation in the West tends to be rather different, the 'simple dichotomies of force versus choice' failing to capture the complexities of the decisions those working in various roles within sex markets make (Pitcher and Wijers, 2014). As we explain, below, the research evidence suggests that more typically women who have made conscious decisions to enter the sex industry become enmeshed in increasingly exploitative circumstances as their work fails to generate enough funds to cover debts, pay bills, raise children or send remittances back to parents or other relatives. It is in these circumstances that desperate people typically come to rely on entrepreneurs within illicit economies; entrepreneurs who promise, sometimes in good faith, to assist them with finances, somewhere to live and work, and transportation for their migratory journeys and daily working routines.

Defining 'Exploitation' and 'Vulnerability'

Within the countries of the European Union, legal definitions of sex trafficking usually refer to 'the exploitation of the prostitution of others'. 'Exploitation', as defined by the EU Directive 2011/36/EU (and echoing the 2000 Palermo Protocol), can entail the:

> recruitment, transportation, transfer, harbouring or reception of persons, including the exchange or transfer of control over those persons, by means of the threat or use of force or other forms of coercion, of abduction, of fraud, of deception, of the abuse of power or of a position of vulnerability

or of the giving or receiving of payments or benefits to achieve the consent of a person having control over another person, for the purpose of exploitation.

While acts such as abduction and the use and threat of force clearly entrap people, other acts within this list – like transporting those who are vulnerable and/or helping to recruit them into work that turns out to be very poorly paid in the expectation of some later repayment – are less overtly exploitative and might be regarded as relatively commonplace features of everyday life. When the endpoint of the journey is entry into sex work, it is often assumed that sex trafficking has taken place. But this is not necessarily so given that some people do wittingly travel to enter into sex work, either because they anticipate it to be better paid than the sex work or other work they are currently undertaking or because it is easier to escape the stigma of being a sex worker if one relocates to somewhere no one knows you (Weitzer, 2018).

Consequently, to determine whether sex trafficking has occurred one has first to define both 'exploitation' and 'vulnerability'. This is not easy since both concepts involve relative dimensions. Does taking a percentage from the earnings of any sex worker, however well paid, in return for the provision of advertising, transport or accommodation count as exploitation? If not, what counts as a non-exploitative minimum wage for someone who sells sex? Are all women who work in the sex industry – or indeed any industry in gender asymmetrical societies – exploited, or just those who have specific vulnerabilities (Farley, 2004)? It is universally accepted within the European Union that children are, by definition, vulnerable and thus cannot 'consent' to sex work or work in illicit markets. But vulnerability can also be defined in terms of citizenship status, physical and learning disabilities, drug dependencies and health conditions, exposure to the threat of violence, economic precariousness and the absence of an affordable home – all of which are features of everyday life for many adult women who sell sex for a living.

Anti-trafficking campaigning groups often assert that vulnerability can be discerned from visual tell-tale signs. Hence, the NGO Stop the Traffik[1] distinguishes between 'sex work' – when 'a person willingly takes part in the sale of sex' that is 'consensual' – and 'sex trafficking' – when 'a person takes part in the sale of sex through threat, abduction or other means of coercion'. People exposed to the latter, Stop the Traffik suggest, are likely to be identifiable as such because they are: closely guarded; may have bruises or scars from being assaulted or burnt with cigarettes; have 'tattoos indicating ownership'; are not allowed to keep their own money; or because they sleep in premises where sexual services are sold or homes that are 'poor or unsanitary'. The problem with such checklists is they overlook the social and legal contexts in which most sex work takes place, that is, where cash is exchanged but no records are kept or tax paid, where recourse to the police is severely hindered by the risk of social stigma and criminalization, and hence where dependence on hired protection is often necessary (Agustín, 2007).

Some countries, like Germany and the Netherlands, have adopted legal positions that provide for the regulation of sex work through the provision of licenses. Within this context, sex workers have secured minimal rights and hence not all financial exchanges pertaining to sex work are deemed 'exploitative'. Other countries, like Sweden, Norway, Israel, France, Eire and Northern Ireland, have adopted models that decriminalize the selling of sex while criminalizing its purchase. How effective this approach is at regulating sex work is fiercely contested. Critics of this legal reform – sometimes termed the 'Nordic model' – suggest it has driven prostitution underground, forced sex workers to operate clandestinely in contexts where they are poorly protected, cannot work collectively with colleagues and are vulnerable to having payments withheld by clients looking to protect themselves from arrest (Pitcher, 2015; Pitcher and Wijers, 2014; Levy and Jakobsson, 2014).

At the heart of these debates are different standpoints regarding the questions of whether sex work is inherently abusive (Farley, 2004) or whether it is simply a form of employment, the harms of which ought to be moderated by guaranteeing workers' rights, safety and minimum rates of pay (Weitzer, 2007). Positions within these debates hardened when modern slavery (re)entered the policy agenda in the 1990s (Broad and Turnbull, 2019), pre-empting the 'almost complete collapse of any discursive boundary between human trafficking and prostitution' (Phoenix, 2009: 7) in many Western legislatures, with policies to curtail 'illegal' migration posited as solutions in the UK, the Netherlands (Pitcher and Wijers, 2014) and Australia (Sullivan, 2010). As organizations representing sex workers routinely argue, laws introduced purportedly to protect sex workers from trafficking have often made their work more dangerous (Adams et al., 2016). In many countries, including the UK, those sex workers who choose to work or travel together risk arrest for running brothels and receiving, harbouring, transporting or transferring those deemed 'vulnerable' (Agustín, 2006). The prohibition of those selling sex from working together 'remains a particularly disempowering element of the prostitution law' which prevents 'crime reporting, disenfranchising workers from legally co-working' and ultimately increasing safety-related risks (Campbell et al., 2018: 18). These risks are compounded variously by aggrieved clients, neighbours who consider sex work a nuisance and competitors who wish to accrue advantage, each of whom know that they need only make an anonymous online report about suspected trafficking to trigger a police investigation or raid (Campbell et al., 2018; Sanders, 2004, 2005; Campbell and O'Neill, 2013).

Law enforcement concerning prostitution in the UK is particularly inconsistent. While exchanging sex for money is not illegal in the UK, soliciting in public is an offence under Section One of the 1959 Street Offences Act, though often tolerated in specific locales. The selling of sex in 'private' is generally not criminalized, unless done in collaboration with other parties, as it is an offence to run a brothel (under the 1956 Sexual Offences Act), with brothels defined narrowly in case law as 'when more than one woman uses premises for the purposes of prostitution, either simultaneously or one at a time' (Stevens v

Christy [1987] Cr. App. R. 249, DC). It is also an offence in the UK to cause or incite prostitution or control it for personal gain under Section 2 of the 2003 Sexual Offences Act, causation having been further specified under case law to include either 'fraud or persuasion'. In other words, those who collaborate with sex workers – assisting them in their work, whether working alongside them, providing ancillary services, transport or premises – risk convictions for 'pimping' and 'brothel keeping' as much as those who simply confiscate a percentage from their earnings out of a sense of entitlement.

Purchasers of sex in the UK also have a duty of care to those from whom they buy sexual services. Since the implementation of 2009 Policing and Crime Act, anyone who buys sexual services from someone who has been subject to exploitative conduct – whether or not the buyer is aware of that conduct – can be found guilty of a sexual offence in the UK (Day, 2010). The 2015 Modern Slavery Act further complicated law in this area and, as some of the cases we discuss later in this chapter reveal, further equated the buyers of sex with those third parties who facilitate the labour of sex workers, both of whom can be cast as 'traffickers' when the workers concerned hail from overseas. Such paradoxes pertain because criminal law in the UK has evolved in the absence of considered debate about the nature of sex work and how global migration and the advent of the internet have changed the ways in which sexual services are sold (Campbell et al., 2018; Sanders et al., 2018).

Acknowledgment of this myopia has tended to be expressed in alarmist tones. For example, in his preface to the all-parliamentary group's report on 'organised sexual exploitation in England and Wales', *Behind Closed Doors*, the group's chair, Gavin Shuker MP, wrote:

> Organised crime groups increasingly dominate the sexual exploitation of women through prostitution, regularly moving women around temporary brothel premises, exhorting a high degree of coercion over them as they do. Pop-up brothels are changing migration patterns with huge numbers of women, particularly from Eastern Europe, being brought in by these groups to service British men who have an expectation of an absolute right to buy sex. A handful of explicit prostitution procurement websites enable this trade, making sizeable profits, directly benefitting from the exploitation of others. But rental landlords, online booking companies, and hotel sites all indirectly profit from the practice as exploiters take advantage of poor safeguards to hire new sites for pop-ups. The result is a trade that is organised, industrialised and highly damaging for those whose consent is purchased.
>
> (Shuker, 2018: ii)

The government briefing goes on to claim that 'third party exploiters, including traffickers and brothel owners, dominate the off-street sex trade, exploiting mainly non-UK national women'; that the 'the largest nationality group identified among potential victims is Romanian' and that 'Romanian suspects constitute the largest nationality group among individuals under investigation' (APPG on Prostitution and the Global Sex Trade, 2018: 1). The suspects who exploit these victims are assumed to use methods of 'deception, coercion and the exploitation of pre-existing vulnerabilities' such as 'debt bondage; sexual and physical violence; threats; surveillance; and isolation', enabled by adult services websites (p.2). The websites Vivastreet and Adultwork, hosted by companies located in tax havens – Jersey and Panama – are singled out by the APPG as the most significant 'third party profiteers of commercial sexual exploitation' and 'trafficking in the UK' (p.18) and sites that have provided account managers to customers who spent copious amounts of money purchasing advertisements that sell prostitution.

Internet Sex Work

There is no denying the scale of sexual services available online. In November 2017, Adultwork, for example, hosted 178,000 adverts selling sexual services with women and 6,000 adverts selling sexual services with men, alongside smaller numbers of adverts for services offered by couples and LGBTQ+ sex workers. Of course, some of these adverts may well have been obsolete, while others promote the same worker under alternative pseudonyms and photographs. Nevertheless, even allowing for some duplication, the site reveals a vast sector. To the purchaser, these sexual services are searchable in terms of location as well as by the demography (age, ethnicity) and physique (bust size) of the sex worker sought. Each sex worker advertises their own profile, in what can be read as competitive sales pitches, outlining likes and dislikes, which services they will and will not supply, times of availability, rates and means of contact and mode of payment.

Many offer purchasable extras, including access to souvenir images and videos, as well as gifts that can be bought for the sex worker, and some advertise 'tours', indicating in which localities they will be on particular days. As with Amazon and eBay, some sellers secure premium slots that are highlighted on the page and supported by sophisticated pitches and seller ratings. Indeed, Vivastreet is in some ways a competitor to eBay in that, in addition to selling sexual and massage services and promoting swingers and fetish clubs, it also advertises a range of second-hand goods, travel and property rentals and job opportunities. The adverts it hosts for sexual services are like those found on the back pages of tabloid newspapers and reveal a market divided between independent sex workers and agency workers (who often appear younger). The site also hosts adverts for the agencies looking to recruit sex workers, webcammers, receptionists and drivers – both for sex workers and clients – outlining possible rates of pay and salaries, as well as the percentage taken by brokers.

What is less certain, however, is the degree to which the majority of those selling sex on the internet consider themselves to be deceived and entrapped by traffickers, and whether the advent of web-based adverts and 'pop-up brothels' – short lease properties used for prostitution – are compounding the exploitation many workers in this industry face. In her ethnography of sex workers in London (1980–2002), Day (2010) discovered that many migrant women went 'on the game' because they had:

> lost their jobs and welfare entitlements and then shifted of necessity into the informal economy as they benefited from a new, albeit highly partial, freedom of movement. Many worked in appalling conditions, with no English, and keeping little of their money. Yet, situations changed and it often took less than a year to become a manager in turn and send remittances home.
>
> (p.824)

Only a very small minority of Day's participants 'spoke of deception or coercion' (p.825). Unlike those women who had entered prostitution via contacts with other 'girlfriends', deceived and coerced women were more likely to have entered 'sex work through boyfriends who turned out to be pimps' whom they did not recognize as such until years later, in part because they were unsure if they had initially chosen the work freely and whether they could have subsequently walked away: 'The differences between a close friend and a vicious manager were only drawn in retrospect, once the relationship had fallen apart' (p.825).

Similarly, Agustín (2006, 2007), drawing upon interviews with migrants who sell sex, has warned against the tendency to dichotomize the relationships between those selling sex and those facilitating their movement, the word 'trafficking' and its glossary of perpetration and victimization a 'woefully inadequate way to conceptualise them' (Agustín, 2007: 48). Against this backcloth, Sanders et al.'s (2018) survey (n = 642) and follow-up interviews (n = 62) with sex workers based in the UK reveal that the movement of the market online – though not without new risks, including having web content stolen and reused or used to blackmail has given many sex workers: more freedom to work flexible hours; greater opportunities for profit through group webcasting and the release of videos; a greater level of control in terms of screening customers and sharing information about men who are violent, remove condoms or attempt to avoid payment; escape from the dangers of street-based sex work; and energized activism that campaigns for workers' rights and decriminalization. Only a quarter of the participants in Sanders and colleagues' study used 'third parties' such as protectors, door staff, drivers and receptionists. But foreign national women were more likely to have someone present in their working location than UK nationals. Sanders et al. suggest this greater dependence on third parties among foreign national women could be because those with limited literacy in English find it 'harder to navigate websites and applications' and/or to 'utilise safety information without translation function' (p.109). It could also be because: foreign national sex workers are less likely to be aware of the complexities of UK law; assume it to be consistent with that of other EU countries; and experience more violence but are less likely to report this to the police (Brown and Sanders, 2017). Sanders et al.'s (2018) research suggests that migrant sex workers, as law violators, are more likely to attract the attention of the police than UK-born sex workers and that the British police often put the onus on migrant sex workers themselves to demonstrate that they have not been trafficked by third-party exploiters.

Traffickers, Pimps, Mamis and Other Third Parties

Inevitably there are relatively few recent studies that address who these third-party exploiters are and what they do. Copley's (2014: 51) international over-view of secondary accounts from soldiers, politicians, pimps and madams attempts to show how 'traffickers utilize techniques of neutralization based on vulnerabilities exacerbated by social influences, cultural norms, and glo-balization'. Bosnian soldiers who trafficked women to 'bordello camps' where they were raped denied responsibility by claiming they were 'only following orders' relayed by 'their President'; Indian madams deny causing harm to sex workers by rationalizing that they are safer in their brothels than at home; Eastern European sex traffickers deny the humanity of young sex workers by referring to them as their 'property'; defenders of the abduction and exploit-ation of Korean and Chinese 'comfort women' during Second World War jus-tify their country's actions as necessary to *reduce* sexual assaults perpetrated by soldiers away from their wives; and those convicted of sex trafficking crimes the world over condemn their condemners by accusing the criminal justice professionals and politicians who have exposed them of being more corrupt than they are.

Such rationalizations are certainly evident in the few primary studies of those who might be deemed 'third-party' exploiters, but these studies also reveal the importance of grappling with the cultural and economic specificities of the relationships between sex workers and those who profit from their labours. In the US, where prostitution is more heavily criminalized and online classified advertising sites that are viewed as 'enabling prostitution and the sex trafficking of minors' have been outlawed (Savage and Williams, 2018), the stratifications of a fiercely competitive sex work market shape relationships between sex workers and the third parties who support and profit from their work. Marcus and colleagues' (2016) participant observation study of over 150 sex workers in New Jersey found that those sex workers who commanded high prices secured more proficient pimps, who treated them well and found them new and better clients and venues. By contrast, those sex workers who were less accomplished, those whose work was predominantly street-based and those who were minors were more reliant on 'spot pimps' – 'street hustlers and drug dealers who refer walk-up customers to sex workers for tips', but with whom sex workers do not have an 'exclusive relationship' (p.50). Spot pimps offered physical protection in return for sex and money, often on a 'pay upfront per transaction' basis. Marcus et al. (2016) found that 'controlling pimps' were a very small minority and that all parties tended to agree that supporting consensual sex work generated better profits than forced prostitution. Pimping for minors was regarded by many as high-risk and unprofitable, not least because of the greater chance of clients refusing to pay.

By way of contrast, Shen's (2016) ethnographic study of Chinese sex workers reveals that caring relationships can and do develop between some female prostitutes and the older female *mamis* who help organize their clients – both groups of women tending to be predominantly rural migrants who collaborate for small margins to retain a degree of self-sufficiency in grindingly competitive, male-dominated business worlds. Similarly, Kay Hoang (2015) depicts mutually supportive relationships between the women who manage gentleman's clubs in Vietnam and the women who drink, flirt and sometimes have sex with patrons of these clubs. Together, both conspire to exploit the (often failing) businessmen from the West, who are there being tested by Vietnamese business partners. The women in this study revealed how they work to dupe businessmen who need to appear generous into providing funds to 'rescue' them by finessing stories of hardship, darkening their skin colour to appear more authentically Vietnamese and even hiring pseudo families in nearby rural enclaves to illustrate how hard they have tried to better themselves. Some Vietnamese sex workers in Kay Hoang's study had escaped compulsory rehabilitation, in the form of menial manual labour, imposed on them by the state and supported by NGOs that previously 'rescued' them. Some were also highly attentive to the investment decisions being made by the men who solicited their attention, following the advice their customers shared with each other and reinvesting their own earnings in the stockmarket accordingly.

A similar emphasis on the intersections of markets with rapid cultural change can be found in Mai's (2012) ethnographic documentary, *Normal: Real Stories from the Sex Industry*, and the various supporting publications upon which it is based (Mai, 2010; see also Mai, 2016). Mai's interviews reveal that sex workers and the third parties they work with in Europe – including men and women, gay, straight and transgender people – tend to share an aspiration to be 'normal'. As a result of disadvantage and discrimination, some willingly enter relationships that are illicit and exploitative as a way of holding onto this promise of future 'normality', social acceptance and/or citizenship. The most brutal character in *Normal* is Besnick, a 27-year-old Albanian soldier's son, who deceives women into working as prostitutes because he wants to be wealthy like a 'billionaire' friend of his. Besnick thus avoided falling in love with the women who worked to pay his fines lest their tears 'fuck' with his 'brain'. But others depicted in *Normal* defy social stereotypes of traffickers and their victims. Adrian, a 24-year-old Romanian living in Rome, had run away from home as a teenager before selling himself to 'queers'. Adrian was then approached by a woman who proposed they do 'some business together', which entailed him providing protection to her while she engaged clients. The woman needed the respectability of having a boyfriend while Adrian needed to earn enough money to return to Romania to seek forgiveness from his father and open a pizza business. By contrast, Candy, a 19-year-old Romanian woman with aspirations to marry, go to 'university and teach in high school', had served a custodial sentence for trafficking women who she and a 'boyfriend' (who had deceived Candy into working as a prostitute) had brought from the Netherlands to London. Others who were sharing the proceeds of sex work with third parties did not necessarily perceive themselves as exploited. Catalin, a 17-year-old man, left behind a life of begging in Romania to sell sex in Rome and shared his income with his wife and parents who knew what he did for living. Similarly, Cynthia, a 37-year-old transsexual Venezuelan, was repaying money she had borrowed from a European woman she regarded as a pseudo mother figure (her own mother having disowned her) in the expectation that one day she could 'be normal here in Europe' and free of the 'fear of being deported'. Finally, Alina, a 32-year-old Moldovan who worked as an 'independent' sex worker to support her legal training, had previously been tricked into prostitution after seeking work as an 'escort'. Alina had, nevertheless, provided false evidence against purported 'traffickers' in order to secure leave to remain in the UK after she was threatened with deportation.

Case Studies

These examples make the point that while sexual exploitation usually involves profiting from the vulnerabilities of others caught at the intersections of multiple inequalities and the restrictions of global migration flows, those third parties who profit from sex work tend to be 'individually motivated, morally complex, and culturally embedded' as Choi-Fitzpatrick (2016: 2) explains. In what follows we present summaries of interviews with three of our participants who were involved in sexual exploitation. All three were charged with, or convicted of, trafficking for the purposes of sexual exploitation offences. All three served custodial sentences of three or more years' imprisonment. We use these cases to illustrate the diversity of roles undertaken by those engaged in pimping and running brothels; to problematize presumptions about victims and victimizers and the relationships between them; and to argue that the exploitation in question is better understood in terms of employment relationships in an industry that depends, because of its complex illegality, on a division of labour comprising kin, intimate partners and acquaintances, marred by degrees of desperation and dependency that are accentuated by gender, poverty and immigration status. These insights make the distinction between 'sex trafficking' and 'migrant sex work' somewhat arbitrary in the UK context. They also make greater clarification of the obligations of those who *provide services to sex workers and/or others in highly exploitative industries* essential if law enforcement is to contribute effectively to reducing sexual exploitation.

Adam: Gangster, Pimp and Rescuer

Adam was a Hungarian man in his 20s serving a custodial sentence for trafficking for sexual exploitation who had been convicted alongside both of his parents and one of his brothers, Dominik. While he pled guilty to the trafficking charges, Adam denied sexually assaulting the victim – Jenny – who had sought a sexual relationship with him when she fled another family who were exploiting her. Adam explained that while he had been charged with multiple counts of rape, he had not been convicted of it: 'if girls feel no like sex I no touch girl. Never'.

Until he was ten years old, Adam lived in Hungary with his parents with whom he was 'very, very close', particularly his father. Aged ten, Adam and his family moved to the UK for a short time and then returned to Hungary before relocating temporarily to Canada after his father was beaten up by former associates in the Hungarian 'mafia'. His dad, Adam explained, was a 'big gigolo' who had numerous affairs which he, Adam, attributed to his mother's gambling problem. By way of contrast, Adam had a difficult relationship with his brother Dominik and, by extension, Dominik's wife Sarah, both of whom had been drug users since their early teens and who had become 'lazy' and reluctant to work.

Adam had also begun taking drugs at the age of 13, progressing from weed to ecstasy and amphetamine. With help from his father, he became a dealer during his teens. This drug use and dealing caused the end of Adam's relationship with his fiancée and 'first love', Hanna, who broke up with him after he served 18 months in prison. Having made the 'biggest mistake' of his life, Adam responded to the break-up by intensifying his drug use, which induced in him psychotic symptoms which he tried to overcome by moving to the UK where his brother and parents had relocated after Hungary's accession to the European Union. In the UK, aged 20, Adam consumed up to £700 worth of amphetamine and crystal meth per week, sometimes with his parents. After a series of casual sexual relationships, Adam met Jenny at a party. She had been living with the family of one of Adam's best friends, making money for them through a sham marriage to an Asian man and as a sex worker. The family kept all her earnings and retained her passport. Jenny 'fell in love' with Adam instantly and asked to live with him and his family instead. Three weeks later, Adam began a sexual relationship with Jenny although maintained that he did not 'love her'. 'She use me, I use her, because she use my family, she never have a family'. Adam argued with Jenny about her 'crazy' behaviour, and criticized her for not taking care of her son, who remained in Hungary – arguments in which Adam slapped and hit Jenny.

'They' or Adam alone – it was unclear – nevertheless spotted a 'good opportunity' for Jenny to work as a prostitute for him in another property, along with two other 'girls' who had been working for his dad's friend. Here, Jenny and Adam were joined by Sarah, Dominik's wife, who had not long given birth and earned money for his brother as a sex worker, an occupation she chose over being made, by Adam, to return to Hungary for failing to contribute to the family's expenses. Adam explained that working in the sex industry in the UK was a way for him to make 'easy money' as people 'spend' and 'party' there, unlike in Hungary where people had no money, and just 'pay the rent, pay the bill'. The 'girls' were advertised on Adultwork and Vivastreet and clients contacted them via mobile phones. Adam's role was to wait in the lounge and deal phys-ically with any clients that got 'crazy'; violence that was a rarity but which he was very prepared to enact. The 'girls' would have between 8 and 12 'clients' on a night, earning around £80 an hour. Adam retained all of Jenny and Sarah's money, maintaining that they could have 'everything' through the family. He retained half of the other two girls' money and kept their passports. Adam spent his money on 'drugs, clothes' and a 'car'. In addition, when an 'aunty' contacted him from Hungary about another 'girl' who had been working for some time as a prostitute, Adam obliged and bought a flight ticket, the cost of which the 'girl' repaid Adam at £50 per week over the course of six weeks.

Aged 21, Adam decided to move back in with his parents, feeling that working with four girls was 'too much risk' after his dad's friend was subject to a police investigation. When Jenny then 'grassed' on Adam, his family were arrested. Although he accepted the charges, he disputed Jenny's status as a victim; 'I am no the victim, but Jenny is no victim as well'. Upon release, Adam expected to return to Hungary 'free', 'no licence, nothing'. Rather than recommence dealing in drugs, as he expected his father would want him to, Adam intended to work with his 'uncle' and 'nephew' in the Netherlands, employing a single sex worker, a 'good girl' who did not use drugs and who might earn him 'about 1000 euros a day'. He surmised that he had learnt from his 'mistakes', explaining that if you 'just look after these girls, just live together, no one else, you have a good life'.

Sandra: Sex Worker Turned Brothel Keeper

Sandra was a 47-year-old British woman sentenced to nine months imprison-ment for keeping a brothel. She was raised in a family of nine children, two half siblings on her dad's side preceding her and six younger siblings, including a brother, Martin, who was two years her junior and whom she had come to regard as her 'son' because she had cared for him when the family was in crisis. Sandra's father – a man of south Asian heritage – had battered his wife and sexually abused his children until Sandra turned 18, when her parents separated. Thereafter, Sandra studied for a diploma in social work and secured a job working with children with behavioural problems.

Aged 27, Sandra's life was again thrown into turmoil when Martin committed an armed robbery and she was found to have committed perjury to cover for him. The loss of her job led to financial difficulties for Sandra, which she attempted to redress by working 'cash in hand' as a nanny by day and a bouncer by night, but to little avail as Martin's drug debts in prison escalated. Because of these debts, Sandra became homeless and was arrested on several occasions for drunk and disorderly behaviour. She fell pregnant to a 'Jack-the-lad' and entered prostitution, having conceived the idea with a friend after watching a television drama that convinced them they could earn a lot of money from 'hand jobs' alone. But, within a day, Sandra was 'doing sex' for money and, in the years that followed, she raised her daughter alone, moving between refuges and brothels, never taking drugs, and keeping herself to herself, before she was helped to settle into a flat of her own. Sandra believed that she had juggled motherhood with sex work ably, 'earning as much in a night as many other people make in a week'; the night-time working, mostly at weekends, enabling her to be back home for 6 am when her daughter woke up.

When Sandra's daughter entered nursery, Sandra began to fear what would happen if any of the parents of other children learnt of her work, so she began to commute to a parlour in a neighbouring city. At this point, sex work became more difficult for three reasons. First, Sandra stopped doing hotel visits, dangerous work which she nevertheless 'loved'. Second, the brothel would fine her £10 for leaving early, something she often needed to do in order to be home in time to collect her daughter from nursery. Third, the sex industry became more competitive as more Eastern European sex workers began to arrive in the UK, selling sex from the street at lower prices than UK sex workers, being more willing to hustle punters, and benefitting, in some places, from police protection in unofficial red-light districts.

By her late 30s, Sandra had enough of handing half her earnings over to men. 'Mentally' she did not want to sell sex anymore. She decided to go into business herself, setting up her own pop-up brothels and negotiating with landlords who she suspected charged her a higher fee than ordinary tenants, but who were aware of her line of business. Some customers were local, but most arrived by black cab, the drivers having been given cards advertising the brothel and taking a commission of £30 for each passenger they delivered. Customers then paid a further £60 on arrival: £30 of which went to the sex worker, £20 of which was retained by Sandra and £10 of which was also taken by Sandra as a door fee. A manager was hired by Sandra to work on the front desk and sometimes her brother, Martin, also helped remove difficult clients, though Sandra was able to do this herself 'being a tough cookie'.

Sandra had hoped that delegating in this way would enable her to provide her daughter with a 'nice life' she herself had been denied as a child, but now having been imprisoned for keeping a brothel she felt she had let her daughter down. When the police first investigated Sandra's brothel business, she was arrested but not charged. Sandra suspected that a rival or disgruntled sacked worker had reported her brothels to the police, who, when they raided her other premises three months later, discovered a victim of trafficking, despite her being 'so careful' about the 'girls' she had working there. Sandra was incredulous: all her 'girls' were 'grown women' not minors, ID checked, who had to abide by the house rules of 'no drugs' and alcohol in the rooms or be 'sacked'. 'I never, ever employed Eastern European girls because I knew from brothels I'd worked in where the pimps are waiting for them, and they're working 24 hours, not going home, just horrible'.

Andrei: IT Assistant or Ringleader?

Andrei was a 35-year-old Romanian man convicted for running and maintaining a brothel, facilitating trafficking and gaining from the benefits of prostitution, offences he initially surmised, with some bravado, were about 'selling pussy', only to insist subsequently that 'trafficking' was 'unthinkable' to him and to explain that his crimes had been motivated by a desire to make money against a backcloth of hardship, addiction and legal ambiguity. Raised by a father who was a high-ranking military officer and a mother who was an army computer technician, as a child Andrei's family 'had money' and were able to afford his training as an accountant in Bucharest. Andrei never practised, however, and instead worked as a barista until he was 25, his tips spent on heroin consumption that became increasingly habitual after he tried it with friends aged 16. After his female partner of seven years ended their relationship and the coffee shop where he worked lost custom, Andrei's 'double life' became unsustainable, neither a holiday nor the consumption of opioid substitutes enough to quell his 'addiction' and return to a 'normal life'. He thus welcomed the offer of a 'normal job', made by a childhood friend, to join him in opening a 'computer business' in the UK, where he would make 'better money' and escape the circle of drug users who sustained his 'addiction'.

Upon arrival in the UK, Andrei discovered that his friend had 'lied' about the nature of the work available. The friend was working with a woman who was running a brothel. They needed Andrei to produce websites for two Romanian 'girls' advertising 'professional massage' services and assisting with renting a house and securing a bankcard, not least because neither of them was fluent in English. The sex workers shared half their income with the brothel keepers who, in turn, provided Andrei with a room in the house to live in and paid him up to £200 per advert. Andrei's heroin consumption then escalated, withdrawal from the methadone treatment he had undergone proving too painful for him. When, three months later, his best friend left the brothel suffering mental health problems caused by his own drug use, Andrei welcomed the invitation to be employed directly by the pimps whose 'wives with benefits' worked on the premises (and who were working in partnership, in some instances post-divorce, to save up enough money to buy properties together in Romania for themselves and/or their children). He was also pleased to expand his services to two of their brothers who were in the same line of work, and other couples who approached him from Romania looking for help to buy travel tickets and support with their websites.

Andrei established his own computer repair business on the premises and divided his time between doing that, getting high and making the adverts, mostly leaving the sex workers' partners to the day-to-day work of acting as 'bodyguards' to protect the women from abusive clients and rival sex work firms who rang up to check out whether or not the women were working alone. But, after his friend left, Andrei also came to see the 'company', together with the car and home it provided him with, as his. Andrei had acted as a guarantor on the properties leased on three-month lets that became the pop-up brothels where sex was sold in neighbouring towns. Sometimes he would provide lifts to the 'girls' when they needed to return to these properties to meet regular customers, or when taxis were unavailable. And when Andrei and two of the men were arrested, he secured them a lawyer who advised the sex workers to 'give better statements' clarifying that they were not victims.

Since Andrei's conviction, the women had moved to Germany where they had secured licenses as masseurs and were waiting for him to return to their firm. In the UK, the police and immigration services had been aware of their business and had previously been satisfied that the women were not being threatened or having their money taken. The police's response changed, however, when an aggrieved punter who was in love with one of the sex workers made a malicious complaint. It was only after two of his co-accused were cajoled into accepting lesser charges in return for giving evidence that depicted Andrei as the 'ringleader' that he had accepted the charges against him. Andrei denied any such coordinating role, explaining he only had a few hundred pounds in his bank account, insisting that none of the sex workers had been 'forced' and that all of them came to the UK seeking sex work of their own volition:

> I never forced for them to do it. It's like, a girl who loves sex and she loves money, she will do it, she will do things without money, money is better.

While he accepted that he had been the 'manager' of a brothel, Andrei asked: 'How' he could 'traffick someone when that someone brought me here, paid for my ... coming here and pay me for what I am doing?'. He nevertheless lied to his family about why he was in prison in the UK, telling them only that he had got into a fight in a pub.

Discussion

In this chapter, we have presented three cases of individuals who were profiting from the sex work of others. Adam was perhaps the most stereotypical case, working within a family business in which prostitution was regarded as a normal way of earning a living and financing drug use. The family business moved from one location or country to another when the going got tough and relied upon networks of male contacts and relationships with women in which sex and business were routinely mixed. The women Adam and his brother employed faced dire straits – return to original traffickers, risk of homelessness, separation from a new-born child, being returned to their home countries – if they could not repay debts incurred through the purchase of travel or pay their way within the house Adam's family provided. The pressure to continue working for Adam and his family was exacerbated for some of these women by their need to send money back to their home country for their children and by the threat of domestic – if not sexual – abuse from men in the family who felt free to physically reprimand them. While Jenny had pursued a sexual relationship with Adam and had agreed to enter sex work for money, she had done so from the position of wanting to be rescued from another family who were exploiting her more acutely, and from which Adam assumed he had saved her.

For Sandra, engagement in prostitution was more shameful, though perhaps not as shameful as the sexual and domestic violence to which she and her siblings had been exposed as children, and which she tried to keep out of mind. Having shared the profits of her sex work with men for many years, she had made a conscious decision to move up a rung and open her own brothel; a decision that was inspired by her desire to build a better life for her daughter, though one which, paradoxically, also helped justify her business-like approach to the management of the other younger women who worked in her brothels. Like Adam, and the taxi drivers who tax brothels for the customers they deliver, Sandra took a substantial cut from the women working on her properties. In return, however, she sought decent working conditions for them and set firm rules prohibiting the consumption of drugs and alcohol. She nevertheless failed to notice that one of the women in her employ was also being exploited by another third party, until the alarm was raised by a competitor or disgruntled customer who alerted the police.

Finally, Andrei had become involved in organizing sex work as a website developer after he was offered the opportunity to work in the UK, which he assumed, incorrectly, would enable him to overcome his heroin dependency. While Andrei offered a misogynistic rationalization for working in the sex industry and became, to some extent, personally invested in the business of 'selling pussy' and 'managing a brothel', he had also been dependent on the couples who hired him and provided him with accommodation in order to support their dreams of buying properties in Romania. They, as he noted, had brought him to the UK, rather than vice versa, and he had had to prove his worth to them before he began to profit from their business. He nevertheless provided the financial and web-based services that enabled their business to grow as well as paying for the legal advice that enabled the women to present themselves as acting freely, exempting themselves from giving evidence against him and the other men they worked with.

In sum, while their trajectories into sexual exploitation varied, Adam, Sandra and Andrei had comprehensible reasons for profiting from the sex work of others: reasons that derived from the various misfortunes in their own lives. Their actions involved exploitation, and sometimes a degree of manipulation and threat, but they were not devoid of all morality. Adam entered a partnership that enabled Jenny to leave a family who had trafficked her. Sandra attempted to provide better working conditions for the women in her brothels than she had encountered as a sex worker herself. Andrei confined his work to the provision of ancillary services requested by sex workers and their partners in order to fund a heroin habit he could not overcome. These 'third-party organizers' of sex work did bare some semblance of similarity to the caricatures routinely presented of them in journalistic reworking of police press releases, in that their engagement with sex workers was for personal profit, underscored by limited empathy, and sometimes finessed with sexism, and supported by connections with others engaged in illicit industries from their countries of origin. All of the women selling the sex were referred to as 'girls', even while their freedom to choose sex work was emphasized, overly so, given the circumstances in which such work was entered.

To suggest that these women were being kept as 'slaves', however, would be to simplify the cases. While we cannot know whether the women from whose sex work Adam, Sandra and Andrei profited worked for them on terms they regarded as 'fair' (in spite of conditions that were for some inescapable given their aspirations and indebtedness), the bigger picture is that all parties operated in what might be thought of as largely unpoliced illegality that only attracted the attention of law enforcement when migrant sex work was framed as modern slavery. Sex work organized in ways that would have been legal in other countries, which had long been part of their daily employment, and which was typically entered into as a 'deal' to cover costs, repay debts, or build a better life, was then recast as something much more sinister, with organized networks of traffickers keeping women captive to secure vast profits for their ringleaders. Our participants saw themselves in different terms. While accepting that they were profiting from the sex work of others, they saw themselves not as 'traffickers' but as fulfilling necessary roles in the facilitation of sex work, enabling women to earn better money and/or work in safety.

Perhaps the strongest conclusion to be drawn from these examples is that modern slavery law operates to demarcate victims from traffickers in settings where those concerned typically see many more shades of grey: where female sex workers actively seek out those who become the 'third-party organizers' of their labour – the providers of properties, protection, working conditions, customers and websites – who they need in order to work, however unpalatable that might seem. Discerning what counts as 'slavery' in these contexts is incredibly difficult, since the sex industry itself ultimately relies upon the exploitation of the bodies – predominantly female bodies – of people whose choices are limited, who are willing to risk their physical and mental well-being for the chance of being able to settle debt, send money to support their children or secure better lives (O'Connell Davidson, 2014). Exploitation in the sex industry is compounded both by laws that prohibit collaboration between sex workers and immigration controls that limit the protections afforded to foreign national workers. This is where third-party organizers who are willing to risk criminalization in return for instant cash profits take advantage, charging fees for the provision of services to those who sell sex (Orchiston, 2016).

For this reason, the blanket decriminalization alone of prostitution risks exacerbating some of the dangers sex workers – especially foreign national workers – face – even while it alleviates others. In the absence of legal protections, minimum wage provisions and trade union representation, decriminalizing the selling and purchase of sex could leave sex workers dependent on an illicit free market of criminal entrepreneurs against whom there is even less recourse to law than the already very patchy provision modern slavery rescue missions provide in extreme cases of exploitation (Phoenix, 2018). Punters who refuse to pay or threaten violence, rival firms and love-smitten and disgruntled clients leave sex workers vulnerable to exploitation that is tempered by people like Adam, Sandra and Andrei, however questionable the morality of their business models. Criminalizing them does serve a symbolic function in terms of condemning relationships that are inherently damaging, exploitative and demeaning. But it probably does little to redress the global structural inequalities that have seen sex work interface with the gig economy in ways that render flexible working a necessity and which create the market for 'pop-up' brothels that are incredibly difficult to inspect and regulate, given how quickly they can be established and relocated in a marketplace that is organized online, if not necessarily by 'organized criminal' masterminds.

Progressive change in this area ultimately means providing rights and resources to sex workers and indeed everyone whose lives are so precarious that sex work appears to be a better alternative than the other limited opportunities on offer. This may seem like a utopian vision but given the expensive failings of modern slavery law to secure justice for victims on any meaningful scale and the relative dearth of prosecutions of those who profit from sexual exploitation, it might be a more realizable alternative than the legal remedies currently on offer. Establishing rights to pay and profit for sex workers might also have the advantage of speaking more clearly to those third-party organizers who see themselves as merely mixing business and family life with pleasure, enabling themselves or others to escape from more acute forms of exploitation, or having made private agreements with women who have few other choices. As the stories we have relayed reveal, sex work entered into consensually at one time can be reappraised later, when it is sometimes deemed exploitation. Clarifying the terms upon which sex workers and others can legitimately work together in ways that reduce the chances of the former becoming further entrapped in enduring exploitation has to be a better starting point than legal interventions that attempt to differentiate acceptable (prostitution) from unacceptable (modern slavery) forms of profiteering from sex work after the event.

Note

1   www.stopthetraffik.org/sex-trafficking-vs-sex-work-understanding-difference/

9 Child Sexual Exploitation

> Tackling sexual exploitation must address the perpetrators – not only preventing their activities but *understanding their motivation*. A common experience of reviews … has been the *lack of meaningful engagement of perpetrators*. Often when they do participate it is in order to protest their innocence and derogate the victims. This should not prevent attempting to *develop an understanding of what has led them to be involved and what might have helped prevent their offending.*
>
> (Spicer, 2018: 146, our emphasis)

In this chapter, we focus specifically on the phenomenon of child sexual exploitation in the UK, exploring how, since the ascendency of the modern slavery agenda, 'Asian grooming gangs' have been recast as the central problem. We look first at whether this term is an accurate depiction of the perpetrators of the many high-profile child sexual exploitation cases reported in the British media between 2015 and 2020. We highlight how the evocation of ethnicity has distracted attention away from the failures of government agencies to protect those for whom they had assumed 'parental responsibility'. We then look at five examples of people we interviewed who had been convicted of offences of sexual exploitation involving children and young people. While conscious of the dangers of appearing to give voice to people who have committed such crimes – and the offence this could cause to survivors – our argument is, as reflected in the quote above, that unless representations of perpetrators are recognizably 'real', efforts to deter offenders and safeguard potential victims will continue to be misdirected. The chapter concludes by flagging the need to situate the analysis of sexual exploitation within an understanding of the intersection of complex inequalities that is alive to the role played by victim agency. The silence around victim agency, we suggest, enables perpetrators to satisfy themselves that women who are much younger than themselves and/or not well looked after have consented to sex acts in the contexts of 'parties' in which acutely transactional relationships are enacted.

DOI: 10.4324/9780429053986-9

Sexual Exploitation and the Modern Slavery Act

As we explained in the last chapter, how and when adults' engagement in sex work gets defined as 'exploitation' complicates the policing of modern slavery in the UK. Such complications should not in theory hinder interventions to tackle child sexual exploitation, as children – unlike adults – cannot legally consent to 'prostitution'. The 2015 Modern Slavery Act added another layer to the safeguarding of young people in the UK, by providing for the creation of Independent Child Trafficking Advocates. However, the government's approach to Independent Child Advocates has appeared reticent. A pilot scheme was launched in January 2017 to see what 'added value' Independent Child Advocates could bring to 'early adopter sites' in Greater Manchester, Hampshire and the Isle of Wight (Keeble et al., 2018). The pilot revealed what had already become apparent from a number of enquiries into the failures of social services to protect children in care from sexual exploitation. In short, the pilot showed that it is not only foreign national or asylum-seeking children who are vulnerable but also British young people, often already known to social services as vulnerable or 'looked after', many of whom go missing from care arrangements when abuses against them are formally investigated.

Public debate in the UK has, by contrast, focussed much more on the ethnic origins of 'grooming gang' members than it has on the failings of the care system. Before spearheading the Centre for Social Justice's response to 'grooming gangs' in 2020, in 2018 as Home Secretary, Sajid Javid had outlined his commitment to answer questions about the ethnic backgrounds of such offenders. Javid advocated for law enforcement efforts that investigated a 'direct link' between 'child sex offenders' and other forms of 'serious and organised criminals' who rely on 'corrupt accountant laundering' and 'international criminal networks' (HM Government, 2018: 3). The British prime minister Boris Johnson subsequently capitalized on the reframing of child sexual exploitation as a problem of infiltration by foreign mafias. Johnson promised to hunt down, deport or even (metaphorically) decapitate perpetrators, hence detracting from the offence caused by his earlier dismissal of investigations into historic child sexual abuse as being akin to 'spaffing' money up the wall (Cowburn, 2019; Tapsfield, 2020).

The Advent of 'Grooming Gangs'

The first use of the term 'grooming gang' in the UK is often attributed to an article written by the journalist Andrew Norfolk for the *Sunday Times* newspaper in 2011. Norfolk claimed that sexual crimes committed by 'predominantly Pakistani' men against white girls aged 11–16 in Rotherham were not being exposed because of a 'conspiracy of silence' (Norfolk, 2011; see also Stephens, 2019). Subsequently, the term 'Muslim grooming gang' became the shorthand for discussions of sexual exploitation in the British media (Cockbain and Tufail, 2020). The term reverberated in parliamentary debates and then across social media as far-right groups claimed that an epidemic of sexual abuse against 'our white girls' was being concealed from the public because of misplaced political correctness that silenced acknowledgement of the adverse consequences of multiculturalism and the 'Islamic jihad' being waged against white people (Britton, 2019). Such narratives have their roots in a long history of racializing crime problems and attributing them to immigration in the UK to detract from other failings of the state. They have been the mainstay of Conservative governments in the UK since at least the 1970s (Jefferson, 2008). They also became a feature of New Labour's response to inner-city riots in the early 2000s, with disorder constructed not as a response to enduring racial discrimination but as a consequence of allowing Muslims to live 'parallel lives' (Cantle, 2001). Thereafter, constructions of Muslim men as fundamentalist, patriarchal and a threat to Western women in particular proliferated amidst the justifications for the War on Terror waged by the US, UK and Australia as justifications for removing Saddam Hussein from power in Iraq in the absence of evidence of weapons of mass destruction (Poynting et al., 2004). References to grooming gangs by politicians on the left and right of the political spectrum thus extend the scapegoating of 'homegrown' 'gangs' of 'Asian' men who were cast (unjustifiably) as a menacing threat deserving of increased police attention in the wake of a rise in racist incidents post 9/11 (Alexander, 2004; Gadd and Dixon, 2011; Gill and Harrison, 2015; Cockbain and Tufail, 2020).

The Independent Enquiry into Child Sexual Exploitation in Rotherham

In 2020, the UK government's continued refusal to publish the findings of its own 'review of grooming gangs' compounded suspicions of a 'cover-up', perhaps intentionally, with then Prime Minister Boris Johnson cryptically implying that the information within the report could be 'misleading if … used out context' (Dearden, 2020). Given earlier acknowledgements of how Northumbria police had paid a convicted child sex offender to act as an undercover informant to gather evidence against those exploiting vulnerable young women (Farthing et al., 2017), the real reasons for keeping the government's review confidential most likely had more to do with contents pertaining to 'operationally sensitive' details about *policing practice* than anything that would further explain the role ethnicity plays in the perpetration of child sexual abuse (Dearden, 2020). The reports of various public enquiries about the numerous cases of localized grooming in Rotherham, Rochdale, Oxford, Peterborough and Newcastle-upon-Tyne had already been published, generating extensive news reports pertaining to the men arrested, prosecuted and convicted for trafficking children for the purposes of sexual exploitation. Indeed, while aspects of its findings may not have been easy for service providers to accept (Casey, 2015), there was no sense in which Alexis Jay's (2014) report into the handling of child sexual exploitation cases in Rotherham between 1997 and 2013 could be accused of silencing debate about the ethnicities of the offenders. Jay's report, as Louise

Casey's inspection report the following year was to surmise, made plain – arguably to the point of oversimplification (Tufail, 2015) – that the 'majority of the perpetrators were *described as "Asian" by victims*' (Casey, 2015: 6, our emphasis).

Jay estimated that at least 1,400 children had been sexually exploited in Rotherham over a 16-year period and that the scale and seriousness of this abuse had been 'underplayed by senior managers' in the police, local government and social care system for at least 12 of these years. Youth workers had been disbelieved and their services discontinued, while there were hints of a police 'cover up' (Jay, 2014: 1). Austerity and unprecedented cuts to social care impacted the most disadvantaged, often leaving families who were struggling with multiple problems to deal with all but the most vulnerable children themselves (see also Ridge, 2013). Children's social care services were 'acutely understaffed and over stretched' (Jay, 2014: 2), leading to the deprioritizing of interventions addressed to a problem that was misconceived as one of 'under-age sex' and 'teenage prostitution'. In Rotherham, as was soon to become apparent in many other English towns and cities, there had been multiple 'collective failures' (p.1) by the police and social workers to deliver services to young people at risk of sexual exploitation and to South Asian populations, which included both perpetrators and victims, whom even the enquiry struggled to reach, principally because service providers tended to treat 'traditional' male 'community leaders' as brokers for 'Pakistani-heritage women' (p.91).

Perpetrators had apparently targeted 'local residential units' where they were able to take advantage of children who were socially isolated from families and 'placed out of area for their own protection' (p.45). The predominantly white female victims the enquiry did reach had complex problems of their own, which were exacerbated as they were sexually exploited:

> Addiction and mental health emerged as common themes in the files. Almost 50% of children who were sexually exploited or at risk had misused alcohol or other substances (this was typically part of the grooming process), a third had mental health problems (again, often as a result of abuse) and two thirds had emotional health difficulties. There were issues of parental addiction in 20% of cases and parental mental health issues in over a third of cases … Truancy and school refusal were recorded in 63% of cases and 63% of children had been reported missing more than once.
>
> (p.31)

Critically, some vulnerable young women were 'courted' by older men whom they considered 'boyfriends', who supplied them with gifts, alcohol and drugs (p.37). Gradually those being groomed would become more isolated from friends and family, while being encouraged to get drunk at parties and 'stay out all night' in houses or rooms where they were not 'bound by any rules' (p.36). Even though some were as young as 11 when they met these 'boyfriends', some victims refused to accept that they had been groomed, while others ultimately returned to the perpetrators out of fear for their families (p.36). Yet social services tended to regard these youths as lower 'priority' than infants in social care, even while the men involved in grooming were known to the police. At least four were brothers thought to be connected to a wider network of men with histories of drug dealing (p.88), some of whom also worked for local taxi firms or takeaway outlets. Arguably, these social connections between perpetrators were more relevant than what victims took to be their 'Asian' appearance. While five of those convicted in Rotherham had some Pakistani *heritage*, an Afghan national, Iraqi Kurds and a Kosovan were identified among the other offenders (p.92).

Regional Reviews in England

Similar findings, including imprecision in the reporting of the mixed ethnic backgrounds of the perpetrators involved, featured in the reports of enquiries into localized sexual exploitation in other English towns and cities published between 2014 and 2020. In Rochdale, eight of the nine offenders convicted of grooming vulnerable young women were British men of Pakistani descent, while one was Afghani, leading the House of Commons Home Affairs Committee (2013: 57) to the view that there had been 'a model of localised grooming of Pakistani-heritage men targeting young white girls' similar to the one in Rotherham. The contexts in which young women experienced sexual exploitation was, nevertheless, demonstrated in other official reports to be more diverse than this. The report of the children's commissioner, *If Only Someone Had Listened* (Berelowitz et al., 2013), revealed, for example, that there had been some selective reporting with regard to the profiles of perpetrators and that many victims had been abused by male members of their own peer groups – including white boyfriends in the same schools – before they became acquainted with older men who subsequently exploited them.

> Peer-groups were routinely involved in sexually assaulting girls who lived near them, often in public places such as stairwells and alleyways, as well as in their own homes. In some cases, boys would use text messages or the Internet to invite their friends to join them. On other occasions this type of group-based activity took place in parks and involved the use of alcohol.
> (p.105)

Some practitioners unwittingly forgot to mention the abuse committed by both younger and older white men when asked about 'grooming':

> During a meeting with two health workers, the Inquiry asked about the profile of perpetrators in the local area. We were told that they were exclusively 'Asian males' … They said the victim had first been exploited in school by her peers, who were all white boys. She was then exploited by an older boyfriend who was an Asian man in his twenties. Following this, she was exploited by an older white man who filmed her having sex with his

friends. She was then exploited by a group of older Asian men who sold her at parties. Finally, an older white man, who was addicted to drugs … took her to the homes of much older, disabled men, and sold her to pay for his drug habit. These health workers had mentally screened out the white perpetrators.

(p.28)

Perpetrators were not necessarily part of organized 'gangs'. Rather some men involved in grooming were active in the networks and places occupied by vulnerable young people:

The Inquiry was told of bus and coach stations being used by perpetrators to spot and recruit children and young people for sexual exploitation. This was particularly the case where they were running away from home and living on the street as a result … In cases like these, individuals involved were connected through the one victim, and their use of bus shelters, rather than their own network, to find vulnerable children and young people … [with] bus or taxi drivers offering lifts, in exchange for sex, to children and young people who were homeless and standing at bus shelters.

(p.103)

Why these young people rarely reported these 'exchanges' is not difficult to understand. Coffey's (2014) interviews with young women in Greater Manchester revealed that some young women experience unwanted sexual attention in public places 'so often' that they do not see any point in going to the police (p.9). Similarly, those in care often expect social workers to 'look down' on them or even blame them for inviting their own victimization (see also Ashurst and McAlinden, 2015). In the absence of parents or teachers they can disclose to, young people with multiple problems can become receptive to offers of 'help' from older men who promise to be 'there' for them emotionally or invite them to flats where they are allowed to consume alcohol and other drugs in order to relax (Coffey, 2014: 25).

The enquiry into the death of Victoria Agoglia – a 15-year old, originally from Rochdale, who was 'repeatedly threatened, assaulted' and 'returned to her residential unit intoxicated and in distress', before a 50-year-old man injected her with a lethal dose of heroin – revealed the intrinsic failings of a multi-agency strategy in Greater Manchester that relied upon the capacities of 'young people to protect themselves' (Newsam and Ridgway, 2019: 8; 14). The strategy depicted young women who were being coercively controlled, like Victoria, as putting themselves at risk by providing 'sexual favours', working in massage parlours and engaging in 'prostitution' to support drug and alcohol dependencies (p.27). Victoria had been taken into care at the age of eight, after her mother died, and her stepfather had been deemed 'unfit' to look after her (MEN, 2013). The men who abused Victoria and a number of other young women were not 'viewed' by professionals 'as sex offenders per se, just a group of men … from one ethnicity taking advantage of kids from dysfunctional backgrounds' (Newsam and Ridgway, 2019: 19). All 26 of the victims of grooming connected to the case had lived in one of the care homes in south Manchester and were in the care of social services. Some had been born with drug dependencies. Detectives explained the failures of their investigations in terms of the difficulties they had engaging 'the Asian community' in which a group of 'predominantly Pakistani men' operated as a 'very organised group of offenders' (p.33 and p.55). But this was not strictly true. Most of the offenders identified worked in the 'Asian restaurant and takeaway trade', but at least one was 'white' and another 'Tunisian'; one was a woman (p.67), and while they were being investigated, a parallel operation was pursuing grooming perpetrated by Kurdish offenders (p.47).

Similar complexities can be discerned in all the other enquiry reports into localized child sexual exploitation in England. In Oxford, a Serious Case Review emphasized that the majority of the perpetrators' Operation Bullfinch identified as responsible for abusing 370 victims of sexual exploitation were of 'Pakistani and/or Muslim heritage' (Bedford, 2015). This framing persisted even after news reportage revealed that of the seven convicted, two were brothers of east African origin and five (two of whom were also brothers) were British citizens with Pakistani parents (BBC, 2013; Guardian Staff, 2013). Their victims had been reported missing over 450 times during a five-year period, but social services had failed to intervene because case workers considered the young women to be 'consenting, or bringing problems upon themselves, and the victims were often perceived to be hostile to and dismissive of staff' (Bedford, 2015: 2). In Peterborough, the boys and the girls who were sexually exploited were already known to social care services (Davies, 2016). Among those who abused them, one was a minor. Among the adult perpetrators were men with Czech, Slovak, Roma and Kurdish backgrounds, connected through a takeaway outlet from which cannabis was sold (Meikle, 2014). Their victims, who were predominantly 14 and under, variously identified as white, Eastern European, Asian and Pakistani. What they had in common were 'difficult home circumstances' including 'neglectful parents, witnessing domestic violence and abuse and substance misuse', together with an experience of service providers that conceptualized 'young people' as 'young adults' liable to make 'unwise decisions' including choosing to enter 'abusive relationships' (Davies, 2016: 8–9).

Likewise, in Newcastle-upon-Tyne, *The Joint Serious Case Review Concerning Sexual Exploitation of Children and Adults* (Spicer, 2018) noted that the defendants in the case were:

> mainly not white but came from a diverse range of backgrounds including Pakistani, Bangladeshi, Indian, Iranian, Iraqi, Kurdish, Turkish, Albanian and Eastern European.
>
> (p.50)

The cases made against them in court found 'no evidence that the defendants were racially motivated in committing the crimes' (p.50). The case review into why victims had been unprotected for so long found 'no evidence … that decisions about taking action' by professionals responsible for safeguarding children 'were affected by lack of concern or interest, misplaced fears about political correctness or fear of being seen as racist' (p.145). As elsewhere, potential victims had initially been regarded as merely 'promiscuous' by social services, before it materialized that young women were being cajoled into sex when intoxicated or raped when 'unconscious' (p.26). In the absence of action on behalf of investigating authorities, some victims did not realize that 'what was happening was wrong' or 'out of the ordinary' and assumed the local men involved were 'friends' who 'bought them drink and drugs', treated them 'nicely' and let them 'sleep over', until they were joined by other men who did 'horrible' things (p.28). Some of these other men were new migrants:

> They left their countries in lorries – they'd done bad things – they have done bad things elsewhere in other countries – they said they had done bad things.
>
> (Victim, p.28)

Others were older men who preyed on young women who were becoming vulnerable due to 'a change of school, lack of friends, bereavement or difficulties at home' (p.28), including sexual and 'domestic abuse', or who had decided to run away (p.29). Young women who tolerated 'exchanges' of sex for drugs, drinks, food, somewhere to stay or taxi rides found themselves trapped in exploitative relationships they no longer had any control over (p.29). Some later had to pursue abortions, became depressed, suicidal or began to self-harm (p.31).

Ethnicity, Professional Failings and Motivation

The Newcastle review was the only review of localized grooming that attempted to speak to those perpetrators convicted of sexually exploiting young women. All but one offender declined the invitation. He was a Turkish asylum-seeker who 'protested his innocence', claiming 'witnesses were paid to lie to the police' (p.20) and explaining that 'he only had sex with girls over 16 years of age' who 'knew what they were doing' and brought their own drugs 'onto his premises', perhaps because one was 'homeless' (p.51). Having failed to elicit explanations from perpetrators, the report into child sexual abuse in Newcastle concludes with the quote with which we opened this chapter: 'Tackling sexual exploitation must address the perpetrators – not only preventing their activities but understanding their motivation' (Spicer, 2018: 146). In the absence of such understanding the shorthand 'Asian grooming gang' has been evoked tautologically as both description and explanation for child sexual exploitation. This term – Asian grooming gangs – has proliferated in part because of the enduring failures of police and social services to protect vulnerable young women whose care had become the primary responsibility of the state, some of whom referred sweepingly to 'non-white groups' as 'Asian'. At the same time, professionals and the media were using a similarly reductionist shorthand to lump together British Pakistanis and Bangladeshis with foreign nationals from Turkey, Tunisia, Iraq, Iran and even Eastern Europe (Tufail, 2015). Because references to 'race' remain conspicuous by their absence in coverage of sexual crimes committed by white men, including those involving high-profile celebrities and public figures, the connection between ethnicity and the social distance between victims and offenders has been over-reified (Cockbain, 2013; Craven et al., 2006). In addition, the question of what brings vulnerable young women into proximity to men working in under-regulated, low-paid jobs in the night-time economy has been overlooked (Cockbain, 2018; Colley, 2019; Kerr et al., 2017; Malik, 2018). In what follows, we address this question through the analysis of interviews with five participants convicted of crimes involving the sexual exploitation of children and young people. Each denied their involvement in grooming for sexual exploitation. However, as we show through the presentation of these cases, each also revealed how behaviour ultimately categorized as 'grooming' became permissible within their lives.

Case Studies

Reshmin: Guilty by Association?

Reshmin was serving a prison sentence for conspiracy to incite prostitution for personal gain and the supply of the class B drug, mephedrone. He was insistent that the case was a 'set up' that he had never consumed nor sold drugs. Reshmin said he had no knowledge of prostitution, his 'association' with other men depicted uniformly as 'Asian' overstated in a court case in which the complainant had been clear that Reshmin was a 'good man' who never abused her: a claim he supported by bringing court transcripts to the second interview.

Before his arrest, Reshmin, then in his late 20s, had been living at his (Bangladeshi) mother's house, following the break up of his ten-year relationship with his wife, a white British woman with whom he had children. His own mother had raised her children alone on a family income that comprised of a weekly benefit payment. Aged 15, Reshmin started working in restaurants to support the family. By his mid-20s, however, the long hours working in the restaurant trade, together with conflict over his wife's expenditure on friends, contributed to the break-up of his marriage. Reshmin moved back into his mother's flat to provide the care that she increasingly needed, while letting a friend – Adi, whom he had known since school – use the council flat he and his wife had rented, holding onto the tenancy in the hope he would eventually acquire the right to buy it.

'Fights found' Adi when he was out drinking because he could not 'hold his tongue'. Having served two prison sentences, Adi now needed to keep out of trouble and Reshmin was sympathetic, not least because he himself had served time for assault, following an altercation in which six white men made advances on one of his friend's ('white') girlfriends. In his 'culture', Rehsmin explained, 'you are not supposed to drink', so he and Adi would play poker at the flat together and 'have a drink and not go out'.

Over time, the poker games expanded to include up to '6–8 lads' – some white British, some British Asian and some of Middle Eastern origin – who would come after working in the restaurants at midnight and play for £10 a game. Sometimes a couple of the men's 'girlfriends would come' to the flat too and 'have a few drinks … listen to music'. Among these girlfriends was a 19-year-old woman – Amy – who became a complainant in Reshmin's trial. She was dating Adi's friend, a white British man. Reshmin said that he had only met Amy a couple of times. He saw her at the white man's flat once, but as with other times he dropped in: 'nothing was happening. Everyone was just chilling out, having a drink … Nobody's having sex with anybody'. Reshmin did, however, go to other parties with Adi where he had seen mephedrone being taken, but it was not his scene and he left soon after arriving. He was clear with Adi that drug-taking was not to happen at his flat and said that to the best of his knowledge it had not, aside from the odd joint smoked on the balcony. In the various police raids on the flat, no 'residue' from drugs or 'paraphernalia' was ever found, and Reshmin was never found in possession of illicit substances on the 'umpteen' occasions the police stopped his car and searched him.

When Reshmin was arrested, it was for 'conspiracy to rape' Amy, who was in the flat with Adi when the police first raided it. The rape charge was dropped when new charges were brought a year later. Then Reshmin became one of 17 men – only four of whom he admitted knowing – accused of conspiracy to incite prostitution and trafficking for sexual exploitation. The court transcripts, which Reshmin brought to the second interview, revealed that Amy was clear that she had not been sexually exploited by him or ever abused in his flat, though she did – in one of her seven statements to the police – implicate him in dealing drugs to Adi, whom she said had supplied her in turn: something Reshmin denied. Reshmin believed that at the trial his ethnicity was evoked merely to incriminate him by association with men who had actually committed sexual offences.

> The way they – they turned around and kept using 'Asian male', 'Asian male' … I used to play poker at my flat with white male. Friends which were white – white male.

Reshmin said it was Adi, not him, who had sent a text to Amy offering her drugs for sex. Amy had told her boyfriend that she was trying to 'come off the drugs', but this was not the whole story, as Reshmin learnt at the trial that Amy:

> was taking all these drugs and things … saying she was going to men's house … so what kind of girlfriend are you if you're doing that? … I didn't know that she was going round … sleeping with everybody … She was going to these different addresses and she'd go take drugs and sleep with

these – these men … there was loads of men in the case which … I've never known … I've never seen them.

Reshmin had never seen Amy or anyone else having sex or being 'sexually … assaulted … and raped' at any of the parties or poker games. But at the trial, he had learnt that after she had called a drug dealer using Adi's phone, Amy was supplied with drugs in return for giving oral sex to a Middle Eastern man (now convicted of rape) who ejaculated in her mouth without her consent, before offering to pay her £30. Convicted by an all-white jury of crimes for which there was little evidence of his direct involvement, Reshmin intended to appeal his conviction once the risk of prolonging his sentence had lapsed. From his perspective, he had simply been found guilty by association, the criminal justice process creating the appearance of a 'gang' that comprised people like him who were merely trying to help out friends, and friends of friends. In short, Reshmin refuted his conviction for conspiracy to incite prostitution on the basis that he was oblivious to the dependencies of some of the women friends in his social circle took to parties, including at his flat, and because he did not have sex with any of these women or really know some of the men in the wider network of party goers who did perpetrate sexual assaults in his absence.

Zahir: Immoral but Not Exploitative?

Zahir was a British Muslim in his late 30s. He described a childhood in which he scuppered a promising start at an almost exclusively white secondary school. Following an assault on a pupil who refused to lend him an inhaler when he needed it, Zahir was expelled and sent by his father to school in Pakistan to re-instil discipline; an experience he found terribly alien. Upon his return, Zahir, then aged 17, fell in with the 'wrong crowd': 'drug taking, drug selling' – cannabis at first, then ecstasy, but 'going up to Class A's', though he did not use heroin back then. A decade of this lifestyle concluded with Zahir being sentenced to four years imprisonment for conspiracy to supply heroin 'whole sale', delivery work that had netted him a 'pocketful of money all the time' and the prospect of a 'flashy car … flashy everything'. A back injury incurred in the prison gym saw Zahir prescribed opiates, precipitating 'daily' 'sniffing' of heroin post-release. He attempted to become a 'reformed', 'family orientated' guy, by marrying a Pakistani woman – a 'virgin … like a family orientated lass' – and talked as if he had 'turned' his life around'. He was, nevertheless, also 'in and out' of methadone treatment and 'getting involved' with other (mostly) Asian taxi drivers or restaurant workers, having a 'drink and smoke', 'taking drugs and going to parties' in flats and houses where his wife and family would not see him.

It was in this context that Zahir was implicated, in his view erroneously, in the abuses perpetrated by a so-called 'grooming gang'. Zahir had brought three white 'girls' – aged '17 or 18 or sommat' – to the first of many house parties in which they alleged they had been 'sexually abused' in exchange for access to mephedrone. Also known as M-Cat, mephedrone is a synthetic 'happy-go lucky' drug that is much cheaper than cocaine, but shared from bags into lines and snorted in much the same way. Zahir had been using mephedrone on the night when he first saw two of the three girls who were allegedly groomed, sat out on a 'park bench' at 3 am in their pyjamas in the 'freezing' cold, 'drunk' and having been kicked out of a 'house party'. That night, Zahir had been to a nightclub with friends. As the 'designated driver' he had not consumed alcohol but had taken mephedrone, which he explained was undetectable by breathalyser. With just one friend left to drop off, Zahir 'got talking' to these girls who 'then jumped in' the back of the car and went with him to another 'mate's house' where a 'party' was being hosted. Upon arrival, the 'girls' entered 'pestering mode', asking for a cut of the drugs divided into lines on the table. The girls whom Zahir had never met before slept over – 'it was just a normal situation' – until the morning so they could get the bus home.

Before catching the bus, one of the girls – Sharon – swapped numbers with Zahir, and over the course of five weeks they began messaging each other. After they dated, Sharon became Zahir's 'girlfriend'. Zahir's recollection was that Sharon was eight years younger than him, but other parts of his story revealed that he was actually at least 15 years her senior. For about 6 weeks, Zahir and Sharon 'obviously had sex' and he took her and two of her female friends to parties he attended. At these parties vodka was consumed and mephedrone was shared, though Zahir would often 'want more … have another bag', the parties becoming 'weekend benders' where he was really 'letting' his 'hair down', routinely consuming an 'ounce' then 'selling a bit' so his 'bit would be for free'. While he was sure the girls were not 'addicted' because the drug was not like that, he himself experienced mephedrone as a 'drug you cannot put down', rendering him 'happy and sociable … the soul of the party'.

Away from the parties, however, Zahir felt 'guilty' for 'going behind' his wife's 'back', for it was 'no way to start a bleeding marriage'. Lacking the 'balls' to tell Sharon he was married, Zahir chose to 'disappear' abroad for six months rather than break up with her. When he returned with his wife, Zahir almost did not recognize his former girlfriend and her friends at the side of the road because they had 'deteriorated' so much. Zahir resumed his attendance at weekend parties in order to support his own 'habit'. He discovered – as he did his drug delivery rounds – that Sharon and her friends were flitting between five or six people's houses, sometimes on the same night and getting themselves 'a bit of a reputation'. It was during this time that Zahir said he twice had sex with Sharon's friend, Rachel, one time in a kitchen and another in a bedroom at houses where there were 'parties'.

From Zahir's perspective, the sex was 'consensual' though casual, for he knew he could not have another 'relationship' with his wife nearby. 'Eye contact' had led to a 'corridor' 'conversation, having a laugh', 'kissing' and then sex against a door to ensure some privacy on the first occasion; while sex in a bedroom of a small house had followed 'chilling and kissing, relaxing, drinking, snorting' to establish a 'connection' on the second. Rachel, by contrast, alleged she had been raped – Zahir argues because the girls were aggrieved that he had concealed the fact that he was married. The charges were reduced to sexual assault at trial because, according to Zahir, the prosecution could only establish that the kissing was non-consensual. The sexual assault charges, nevertheless, helped 'stitch' him up with a conviction for 'conspiracy to incite prostitution'. At the trial it was revealed that some Kosovan men were profiting by getting Sharon and Rachel 'doing things in parks'. The judge deemed it irrelevant whether or not Zahir and his co-accused made any money themselves from the sex work undertaken by the complainants. The court concluded that Zahir had established the relationship with his 'girlfriend to abuse her' and that he had 'gained in sexual favours in "return" for "giving" the girls drugs'. Zahir's view is that 'fucking corrupt' 'police' officers 'showered the complainants with gifts … houses and mobile phones' to 'pressurize' them to come to the view that 'these Asians are fucking bastards'. He did, however, admit that other men – one a registered sex offender and another a prolific drug dealer with whom he was friends – had offered the girls M-Cat in exchange for a 'blow job'. The 'lass' in question had apparently 'changed her mind halfway through', but the drug dealer had 'kept her head down', saying 'I'll give you some drugs', knowing Zahir had gone out to collect the drugs that were to be used to compensate his victim.

Naz: Deluded and Dangerous and Socially Isolated

Another man, Naz – a British Muslim, in his early 40s – did not deny being a sex offender, but insisted that he was not part of a 'gang': to the contrary he was regarded as a 'black sheep' within his family and had been 'ostracized' by the 'Asian community', loneliness compounding his reliance on the company of young white women who wanted to come and drink alcohol in his flat. Serving a lengthy prison sentence for trafficking for the purposes of sexual exploitation, inciting prostitution, supplying cannabis and sexual assault, Naz argued that the 'racist' police had 'twisted everything' around to make it look like he was 'a horrible lad, raping our women, abusing young kids'. Naz had endured a series of losses in his mid-teens including the deaths of his (Bangladeshi) mother, then father, with whom he had an unresolved rift, and his estrangement from his older siblings who refused to take him into their homes when he fell in with the 'wrong crowd'.

Naz had started taking 'cannabis', 'drinking' and using a 'bit of coke … and … crack' when his 'world fell apart'. A man called Daarshik helped him find casual work in an Indian restaurant, enabling him to find somewhere to live. This was followed by a decade of very low-paid (£2–3 an hour) work as a trainee waiter, compensated by living in a 'staff house' that facilitated the unsociable working hours and access to leftover curries. Given the 'dirty jobs' and denied a day off, Naz got into physical conflict with various bosses who treated him badly and lost his job on multiple occasions. He acquired a 'taste for drinks' to moderate his drug use and overcome his loneliness: 'I loved drinks … no-one knows me, so I was just buzzing … And the women come and talk to you all the time'. In his late 20s, he 'fell in love' with a 'radgy type of girl', 'a charmer', who 'basically needed money' as she had a child to support. This relationship came to a swift end one night when Naz was still out on the streets feeling 'very horny', drunk and 'high on coke'. He rang his girlfriend for phone sex and, even though he was caught by police 'masturbating behind a bin' with an 'erection' and his 'penis' out, he did not consider this indecent 'exposure', because he 'didn't cum or anything basically'. A subsequent incident of 'indecent exposure' occurred when some '16-year old girls' – 'they were old enough' – reported Naz for asking 'Do you want a piece of this?' when he was taking a 'piss' – in his view, 'like a normal bloke' – on a hot summer's day.

Naz was put on the sex offender register and a sex offender treatment pro-gramme in the community. It was then that Daarshik started coming round when Naz was 'drunk', to hoover, clean and tidy his 'broken' flat. Daarshik wanted to 'sober up', have a 'little break' from his 'nagging' 'wife and kids' and be a bit of a 'Jack the Lad'. Typically, Daarshik would take 'phone calls' in the flat, then 'disappear', but Naz had since learnt that Daarshik had profited financially from taking young women he met at the flat 'from one house to another, Jack the Lad and all that'. Naz also let slip that Daarshik had been in the flat with young women, despite denying this had ever happened. The young women had started coming to the flat the day Naz completed his sex offender treatment. Naz had been 'celebrating' and was 'drunk'. 'Feeling sorry for himself' and in need of 'company', he spotted Bethan (aged '17' or '19') at the tram station and invited her back. Naz and Bethan had a few drinks and sex at the flat because she was 'like him': needing 'someone to talk to', 'wasn't all that in the head' and 'getting abused by her dad'. Bethan, he said, 'came onto' him, only to dismiss their acquaintance as a 'one night stand ... that meant nothing' the next day, revealing herself to be a 'dyke'. She nevertheless returned to the flat on multiple occasions with other young women, most of whom were 16, but one of whom was a 15-year-old who was having a hard time with her mum. Naz provided all the girls with free curries from his work and a 'roof over their heads' and would sometimes share spliffs with them. The girls would be 'high' on Lambrini and vodka talking about their relationships, often arguing in ways that Naz found 'hilarious' – 'I was just laughing and chilling because it's just so funny when these are fighting each other'. Despite the mess, the girls, Naz said, 'found it a luxury' being drunk in his flat and being able to sober up there before going home: 'they were just growing up ... enjoying life and all that', being in a place 'where ... they can do whatever they want': 'they thought it was ... safe and all that'.

Naz explained that the girls would sometimes stay over, with four 'cuddled up' in his double bed – though there were no bedsheets at that time – while he 'watched DVDs' in the lounge with his 'Kestrel and a little spliff and all that'. As he repeatedly rationalized, both he and they were 'having a laugh': 'it just made my day and night go ... for my loneliness', so many of his 'Christmases and Eids' had been spent in drunken and depressed solitude. He denied the sexual assault on one of Bethan's friends for which he was convicted: 'I've always looked out for them girls. I gave them food … whatever they wanted ... I've never done anything sexually'.

This qualification has to be read in the context of Naz's other denials about indecent exposure not being sexual if you did not ejaculate. For example, Bethan had alleged that Naz and another man sat next to a girl on Naz's sofa while she had her 'pants down'. Naz explained, 'It was just a normal thing, there was no sexual activities, apart from the girls touching each other'. He explained: 'I was just pissed. I was just watching. I was laughing … And then I used to tell them, yeah, "Go to the bedroom"': 'these girls' were all 'dykes', 'lesbians' and he had only done what a 'normal lad would do when he's lonely': 'nothing really hardcore ... because I'm not a pervert and I wasn't one of them, you know what I mean'. These somewhat convoluted denials were reinforced by Naz's recollection of how the police had attended the flat after he and Daarshik had picked up four girls in a car and taken them back there. The two men were cautioned for supplying cannabis to the girls, while the girls were advised that Naz was a registered sex offender. No further action was taken and some of the girls continued to 'come and go' for a further three years, despite Naz saying (at least sometimes) 'you can't come here because, I'm, I'm like a father … to you', a precaution he equated to 'having done everything right by the books'. Indeed, after the police caution, another man who was subsequently convicted of rape – a migrant who spoke little English and had few friends – also attended the flat to 'have a normal conversation' with the girls when they were 'high on drinks' and 'touching him and all that … just having a laugh … just a normal thing'. From Naz's perspective this 'normal thing' involved 'no sexual activities … apart from the girls, you know, having, touching each other'. Amidst this convoluted denial of sexual touching that he did not regard as 'sexual', Naz concluded that the girls had taken 'advantage' of his 'good heart' and 'used him', when all he was doing was trying to 'help' them 'out'.

Linda: Turning a Blind Eye?

How some young people end up at such parties was partially explained to us by two women who had been convicted of trafficking children for the purposes of sexual exploitation. Linda was a white Zimbabwean woman in her 40s, serving a six-year sentence for trafficking her daughter and her daughter's friends. Linda's own childhood had also been emotionally desolate. Although part of a large family, 'no one ever showed' Linda 'love'. Her father left when she was four, having been abusive to her mother. Linda's stepfather sexually abused her for a decade thereafter. Linda's mum was often absent with work, so Linda became 'the mother of the house', left school aged 12 and then took on the running of the family farm. She had three children to a man who encouraged her to migrate to the UK to escape the political violence in Zimbabwe, but her husband proved coercively controlling, and Linda was left homeless and had to move into a women's refuge after her husband assaulted their son. By her 30s, Linda had had two more children to another man from whom she separated because he was 'using' her. Sophie, Linda's eldest daughter – around 15 at the time she was sexually exploited – was 'a very bright kid' who was being bullied at school 'because she was a virgin'. Sophie 'went off the rails' and began running away from home, perhaps because she was questioning her identity: 'she wasn't really a girl if that makes sense; she was a boy'. It was then that Linda met two brothers – who were white British – Howard and Samuel – who persuaded her into taking Sophie and friends to a series of 'hotel parties'.

The first time Howard (aged 19) came to Linda's house, Sophie asked if he could stay over because he was 'tired' or 'drunk'. Howard told Linda that he and Samuel had a 'horrible childhood' and were 'never shown love', much as she herself was not. Linda 'felt sorry' for them and became 'more or less … friends', not minding that they did drugs, perhaps because she had also started using cocaine with them. Linda began 'seeing' Samuel (aged 28 and over ten years her junior), but discovered he was 'just using' her 'as well'. He was seeing other women and when she confronted him he threatened to 'smash' her daughter's face in and emptied her bank account.

Indebted and possibly drug-dependent, Linda became complicit in her daughter Sophie's sexual exploitation, taking her to hotel parties she had also attended when together with Samuel. Three of Sophie's friends, aged between 13 and 15, went to hotel parties with the brothers where they would 'stay up all night' and 'listen to music'. Linda said she 'couldn't understand it', but became 'exhausted' with warning Sophie and 'gave up', for she 'didn't know it was trafficking'. She nevertheless worried that if she reported her concerns, 'social services' would 'take' her 'kids away'. A family support worker engaged with one of Sophie's friends raised the alarm, revealing that Linda had driven the four girls to hotels on at least four separate occasions. At the bequest of one of Howard's friends, the girls had to send photos of themselves before they were approved to come to a (cheap) room booked on a fraudulent PayPal account.

The first time, Sophie and two of the girls 'came begging' Linda to take them there. Linda told them to 'find your own way', but Howard persuaded her to offer a lift. One of Sophie's friends 'had sex with Howard' that night and it was alleged in court that Linda had encouraged her to do so. On another occasion, Linda delivered vodka to the hotel at the request of the brothers but claimed to have 'slapped' Sophie in the 'face' because she was 'shocked' to see her drinking alcohol at the party when she had promised not to. On the final trip, Howard and Linda drove the girls to a hotel, and Linda delivered cigarettes to the party, following a request from the friend of Howard's who had booked the room, where she saw all the men and girls 'listening to music'. The next day, the men had left the girls at the hotel with no money, so Linda returned to collect them. Subsequently, when the case went to trial, the men tried to 'blame everything on' Linda, the prosecution implying that Linda must have known about the rapes of minors that Howard had perpetrated before she met him and that she knew what was happening in the hotels. 'How stupid was I?' she asked rhetorically.

Susan: Exploited or Exploitative?

As Linda's case reveals, some women who have been sexually exploited become complicit in the victimization of others. This was also true of Susan, a white woman from the UK in her 20s, in prison for sexually exploiting her younger teenage sister and a mutual friend of theirs, both of whom had lived in institutional care. After becoming pregnant, aged 14, Susan had been taken into care. The father of Susan's child and her first boyfriend was 'very violent': 'hitting' her 'all the time'. This boyfriend had broken Susan's nose and taken her hostage, while she was pregnant, telling her she didn't 'deserve this baby' and calling her a 'fucking slag'. Aged 18, Susan's baby was taken into care by social services – 'horrible kiddie-snatching people'. Susan then became 'really depressed' and started drinking heavily and taking drugs – weed and cocaine and M-Cat. Susan became pregnant again to the same abusive man. When her second child was taken into care, Susan began drinking a 'bottle and a half of vodka every day' on top of prescription medication for depression and illicit drug use. Owing money to her 'drug dealer', she went 'on the game'.

It was then that Susan started dating a Kurdish Muslim and car wash worker in his thirties, who asked her to convert to Islam. Susan agreed because she 'loved him' and started going with him to 'house parties' attended by other 'Asian' men: 'Asian' a term Susan used to include Kurdish men as well as British Pakistanis. The men, she said, 'weren't always' 'rough' when she was alone with them, but some became 'horrible', giving drugs to other girls instead of her and boasting that they were 'gonna fucking sleep with this one now and then give her everything'. After falling asleep at a party, Susan awoke to find she was being raped by a friend of her new boyfriend. Thereafter her depression deepened – she was 'crying all the time' and having 'flashbacks' – while the sexual exploitation intensified. Male friends of her boyfriend gave Susan alcohol and drugs to use her 'vagina', 'demanding' sex by threatening her 'if you don't do this, you're not getting [drugs]'. She became pregnant for the third time, whereupon her boyfriend told her to 'kill' the baby.

Susan suspected that her boyfriend had been 'shagging' other girls, including some who were 'underage', but he persuaded her to continue in the relationship with him. It was at this point that Susan became implicated in the exploitation of her sister and another young woman they were both friends with. Susan had also taken her sister, then aged 14, 'to sleep with men' at the parties. She also encouraged another young woman – whom she believed to have had sex with her boyfriend, though it later materialized had actually been raped by her boyfriend – to attend the house parties alongside her. Susan's motives for exposing her sister and this other teenager to the abuse she herself was suffering appeared mixed. At the time she had come to regard the friend as a 'slag' and so was willing to accompany her in her boyfriend's car 'here, there and everywhere', whereupon the friend was delivered to men who paid to have sex with her. Susan's explanation for bringing her sister was less clear. Initially, Susan had found the parties a way to 'chill and get high' though they were also risky given the drug-taking that took place there, so it seemed plausible that she wanted someone close to her there to keep her company, especially given how lonely she sometimes felt. However, after Susan had been raped the dangers would have been all too apparent. Susan took some pleasure in hearing her sister unnerving the men who had raped her too when she exclaimed: 'haha, you've shagged an underage girl'. Post her conviction for trafficking for sexual exploitation, Susan felt grossly let down by social services and her family. She knew what she did was wrong, but was aggrieved that there had been no official recognition of how she, like her sister, was also repeatedly abused and 'fucked up' by 'Asian' men.

Discussion

In this chapter, we have presented five case studies involving people convicted of trafficking for sexual exploitation involving children and young people. While all reveal that some element of grooming occurred, they each cast doubt on whether this was the orchestrated activity of criminal 'gangs'. Rather what emerged from their stories were accounts of loose groups of acquaintances – some of whom were relatives, but others of whom were work colleagues or 'friends of friends' involved in the buying and selling of drugs. Their social circles extended to include vulnerable young women and children, some of whom were already involved in exploitative and transactional relationships and who were attracted to the idea of partying because of the prospect of free alcohol, illicit drugs and/or somewhere to sleep for the night.

Minority ethnic groups predominated in some, but not all, of these networks, not because they derived from religious cultures that promoted child sexual abuse – indeed, none of our participants were particularly devoted to any faith – but for a multitude of social and cultural reasons. These reasons included participation in low-paid, low-skilled work that took place in the night-time economy, pushing leisure time into the early hours of the morning; cultural prohibitions against drinking in licensed venues; illicit drug use; and the desire for casual sex outside of committed relationships. The parties described by our participants appeared in many ways to be pale imitations of the elite soirees that have become associated with the #MeToo scandals that have implicated powerful men (Jeffrey Epstein, Max Clifford, Prince Andrew and Harvey Weinstein) in sexual abuse and harassment. Our participants described 'parties' that took place in run-down flats, council houses and cheap hotels – rather than penthouses and private manors – but the exchanges of drink and drugs for sex in the context of very unequal power relations were not radically different.

Sexual relations at the parties Reshmin, Zahir, Naz, Linda and Susan described were seemingly casual from the perspective of the men, with many of the young women consenting to sex, at least superficially, because they were persuaded it would cement mutual love and exclusivity. The deceptions and self-deceptions of heterosexual intimacy were amplified by differences in age and experience. Consent was thus negotiated on unequal terms. Some of the men assumed that where consent had been negotiated on one occasion it could be presumed on subsequent occasions. They also assumed, wrongly: that children can legally consent to sex in the UK; that people who are intoxicated and/ or drug-dependent can legally consent to sex in exchange for illicit substances or alcohol in the UK; that women below the age of 18 can legally consent to being paid for sex in the UK; and that tenancy-holders bare little legal responsibility for what happens within properties they let. Many of the men became drug and alcohol dependent themselves, but because they were working, albeit in low-paid jobs, they could afford to finance their habits, while the women were cajoled into trading sex directly with themselves, their friends or (in Linda's case) their children, for intoxicating substances, some of which were new synthetic drugs they had little prior knowledge of. While lacking employment and the financial means to fund their leisure activities, the young women and girls also lacked capable guardians who could protect them. They typically had parents who were struggling to care for them or were dependent on either a care system working with inadequate resources or 'pimps' who took a cut of their earnings. The men who abused them assumed that, because the women returned to the parties, they had chosen to be there and to participate in the exchanges of sex for drugs and alcohol that became 'normal things' to do there. Some of the young people who attended these parties may have initially held views similar to those articulated in Hallet's (2016) study of young people in care, who explained how attendance at risky social gatherings can reflect:

> their best attempts … to cope [and] to assert themselves – even when to cope meant controlling how out of control they could get … [F]or some young people, the exchange of sex appears as an expected condition or a viable option – perhaps the only or best one available at that point. In short, the seeming contradiction of feeling in some ways visible as a person (being appreciated, looked at, 'looked after'), whilst also being exploited, can occur because the objectification in exchanging sex is cast as something expected, acceptable or a least-worst option. For young people who consider themselves to be vulnerable and without care – without attention, acknowledgement and help – 'sexual exploitation' can be a solution of sorts: 'help' and recognition, of some form, from someone. In being taken advantage of, they were simultaneously acknowledged and felt wanted or were coping, whilst also being abused and exploited … When the young people talked of 'people who take advantage', they spoke of them as 'dirty horrible men', 'predators', 'mingers' and as people who 'completely fucked me up'. Yet they also spoke of them as 'someone who was there', who made them 'feel safe' and of 'people who put you up' and 'who relieve one kind of strain on you'. 'People' who take advantage and 'people' who help can be one and the same'.
>
> (Hallet, 2016: 2141–2142)

And this was part of the paradox the men depicted in this chapter failed to grasp. They were both 'good helpers' of young people in need and 'horrible men'. They were people who could make young women 'feel safe' and 'people who fucked them up'. They had needs of their own that they could barely face up to; needs that were obscured in the re-enactment of pornographic fantasies of sexual encounters that 'just happened' at parties, often with little dialogue beforehand and no sense of care or commitment afterwards. In turn, they left those they invited to 'parties' vulnerable to other men who were much more predatory and who destroyed their capacities to enjoy the few freedoms they had. The parents of the young people who were abused had problems of their own too – as Linda's case clearly illustrates. In turn, some women who are abused feel unable to turn to the authorities for fear of implicating themselves or losing their children. And some women who are abused engage in exploitation too, as Susan's case illustrates, perhaps to normalize the horrors they are living with and to achieve some semblance of control by sharing the risks and having someone else witness what they are going through.

As all the enquiry reports we discussed in the opening of this chapter reveal, we need to better understand how such behaviour also becomes normalized in the lives of perpetrators. The salacious and typically racialized reporting of their crimes was one reason why all the research participants whose stories are retold above continued to protest their innocence, for none regarded themselves as members of 'grooming gangs'. If we are to better prepare over-stretched police and social service professionals to intervene more effectively in such cases, we will need to refocus attention on the ways in which age, gender and ethnicity are 'read' by victims and perpetrators living in the same localized communities through narratives that redefine transactional relationships – in which power inequalities are stark – as 'safe' and 'exciting'. One of the things that renders relationships in which power relations are exploitive to young people uniquely enticing is the way in which they are constructed by perpetrators as beyond the comprehension of those in positions of authority, of whom victims are already mistrustful. 'Party' narratives compound the receptiveness of those deprived of the care they are formally said to be receiving to the advances of adults who promise to 'look after them'. Highlighting this has surely got to be a more effective response to the sexual exploitation of children and young people than erroneously framing the problem as one of ethnic difference.

10 Conclusion

In this book, we have reported findings from the first-ever primary study of modern slavery offenders. All of our participants, except one, had been incarcerated as a consequence of their involvement in modern slavery and related offences. As we explained in the introduction, 'modern slavery' is a term that captures an ever-expanding range of crimes, more reflective of the political contours of debates about 'organized crime' and immigration than common features of the offending behaviour the policy umbrella has come to refer to. Throughout this book, we have tried to locate modern slavery offenders' behaviour in historical, legal and social contexts. In so doing we have attempted to render crimes of exploitation comprehensible against backdrops of destitution, marginalization, substance use, abuse and trauma, migration and choices limited by multiple structural disadvantages, including those wrought by the legacies of colonialism.

In re-articulating offenders' explanations for the modern slavery offending of which they were accused, we have sought to cut through the discourses of 'evil' that mystify extreme forms of exploitation as inhuman behaviour that defies social scientific explanation. We have done this not to diminish the considerable harms that victims of modern slavery suffer but to illustrate the kinds of social change that are required if these harms are to be prevented. We are in no doubt about the seriousness and impact of the harms inflicted on others in the commission of the offences described in this book. Nor do we wish to understate the considerable efforts of the many professionals who have worked to bring the exploitation such offences entailed to an end. Rather, in demystifying the choices made by perpetrators and moving beyond the binaries of 'good' and 'evil', we have attempted to show why some people become involved in modern slavery, what backgrounds and pathways contributed to their offending, who helped to facilitate their crimes and what motivated them. The value of our analyses needs to be judged against its capacity to explain this offending, to inform better responses to modern slavery, including what it reveals about how to deter prospective offenders and prevent modern slavery from occurring in the first place.

It has become commonplace in political speeches, journalistic reporting and in the campaigning material of anti-slavery charities to assert that modern

DOI: 10.4324/9780429053986-10

slavery is everywhere, that it is a growing social problem, cultivated by trans-national organized crime groups who have infiltrated local communities, super-market supply chains, car washes, nail bars, houses where drugs are cultivated and sex is sold, exploiting the most vulnerable British women and children as well as migrant workers. Currently, there are almost 13,000 people in the National Referral Mechanism (Thompson, 2022). But offenders remain largely elusive – only 132 people were convicted in England and Wales for offences involving modern slavery, human trafficking, servitude and forced labour between 2017 and 2020 (IASC, 2021: 77). Despite these small numbers, we were able to find 30 offenders convicted for modern slavery and related offences willing to be interviewed by us. Given that many such offenders are deported on conviction, this was not an inconsiderable sample, though it is virtually impossible to know to what degree it is representative of the evermore ill-defined population of modern slavery offenders. In the preceding chapters, we have organized these accounts by 'exploitation type' for ease of understanding. Within these chapters, there are some commonalities between the different case studies presented which reveal how the behaviours of offenders and victims are shaped by the markets in which exploitation occurs. There were also, however, some stark differences between our interviewees, revealing that – even within exploitation types – identifying shared causes of modern slavery is difficult.

This complexity, as we explained in Chapter 2, is obscured in policy narratives and the problematic statistical data evoked to support them. This obfuscation, we have argued, has serviced the political agenda of the Conservative Party in the UK. Its leaders have deployed the 'folk devil' of the modern slavery offender – in various guises – to legitimize the implementation of very hostile immigration policies that actually render irregular migrants more susceptible to exploitation within the UK than they were before the implementation of the 2015 Modern Slavery Act. The few pre-existing studies of people traffickers conducted around the world suggest that only a minority resemble the folk devils evoked to justify international law enforcement action on organized crime, people smuggling and people trafficking. Our own study of modern slavery offenders comes to a similar conclusion.

As we explained in Chapter 3, there are overlaps between human trafficking and human smuggling: the smuggled becoming vulnerable to exploitation when their journeys are forestalled. But, as our interviews revealed, those who assist others to cross borders illegally do not necessarily wish to see them exploited. Some smugglers do have connections with international networks with both licit and illicit business interests that generate considerable profits. And yet not all of those who service such networks make much money. Some are jobbing men and women, with histories of crime and criminalization. They are rarely criminal masterminds and perhaps more commonly men who deceive themselves that there is 'easy money' to be made from a small number of driving jobs that will help deserving migrants get where they need and secure paid work. Other smugglers we interviewed had themselves previously embarked on similar journeys, as refugees in the aftermath of wars, seeking a better life through migration and hard work in cash-based labour markets. These interviewees, among others, were also inclined to return favours to friends and acquaintances who had helped them out when they were in need. Such help could involve giving lifts to 'friends of friends' without asking too many questions. Smuggling, then, is organized as much through such informal obligations among the displaced as it is by international crime groups.

This sense of obligation is, in many ways, a response to the 'vicious circle', anticipated by the United Nations (2017: 5–6), in which dangerous border crossings invite more restrictive immigration regimes, forcing irregular migrants to pursue dangerous journeys, facilitated by family and acquaintances, as well as those who routinely profit from providing smuggling services. The ascendency of human trafficking and modern slavery on the international security agendas of the United Nations and the European Union is a direct response to the construction of smuggling and people trafficking as organized crime problems, orchestrated by mafia bosses assumed to also be involved in arms trading, terrorism and drug trafficking. Most modern slavery is indeed consistent with a basic definition of organized crime. Almost by definition, it involves planned and coordinated criminal behaviour conducted by three or more people acting in concert on a continuing basis for financial gain. But little of it is as sinister or insidious as the organized crime narrative conveys. Some of our participants were part of criminal networks that included family, friends and acquaintances able to facilitate illicit activity across international borders. But most of these networks involved only a few connections and generated profits that were modest and short-lived. In some cases, they simply failed to deliver any revenue or were loss-making.

To test the organized crime thesis, in Chapter 4, we presented four case studies where participants were involved in sustained international criminal activity. All four of these men were able to operate legitimate and illegitimate businesses using the skills and contacts they had gathered over the course of their lives. They were involved in multiple crime types – taking opportunities where they arose, including developing relationships with those who depended on them for help with migration and with employment. Such relationships typically became more exploitative than they were intended to be as things went wrong for irregular migrants with debts to pay, underlying vulnerabilities or substance dependencies. Hence, the men we interviewed took pride in their criminal exploits, downplaying the immorality of their illicit enterprises by denying that they ever intended to cause their victims harm and noting, where relevant, that these 'victims' had often been willing accomplices who had sought their 'help' or that of their associates. The four men whose stories are retold in this chapter all had relationships with women that were founded upon traditional conceptions of masculinity, inherited from fathers who they held in exceptionally high regard. They were men who were largely oblivious to the ways in which global gendered inequalities render some women susceptible to exploitation even while they may choose to engage with illicit enterprises. Critically, while some of them presented themselves as successful entrepreneurs or 'Mr Bigs' of a kind, all four of these men discovered, after their arrests, that they were largely replaceable in criminal enterprises in which modern slavery was little more than a side-line or by-product of other illicit activities, like money laundering, the provision of 'escort', 'massage' and other 'sexual services' and people smuggling. Arguably, the downfall of all four men owed a debt to their tendencies to overestimate and overstate their own competencies.

Addressing the global and local inequalities that generate the need among some women to turn to men with criminal connections such as these for work and money is crucial to breaking the business model of crimes of exploitation that are organized across international borders on an enduring basis. This is a point we reiterated in subsequent chapters on sham marriage, domestic servitude and the trafficking of adult women for sexual exploitation. Chapter 5 explored the incongruities entailed in including 'sham' and 'forced' marriage within the modern slavery agenda. Contextualizing the case studies of participants who had entered, or arranged, marriages within the social and legal histories of 'marriages of convenience', we documented how official responses to unions between UK and foreign nationals have introduced racially discriminatory criteria – a moral economy of suspicion (D'Aoust, 2018) – in response to fears about the circumvention of immigration controls. This, as we argue, is not to deny that a minority of those with very limited options to resist deportation or raise money to pay debts do utilize marriage to escape dire straits. We presented two cases where research participants had used marriage as a way of securing money or legal status. Both paid remittances to destitute family members living in countries of origin still blighted by gross structural inequalities of post-colonialism. Legacies of bonded labour, gendered inequality and dependency and traditions of migration and marriage lay behind the criminality of those participants involved in arranging or entering sham marriages. They were encouraged, despite their own misgivings, by others who escaped criminalization to commit what was depicted as victimless law infringements from which all parties would benefit. While the outcomes in both cases were particularly tragic, it was difficult to avoid the conclusion that immigration law and its enforcement had contributed substantially to the harms caused to victims and those ultimately convicted of this form of modern slavery.

Domestic servitude is often considered the form of modern slavery most difficult to detect because victims usually have very limited contact outside the family homes where they live and work. Yet, this very privatized form of labour exploitation can also be understood, as we show in Chapter 6, as a product of the very public histories of gendered inequality, poverty and globalization that inform the history of fosterage and post-colonial migration from Nigeria. Throughout the 20th century, child fosterage has been deployed in West Africa as a means to 'even out hardship' (Isiugo-Abanihe, 1985: 55) by sending children to study, upskill and work with wealthier families. The practice travelled back to the homelands of European colonizers as migration from West Africa to Europe increased, only to become redefined, perplexingly, as a problem 'organized crime' to be solved by raising awareness in

Nigerian communities (HM Government, 2018). As the case study we relay in this chapter reveals, the legal arrangements formulated as part of the UK's Overseas Domestic Worker Visa play a definitive role in organizing this particular form of modern slavery. The case we presented in this chapter showed how the Overseas Domestic Worker Visa, while appealing to those invested in the cultural practice of fosterage, also produces workers who are vulnerable to exploitation that can be lawful. As such, those who come to work in the UK on these visas often have little recourse but to claim they have been trafficked if they wish to avoid deportation after leaving the specific employment they were permitted to undertake. Our case example also revealed how, in practice, UK law also reaffirms patriarchal expectations in terms of who is deemed most responsible for the exploitation of overseas workers that become officially recognized as victims of domestic servitude. This begs the question as to whether modern slavery legislation is the most appropriate instrument to redress practices that are not only culturally normative in some contexts but which also gel with legally permissible forms of exploitation condoned by an immigration system that channels some of the world's most destitute women into very poorly paid work undertaken in the most under-regulated and most privatized employment sector.

Chapter 7 explores other forms of labour exploitation that occur within otherwise legitimate markets. This chapter draws on Box's (1983) analysis of the power imbalances between multi-national corporations and the freedoms they seek to trade unfettered by regulation and taxation and the power of governments to regulate labour and protect workers from breaches of human rights and risks to their health and safety. This tension has resurfaced in the development and implementation of the Transparency in the Supply Chain provisions of the 2015 Modern Slavery Act. These have done very little to temper the market forces propelled by the demand for cheap goods and services that generate opportunities for exploitation at the peripheries of the labour market. While labour exploitation became the most commonly reported form of exploitation in the UK in the mid-2010s, offenders were rarely prosecuted for such offences. Though there were many reports of modern slavery in the supply chains of very large corporations, prosecutions of company directors and chief executives remain almost unheard of. Though exploitation within competitive, global labour markets appears endemic, when particular instances of it are exposed, most companies depict it as anomalous behaviour that had been concealed from them by rogue suppliers and subcontractors and which is highly inconsistent with their brand and the aspirations espoused in their modern slavery statements. The labour exploiters we interviewed, though diverse in terms of their positioning in local, national and international markets, all denied any intentional exploitation of their employees. One reason why our participants rejected the label of the modern slavery perpetrator had to do with the normality of their behaviour in the context of commonplace business practices. In the context of weak regulatory processes and pressures to keep labour costs low that derived variously from poor business management, consumer demand and the requirements of new immigration laws, the labour exploiters we interviewed had cut corners, turned blind eyes and taken advantage of workers with few alternatives but to accept poor working conditions and pay that was much lower than the national minimum wage. As we conclude, protecting workers' rights and supporting employers to redress labour exploitation are likely to prove more effective at reducing modern slavery than approaches that leave both parties afraid to seek help through fear of criminal sanction.

Chapters 8 and 9 addressed sexual exploitation, the former focussed on adult sexual exploitation and the latter focussed on child sexual exploitation. Chapter 8 challenges the stereotype of the evil trafficker enslaving innocent women duped into making migration journeys only to be forced into prostitution. One of the reasons that this stereotype has endured is that it offers a simple explanation for another phenomenon many people neither understand nor wish to comprehend: sex work. Political outrage about sex trafficking has made it difficult to ask sociological questions about the circumstances within which some women, and a smaller number of men, make the decision to engage in sex work in their home countries and abroad. Such outrage has also foreclosed analysis of how the legal frameworks governing sex work and migration combine to render some sex workers reliant on third parties to facilitate their work. And, in conflating sex trafficking with the kidnapping of women from other countries, they have forestalled the dialogue needed to consider why it is that some women choose to travel, knowing they are going to undertake sex work, in the hope of being able to raise money for dependents at home or in countries of origin. While no one can consent to be trafficked, it is important to recognize that many adult women do consent to engage in sex work and that some travel from poor countries of origin to the West where they can secure a better rate of pay. It is the lack of rights and protections these workers face in the places where they work that exposes them to the extreme forms of exploitation that are commonly regarded as 'trafficking' and 'modern slavery'.

In the UK, migrant women involved in sex work have little choice but to approach third parties who are frequently internationally mobile men and women with similar backgrounds to help them overcome barriers put in their way by their own families, poverty, immigration control and sexual and racial discrimination in the labour market. As we show, some women who have worked in sex markets for many years come to view running a brothel as a step up from sex work and a means to stop sharing the proceeds of their labour with men who charge them for premises, security and transport. Once in 'brothel-keeping' roles, the exploitation of others is perhaps less easy for some women to see, or overlook, especially among those who are still contending with abusive partners, who have been socially ostracized or who have significant debts of their own. The men we interviewed who had been convicted for sexual exploitation had provided a range of services for sex workers – security, online advertising, renting accommodation, transport and arranging appointments with clients. Motivated variously by the need to make a living, maintain substance dependencies or participate in a 'party lifestyle', most of these men saw nothing wrong with providing services to sex workers, especially when some of those sex workers had asked for their help, refused to testify against them or even promised to resume working with them after their release from prison. These men were not all completely callous. They were, nevertheless, poorly prepared and emotionally equipped to care for women with few or no legal rights in the UK and difficult to reason with when debts were not repaid, or the women became too ill to work. Such is the nature of illicit markets where workers have limited recourse to law or regulation.

What troubled us most in our interviews with foreign national men convicted of trafficking women for the purposes of sexual exploitation was their interest in returning to this form of illicit enterprise elsewhere in Europe after their deportation. In unregulated markets, workers rely on such people to arrange and assist with sex work. Where those workers are vulnerable for a variety of reasons – including but not limited to migration, poverty, the need to make remittances or care for family – there is very little to prevent the arrangements with third parties from becoming exploitative. This is why conferring rights to minimum rates of pay, decent working conditions, support and assistance to sex workers and those considering sex work is crucial. Without these safeguards, some women see little alternative but continue to be exploited or exploit others. And these women, despite their prior experiences of exploitation, then become criminalized as modern slavery offenders too.

In Chapter 9, we argue that explaining child sexual exploitation as a problem derivative primarily of the activities of 'Asian grooming gangs' has diverted attention away from the multiple failures of government agencies required to provide protection to those in their care. Official inquiry reports that investigated the sexual exploitation of children across England in the late 2010s revealed systemic failures in the social care system, caused by severe resource constraints, poor management and institutional racism. At the same time, these reports illustrated how uncritical references to the ethnicities of perpetrators made by professionals, the media and sometimes victims themselves had clouded an understanding of what motivates adult men to sexually exploited children and young adults and the contexts in which such exploitation arises.

This chapter situates the accounts of those responsible for child sexual exploitation within offenders' own biographies, these also providing a glimpse into the unfortunate circumstances that compounded the vulnerabilities of their victims too. The crimes of our participants were generally not organized for financial gain, or by 'gangs', even though gang membership was officially implied in all but one of the cases we reported on. Rather child sexual exploitation took place at 'parties' attended by loosely acquainted participants looking for places to consume illicit drug or alcohol in the early hours when the adults' employment displaced their leisure time. These exchanges were often viewed by the men we interviewed as consensual, teenagers' repeated attendance misconstrued as consent to continue exchanging sex for alcohol, drugs, food or somewhere to sleep. For women implicated in child sexual exploitation, their own abuse as children contributed to the normalization of male perpetrators' behaviour, partially explaining why they were cajoled into facilitating the attendance of other victims at household and hotel parties where they were sexually assaulted. By way of contrast, none of the men we interviewed fully recognized the power differentials between themselves and the much younger women who were being exploited, though their involvement in these parties varied.

We remain concerned that the discourse on 'Asian grooming gangs', in combination with references to modern slavery, actually makes it more difficult to recognize the dangers posed by serial sex offenders, as well as the misogynistic assumptions of a wider group of men largely oblivious to the ways intoxication, destitution and vast age differentials complicate the issue of sexual consent. This was also true of some of those men within our sample implicated in the sexual exploitation of adults, though it is impossible to discern common features of the motives of all those who took part in our project. Everyone we interviewed admitted some wrongdoing, but no one truly recognized themselves as a perpetrator of modern slavery or human trafficking. All of our participants felt their actions and intentions had been misrepresented in court, and the media and some brought evidence of this in the form of court transcripts to the interviews. Foreign national offenders often had limited understanding of the prosecution processes. Some had been encouraged to plead guilty on the false promise of a reduced sentence if they agreed to deportation. Some British offenders also said they had no opportunity to explain what had happened in court or were advised by judges that there was no value in doing so once a guilty plea had been entered. One participant pled guilty to a charge of facilitating the entry of a non-EU national into the UK – a charge he considered to be informed by a misunderstanding – because the cost and time involved in travelling for court hearings were too prohibitive for his family. Another who had advertised the sexual services of Romanian women online brought victim statements recorded by the police to the interview to evidence his claim that the women involved did not consider themselves to have been exploited by him. All the men involved in 'grooming' cases alleged associations with 'Asian' men they barely knew had helped secure convictions against them in the context of racially discriminatory legal processes and media coverage. Only a couple of participants – both involved in running legitimate businesses – had even the barest knowledge of modern slavery law prior to conviction. Consequently, no one had been deterred by the sentencing powers introduced by the 2015 Modern Slavery Act as no one we interviewed thought this law truly applied to the crimes they became implicated in.

This is why our focus in this book has been on demystifying pathways into modern slavery offending that might otherwise be regarded as unthinkable, not only to the general public but also to many of those convicted of this new crime. Through each chapter, we have sought to situate the stories we heard in our interviews within relevant historical, cultural, socio-economic literature and research. What we have shown is that references to 'evil', 'criminal masterminds', 'organized crime' and 'criminal gangs' oversimplify the complex interdependencies that define the relationships between exploiters and exploited, some of whom do not see each other as such. Certainly, there were many within our sample with long histories of criminal involvement: some of whom were raised in criminal families or were embedded within networks of criminal acquaintances. Much of this prior criminal activity was petty in nature, and some of it was survival focussed. Only a minority – all men – were invested in enduring criminal enterprises. Others within the sample – notably those implicated in domestic servitude and most of those implicated in labour exploitation – were one-time offenders who had never been in contact with the criminal justice system previously. They had become implicated in modern slavery in the operation of otherwise legitimate businesses. Most, but not all of these one-time offenders, had been highly regarded in their local communities, and some were avowedly religious, moral people, who were shocked to discover they had broken the law. Others still had become caught up in criminality in later life – transporting sex workers, running brothels, entering or arranging sham marriages – in part because they were desperate and destitute themselves. They perpetrated crimes of modern slavery and immigration offences to escape exploitation perpetrated against them. This subgroup was disproportionately, but not exclusively, women, none of whom had been formally identified as victims of modern slavery.

Indeed, even some of those who had mobilized transnational networks of offenders implicated in people and drug smuggling operations had endured brutality and disadvantage in their earlier lives: including experiences as a child soldier, being introduced to cocaine by parents as a young teenager and being taken into care due to parental substance use and suicide attempts. These early foundations do not justify the later criminality and exploitation of others, but they are part of the explanation as to why some of those depicted as 'Mr Bigs' considered themselves to be 'fixing' the problems of disadvantaged groups via means they understood to be illicit but not necessarily immoral. Those they were helping would have included people like those others in our sample who lived lives at the sharp end of globalization, who worked long hours in multiple low-paid jobs to send remittances to children and other adults who were economically dependent on them, or whose emotional learning appeared to have been impoverished by childhood histories of abuse and neglect.

In tracing their stories and following their decision-making, it is possible to identify points at which supportive interventions could have prevented many of our participants from engaging in the catalogue of crimes now defined as modern slavery: gaps within systems of support for those at the margins of society, whether because they were lacking parental care, insufficiently protected by social services, not recognized as victims of trafficking or were trapped by an immigration system that forces them to choose between destitution, selling themselves or other forms of cash-based employment. In focusing on the backgrounds and journeys of perpetrators, we are not diminishing or disregarding the harms perpetrated by our participants. In a minority of cases, these harms involved brutal physical or sexual assaults. In most cases these harms were financial – with few of their victims receiving recompense of the perpetrators were convicted. Some of the harms were brief while others were endured for many months. Some victims did experience long-term psychological harm, though there were also a few seemingly 'victimless' cases. And even in those cases where perpetrators had exploited the precarity of victims, it was rarely apparent that the criminal justice process had delivered anything approximating reparation; some victims were also deported or criminalized in the process of bringing modern slavery offenders to justice.

The mystification of modern slavery as an evil of biblical proportions will not serve to reduce the prevalence of the exploitation attributed to those accused of perpetrating such crimes, perplexingly 'in plain sight' while also evading detection and justice. The scapegoating of smugglers, traffickers and modern slavery offenders as folk devils distracts from the role of national governments and international bodies in compounding the plights of those at the sharp ends of globalization through border enforcement, denying them welfare and rights as workers and citizens, and by casting them as 'illegal' by virtue of being undocumented. In redirecting our attention towards sex traffickers, grooming gangs and organized crime, the modern slavery agenda has diverted attention away from the structural factors, market dynamics and legal regimes that make exploitation all the more likely. The lack of choices available to those prospective perpetrators living in destitution, amidst conflict, or with no real way of legitimately improving their situation illuminates this point.

Of course, some, maybe all of those we interviewed, were making excuses, downplaying what they had done, overstating the hardships they too had endured and displacing blame elsewhere. But this does not undermine the need to face the folk devils of anti-trafficking policy. In learning more about what modern slavery offenders do and do not do, and what decisions they might or might not be considered responsible for, we can also more clearly demarcate the circumstances that were not within their control, including those that are the products of global inequality, market imperatives, social policies and law and border enforcement. The interview accounts reproduced in this book need to be seen in this light: as evidence of the dangers of scapegoating a folk devil that bares only a pale resemblance to reality and of being distracted away from the role political economies play in sustaining banal forms of exploitation. These banal forms of exploitation, as the interviews we have conducted reveal, rapidly become brutalizing when new market pressures are introduced, indebtedness deepens, welfare safeguards are withdrawn, workers suffer ill-health or the needs of their dependents become more acute. This is the unthinkable reality that makes the demonizing discourse of modern slavery politically palatable. And yet, as many of our interviewees revealed, the mischaracterization, racial profiling and punitiveness this demonizing enables also make it harder for those implicated in exploitation to accept their part in it and stifles a much-needed public debate about the social, economic and legal interventions that are needed to reduce the growing number of people living at the margins of society and at risk of extreme forms of exploitation.

Bibliography

Aas, K.F. (2011). '"Crimmigrant" bodies and bona fide travelers: Surveillance, citizenship and global governance', *Theoretical Criminology*, 15(3), pp. 331–346.

Aas, K. and Gundhus, H. (2015). 'Policing humanitarian borderlands: Frontex, human rights and the precariousness of life', *British Journal of Criminology*, 55(1), pp. 1–18.

Adams, N., Brady-Clark, M. Michaels, H. and Wills, R. (2016). *Decriminalisation of Prostitution: Report of Parliamentary Symposium*. London: English Collective of Prostitutes. Available at: http://prostitutescollective.net/wp-content/uploads/2017/01/Online-Symposium-Report.pdf (Accessed 31 January 2022).

Agustín, L. (2006). 'The disappearing of a migration category: Migrants who sell sex', *Journal of Ethnic and Migration Studies*, 32(1), pp. 29–47.

Agustín, L. (2007). *Sex at the Margins: Migration, Labour Markets and the Rescue Industry*. London: Zed Books.

Åkesson, L. (2009). 'Remittances and inequality in Cape Verde: The impact of changing family organisation', *Global Networks*, 9(3), pp. 381–398.

Albanese, J. (2012). 'Deciphering the linkages between organized crime and transnational crime', *Journal of International Affairs*, 66(1), pp. 1–16.

Albanese, J.S., Broad, R. and Gadd, D. (2022). 'Consent, coercion and fraud in human trafficking relationships' *Journal of Human Trafficking* [Preprint]. Available at: www.tandfonline.com/doi/full/10.1080/23322705.2021.2019529 (Accessed: 27 January 2022).

Albrecht, H. (2002). 'Fortress Europe? – controlling illegal immigration', *European Journal of Crime, Criminal Law and Criminal Justice*, 10(1), pp. 1–22.

Alexander, C. (2004). 'Imagining the Asian gang: ethnicity, masculinity and youth after "the riots"', *Critical Social Policy*, 24(4), pp. 526–549.

Amnesty International (2017). *Libya: European Governments Complicit in Horrific Abuse of Refugees and Migrants*. Available at: www.amnesty.org/en/latest/news/2017/12/libya-european-governments-complicit-in-horrific-abuse-of-refugees-and-migrants/ (Accessed: 11 January 2022).

Amzat, I.H. (2010). 'The effect of poverty on education in Nigeria: obstacles and solutions', *OIDA International Journal of Sustainable Development*, 1(4), pp. 55–72.

Anderson, B. and Andrijasevic, R. (2008). 'Sex, slaves and citizens: the politics of anti-trafficking', *Soundings*, (40), pp. 135–145.

Annan, K.A. (2004). *Foreword to the United Nations Convention Against Transnational Organized Crime and The Protocols Thereto*. Vienna: UNODC. Available at: www.unodc.org/documents/middleeastandnorthafrica/organised-crime/UNITED_NATIONS_CONVENTION_AGAINST_TRANSNATIONAL_ORGANIZED_CRIME_AND_THE_PROTOCOLS_THERETO.pdf (Accessed 12 January 2022).

Anti-Slavery International (2018). *Sitting on Pins and Needles.* Available at: www.antislav ery.org/sitting-on-pins-and-needles/ (Accessed: 27 January 2022).

Anti-Slavery International (2021). *The New Plan for Immigration Won't Help Victims of Modern Slavery.* Available at: www.antislavery.org/new-plan-for-immigration-surviv ors/ (Accessed: 27 January 2022).

APPG on Prostitution and the Global Sex Trade (2018). *Behind Closed Doors: Organised Sexual Exploitation in England and Wales.* London: APPG. Available at: www.appg-cse. uk/wp-content/uploads/2018/05/Behind-closed-doors-APPG-on-Prostitution. pdf (Accessed: 29 January 2022).

Armitage, J. (2018). '£20m Extra for Scanners to Detect Stowaways on Calais Lorries', *Evening Standard*, 30 April [Online]. Available at: www.standard.co.uk/news/polit ics/20m-extra-for-scanners-to-detect-stowaways-on-calais-lorries-a3827301.html (Accessed: 10 January 2022).

Ashurst, L. and McAlinden, A-M. (2015). 'Young people, peer-to-peer grooming and sexual offending: understanding and responding to harmful sexual behaviour within a social media society', *Probation Journal*, 62(4), pp. 374–388.

Asylum and Immigration Act 2004, c.19. Available at: www.legislation.gov.uk/ukpga/ 2004/19/contents (Accessed: 2 February 2022).

ATMG (2013). *In the Dock: Examining the UK's Criminal Justice Response to Trafficking.* London: Anti-Trafficking Monitoring Group. Available at: www.antislavery.org/wp-content/uploads/2017/01/in_the_dock_final.pdf (Accessed: 5 February 2022).

ATMG (2018). *Before the Harm is Done: Examining the UK's Response to the Prevention of Trafficking.* London: Anti-Trafficking Monitoring Group. Available at: www.anti slavery.org/wp-content/uploads/2018/09/Before-the-Harm-is-Done-report.pdf (Accessed: 5 February 2022).

Aziani, A. (2021). 'The Heterogeneity of Human Smugglers: A Reflection on the Use of Concepts in Studies on the Smuggling of Migrants', *Trends in Organized Crime.* [Online]. Available at: https://link.springer.com/article/10.1007/s12117-021-09435-w (Accessed: 11 January 2022).

Badshah, N. (2019). 'Teenager Fleeing Dutch Asylum Shelter One of 39 Dead in Essex Lorry', *The Guardian*, 23 November [Online]. Available at: www.theguardian.com/ uk-news/2019/nov/23/teenager-fleeing-dutch-asylum-shelter-one-of-39-dead-in-essex-lorry (Accessed: 10 January 2022).

Balch, A. (2015). 'Understanding and Evaluating UK Efforts to Tackle Forced Labour', in Waite, L., Craig, G., Lewis, H. and Skrivankova, K. (eds.) *Vulnerability, Exploitation and Migrants: Insecure Work in a Globalised Economy.* Basingstoke: Palgrave Macmillan, pp. 86–98.

Balch, A. and Geddes, A. (2011). 'Opportunity from crisis? Organisational responses to human trafficking in the UK', *The British Journal of Politics and International Relations*, 13(1), pp. 26–41.

Batalha, L. (2004). *The Cape Verdean Diaspora in Portugal: Colonial Subjects in a Postcolonial World.* Oxford: Lexington Books.

BBC News (2013). *Oxford Grooming Sex Case: Brothers Jailed for Life.* Available at: www. bbc.co.uk/news/uk-england-oxfordshire-23079649 (Accessed: 9 February 2022).

BBC News (2017). *Women Trafficked to Glasgow for Sham Marriages.* Available at: www. bbc.co.uk/news/uk-scotland-39855287 (Accessed: 21 January 2022).

BBC News (2019). *Essex Lorry Deaths: Police Name 39 Vietnamese Victims.* Available at: www.bbc.co.uk/news/uk-england-essex-50350481 (Accessed: 11 January 2022).

Bedford, A. (2015). *Serious Case Review into Child Sexual Exploitation in Oxfordshire: From the Experiences of Children A, B, C, D, E, and F.* Oxfordshire: OSCB. Available at: www. oscb.org.uk/wp-content/uploads/OSCBPressReleaseFINAL.pdf (Accessed: 9 February 2022).

Benson, M. and Charsley, K. (2015). 'From genuine to sham marriage: moral panic and the 'authenticity' of relationships', in Cree, V., Clapton, G. and Smith, M. (eds.) *Revisiting Moral Panics.* Bristol: Policy Press, pp. 221–230.

Bentham, M. (2019). 'UK Must Act to Stop Slavery and Trafficking of Nigerian Girls', *Evening Standard*, 29 November [Online]. Available at: www.standard.co.uk/news/ uk/uk-must-act-to-stop-slavery-and-trafficking-of-nigerian-girls-a4299971.html (Accessed: 22 January 2022).

Berelowitz, S., Clifton, J., Firmin, C., Gulyurtlu, S. and Edwards, G. (2013). '*If only someone had listened' Office of the Children's Commissioner's Inquiry into Child Sexual Exploitation in Gangs and Groups: Final Report.* London: Office of the Children's Commissioner. Available at: www.childrenscommissioner.gov.uk/wp-content/uploads/2017/07/ If_only_someone_had_listened.pdf (Accessed: 9 February 2022).

Bernstein, E. (2007). 'The sexual politics of new abolitionism', *Differences*, 18(3), pp. 128–151.

Bollas, C. (1993). *Being a Character: Psychoanalysis and Self Experience.* Abingdon: Routledge.

Bosworth, M., Franko, K. and Pickering, S. (2018). 'Punishment, globalisation and migration control: "Get them the hell out of here"', *Punishment and Society*, 20(1), pp. 34–53.

Bolt, D. (2016). *The Implementation of the 2014 'Hostile Environment' Provisions for Tackling Sham Marriage*, London: Stationary Office. Available at: https://assets.publishing.serv ice.gov.uk/government/uploads/system/uploads/attachment_data/file/577880/ Sham_Marriage_report.pdf (Accessed: 21 January 2022).

Bosworth, M. and Guild, M. (2008). 'Governing through migration control: security and citizenship in Britain', *British Journal of Criminology*, 48(6), pp. 703–719.

Bowden, G. (2016). *Amazon Working Conditions Claims of 'Exploitation' Prompt Calls for Inquiry.* Available at: www.huffingtonpost.co.uk/entry/amazon-working-conditi ons-inquiry_uk_584e7530e4b0b7ff851d3fff (Accessed: 27 January 2022).

Box, S. (1983). *Power, Crime, and Mystification.* London: Routledge.

Brachet, J. (2018). 'Manufacturing smugglers: From irregular to clandestine mobility in the Sahara', *The Annals of the American Academy of Political and Social Science*, 676, pp. 16–35.

Britton, J. (2019). 'Challenging the racialization of child sexual exploitation: Muslim men, racism and belonging in Rotherham', *Ethnic and Racial Studies*, 42(5), pp. 688–706.

Broad, R. and Turnbull, N. (2019). 'From human trafficking to modern slavery: the development of anti-trafficking policy in the UK', *European Journal on Criminal Policy and Research*, 25(2), pp. 119–133.

Brotherton, V. (2019). 'Class Acts? A comparative analysis of modern slavery legislation across the UK', in Craig, G., Balch, A., Lewis, H. and Waite, L. (eds.) *The Modern Slavery Agenda: Policy, Politics and Practice in the UK.* Bristol: Policy Press, pp. 97–120.

Brown, K. and Sanders, T. (2017). 'Pragmatic, progressive, problematic: addressing vulnerability through a local street sex work partnership initiative', *Social Policy and Society*, 16(3), pp. 429–441.

Bulman, M. (2021). 'Priti Patel's focus on bolstering borders will lead to more exploitation in UK, warns modern slavery tsar', *The Independent*, 29 December [Online]. Available at: www.independent.co.uk/news/uk/home-news/modern-slavery-immigration-exploitation-priti-patel-dame-sara-thornton-b1982124.html (Accessed: 2 February 2022).

Campana, P. (2018). 'Out of Africa: The organization of migrant smuggling across the Mediterranean', *European Journal of Criminology*, 15(4), pp. 481–502.

Campbell, R. and O'Neill, M. (2013). *Sex Work Now*. London: Routledge.

Campbell, R., Sanders, T., Scoular, J., Pitcher, J. and Cunningham, S. (2018). 'Risking safety and rights: online sex work, crimes and "blended safety repertoires"', *British Journal of Sociology*, 70(4), pp. 1539–1560.

Campesi, G. (2018). 'European Border and Coast Guard (Frontex): Security, Democracy, and Rights at the EU Border', *Oxford Research Encyclopaedia of Criminology and Criminal Justice*. Available at: https://oxfordre.com/criminology/view/10.1093/acrefore/9780190264079.001.0001/acrefore-9780190264079-e-354 (Accessed: 11 January 2022).

Cantle, T. (2001). *Community Cohesion: A Report of the Independent Review Team*. London: Home Office. Available at: https://tedcantle.co.uk/pdf/communitycohesion%20cantlereport.pdf (Accessed: 9 February 2022).

Casey, L. (2015). *Report of Inspection of Rotherham Metropolitan Borough Council*. London: Department for Communities and Local Government. Available at: www.gov.uk/government/publications/report-of-inspection-of-rotherham-metropolitan-borough-council (Accessed: 9 February 2022).

Centre for Social Justice (2013). *It Happens Here: Equipping the United Kingdom to Fight Modern Slavery*. London: Centre for Social Justice. Available at: www.centreforsocialjustice.org.uk/wp-content/uploads/2013/03/CSJ_Slavery_Full_Report_WEB5.pdf (Accessed: 5 February 2022).

Centre for Social Justice (2020). *It Still Happens Here: Fighting UK Slavery in the 2020s*. London: Centre for Social Justice. Available at: www.centreforsocialjustice.org.uk/library/it-still-happens-here-fighting-uk-slavery-in-the-2020s (Accessed: 5 February 2022).

Chantler, K. (2014). 'What's love got to do with marriage?', Families, Relationships and Societies, 3(1), pp. 19–33.

Chantler, K,. Baker, V., MacKenzie, M., McCarry, M., and Mirza, N. (2017). *Understanding Forced Marriage in Scotland*. Edinburgh: Scottish Government. Available at: www.gov.scot/binaries/content/documents/govscot/publications/research-and-analysis/2017/01/understanding-forced-marriage-scotland/documents/00513514-pdf/00513514-pdf/govscot%3Adocument/00513514.pdf (Accessed: 21 January 2022).

Choi-Fitzpatrick, A. (2016). 'The good, the bad, the ugly: Human rights violators in comparative perspective', *Journal of Human Trafficking*, 2(1), pp. 1–14.

Choi-Fitzpatrick, A. (2017). *What Slaveholders Think: How Contemporary Perpetrators Rationalize What They Do*. New York: Columbia University Press.

Chuang, J. (2006). 'Beyond a snapshot: Preventing human trafficking in the global economy', *Indiana Journal of Global Legal Studies*, 13(1), pp. 137–163.

Chuang, J. (2014). 'Exploitation creep and the unmaking of human trafficking law', *American Journal of International Law*, 108(4), pp. 609–649.

Cockbain, E. (2013). 'Grooming and the "Asian sex gang predator": The construction of a racial crime threat', *Race and Class*, 54(4), pp. 22–32.

Cockbain, E. (2018). *Offender and Victim Networks in Human Trafficking*, London: Routledge.

Cockbain, E., Bowers, K. and Dimitrova, G. (2018). 'Human trafficking for labour exploitation: The results of a two-phase systematic review mapping the European evidence base and synthesising key scientific research evidence', *Journal of Experimental Criminology*, 14, pp. 319–360.

Cockbain, E., Bowers, K. and Hutt, O. (2022). 'Examining the geographies of human trafficking: Methodological challenges in mapping trafficking's complexities and connectivities', *Applied Geography*, 139, pp. 1–16 [Online] Available at: www.sciencedirect.com/science/article/abs/pii/S0143622822000145 (Accessed: 16 February 2022).

Cockbain, E., & Brayley-Morris, H. (2018). 'Human trafficking and labour exploitation in the casual construction industry: an analysis of three major investigations in the UK involving Irish traveller offending groups', *Policing: A Journal of Policy and Practice*, 12(2), pp. 129–149.

Cockbain, E. and Tufail, M. (2020). 'Failing victims, fuelling hate: challenging the harms of the "muslim grooming gangs" narrative', *Race & Class*, 61(3), pp. 3–32.

COE Convention (2005). Council of Europe Convention on Action Against Trafficking in Human Beings (COE: CETS 197). Available at: https://rm.coe.int/168008371d (Accessed: 5 February).

Coffey, A. (2014). *Real Voices: Child Sexual Exploitation in Greater Manchester: An Independent Report*. Available at: www.basw.co.uk/system/files/resources/basw_103 119-3_0.pdf (Accessed: 9 February 2022).

Cohen, S. (2001). *States of Denial*. Cambridge: Polity.

Cohen, S. (2002). *Folk Devils and Moral Panics*. Abingdon: Routledge.

Cole, H. (2021). 'LOOPHOLE KO child rapists and terrorists will be stopped from using exploiting modern slavery loophole to stay in Britain', *The Sun*, 19 March [Online]. Available at: www.thesun.co.uk/news/14397127/uk-clampdown-depo rtation-law-firms-criminals/ (Accessed: 15 February 2022).

Colley, S. (2019). 'Perpetrators of Organised Child Sexual Exploitation (CSE) in the UK: A review of current research', *Journal of Sexual Aggression*, 25(3), pp. 258–274.

Commonwealth Immigrants Act 1962, c.21. Available at: www.freemovement.org.uk/wp-content/uploads/2018/04/CIA1962.pdf (Accessed: 20 January 2022).

Cooper, C., Hesketh, O., Ellis, N., Fair, A. and Home Office Analysis and Insight (2017). *A Typology of Modern Slavery Offences in the UK*. Research Report 93. Available at: https://assets.publishing.service.gov.uk/government/uploads/system/uploads/ attachment_data/file/652652/typology-modern-slavery-offences-horr93.pdf (Accessed: 21 January 2022).

Copley, L. (2014). 'Neutralizing their involvement: sex traffickers' discourse techniques', *Feminist Criminology*, 9(1), pp. 45–58.

Coroners and Justice Act 2009, c.25. Available at: www.legislation.gov.uk/ukpga/2009/ 25/contents (Accessed: 2 February 2022).

Council Directive 2004/81/EC of 29 April 2004 on the residence permit issued to third-country nationals who are victims of trafficking in human beings or who have been the subject of an action to facilitate illegal immigration, who cooperate with the competent authorities [2004] OJ L261/19.

Council Directive 2011/36/EU of the European Parliament and of the Council of 5 April 2011 on preventing and combating trafficking in human beings and protecting its victims, and replacing Council Framework Decision 2002/629/JHA [2011] OJ L101/1.

Council Framework Decision 2002/629/JHA of 19 July 2002 on combating trafficking in human beings [2002] OJ L203/1.

Cowburn, A. (2019). 'Boris Johnson argues about definition of "Spaffing" in TV interview after being confronted over child sex abuse investigation remarks', *The Independent*, 30 September [Online]. Available at: www.independent.co.uk/news/uk/politics/boris-johnson-spaffing-definition-meaning-itv-news-interview-video-sex-abuse-investigation-a9126391.html (Accessed: 9 February 2022).

CPS (2017). *Violence Against Women and Girls Report: Tenth Edition, 2016-17*. Crown Prosecution Service. Available at: www.cps.gov.uk/sites/default/files/documents/publications/cps-vawg-report-2017_0.pdf (Accessed: 7 February 2022).

CPS (2018a). *DPP Speech to the International Summit on Modern Slavery*. Available at: www.cps.gov.uk/cps/news/dpp-speech-international-summit-modern-slavery (Accessed: 21 January 2022).

CPS (2018b). *Modern Slavery, Human Trafficking and Smuggling*. Available at: www.cps.gov.uk/legal-guidance/human-trafficking-smuggling-and-slavery (Accessed: 21 January 2022).

Craven, S., Brown, S. and Gilchrist, E. (2006). 'Sexual grooming of children: review of literature and theoretical considerations', *Journal of Sexual Aggression*, 12(3), pp. 287–299.

D'Aoust, A-M. (2013). 'In the name of love: Marriage migration, governmentality and technologies of love', *International Political Sociology*, 7(3), pp. 258–274.

D'Aoust, A-M. (2018). 'A moral economy of suspicion: Love and marriage migration management practices in the United Kingdom', *Environment and Planning D: Society and Space*, 36(1), pp. 40–59.

Davies, C.T. (2016). *An Overview of the Multi-Agency Response to Child Sexual Exploitation in Peterborough*. Peterborough: Peterborough Safeguarding Children Board. Available at: www.safeguardingcambspeterborough.org.uk/wp-content/uploads/2016/06/An-Overview-of-the-Multi-agency-response-to-CSE-in-Peterborough.pdf (Accessed: 9 February 2022).

Davies, J. (2020). 'Criminological reflections on the regulation and governance of labour exploitation', *Trends in Organised Crime*, 23, pp. 57–76.

Day, S. (2010). 'The re-emergence of "trafficking": sex work between slavery and freedom', *Journal of the Royal Anthropological Institute*, 16(4), pp. 816–834.

Dearden, L. (2019). 'Sajid Javid says UK will do "everything we can" to thwart asylum claims from people crossing channel', *The Independent*, 2 January [Online]. Available at: www.independent.co.uk/news/uk/home-news/migrant-crossings-sajid-javid-english-channel-asylum-seekers-refugees-home-secretary-a8707646.html (Accessed: 14 January 2022).

Dearden, L. (2020). 'Grooming gangs review was 'internal', government says after 120,000 people demand publication', *The Independent*, 25 April [Online]. Available at: www.independent.co.uk/news/uk/home-news/grooming-gangs-review-sajid-javid-release-petition-home-office-a9483796.html (9 February 2022).

Dearden, L. (2021). 'Home Office triggered unlawful prosecutions by hunting down asylum seekers who steered Channel boats', *The Independent*, 22 December [Online]. Available at: www.independent.co.uk/news/uk/home-news/channel-crossings-unlawful-prosecutions-home-office-b1980960.html (Accessed: 2 February 2022).

Doezema, J. (2005). 'Now you see her, now you don't: Sex workers at the un trafficking protocol negotiation', *Social and Legal Studies*, 14(1), pp. 61–89.

Doezema, J. (2010). *Sex Slaves and Discourse Masters*. London: Zed Books.

Dolz, P.O. (2018). 'Greek court acquits Spanish firemen accused of people smuggling', *El Pais*, 8 May [Online]. Available at: https://english.elpais.com/elpais/2018/05/08/inenglish/1525767878_346157.html (Accessed: 12 January 2022).

Drotbohm, H. (2009). 'Horizons of long distance intimacies: Reciprocity, contribution and disjuncture in Cape Verde', *The History of the Family*, 14(2), pp. 132–149.

Duggan, J. (2019). 'Smuggling Boss Hunt: Millionaire Vietnamese gang lord wanted by cops over 39 migrant deaths', *The Sun,* 30 October [Online]. Available at: www.thesun.co.uk/news/10241144/millionaire-vietnamese-gang-lord-migrant-deaths/ (Accessed: 10 January 2022).

EASO, European Asylum Support Office (2015). *Country of Origin Information Report: Pakistan: Country Overview*. Available at: www.easo.europa.eu/sites/default/files/public/EASO_COI_Report_Pakistan-Country-Overview_final.pdf (Accessed: 21 January 2022).

Edwards, A. and Gill, P. (2002). 'Crime as enterprise? The case of "transnational organised crime"', *Crime, Law and Social Change*, 37(3), pp. 203–223.

Ellison, G. (2017). 'Criminalizing the payment for sex in Northern Ireland: Sketching the contours of a moral panic', *British Journal of Criminology*, 57(1), pp. 194–214.

European Commission (2015a). *The European Agenda on Security*. Brussels: European Commission. Available at: www.cepol.europa.eu/sites/default/files/european-agenda-security.pdf (Accessed: 14 January 2022).

European Commission (2015b). *A European Agenda on Migration*. Brussels: European Commission. Available at: https://eur-lex.europa.eu/legal-content/EN/TXT/?uri=celex:52015DC0240 (Accessed: 17 January 2022).

European Commission (2015c). *EU Action Plan against Migrant Smuggling (2015–2020)*. Brussels: European Commission. Available at: https://ec.europa.eu/anti-trafficking/sites/antitrafficking/files/eu_action_plan_against_migrant_smuggling_en.pdf (Accessed: 11 January 2022).

European Commission (2016). *Securing Europe's External Borders: Launch of the European Border and Coast Guard Agency*. Available at: https://ec.europa.eu/commission/presscorner/detail/en/IP_16_3281 (Accessed: 12 January 2022).

European Commission (2019a). *Progress Report on the Implementation of the European Agenda on Migration*. Brussels: European Commission. Available at: https://ec.europa.eu/migrant-integration/library-document/progress-report-implementation-european-agenda-migration_en (Accessed: 14 January 2022).

European Commission (2019b). *EU Delivers on Strong European Border and Coast Guard to Support Member States*. Available at: https://ec.europa.eu/commission/presscorner/detail/en/statement_19_6237 (Accessed: 12 January 2022).

European Commission (2021). *EU Strategy on Combatting Trafficking in Human Beings 2021–2025*. Brussels: European Commission. Available at: https://ec.europa.eu/home-affairs/system/files_en?file=2021-04/14042021_eu_strategy_on_combatting_trafficking_in_human_beings_2021-2025_com-2021-171-1_en.pdf (Accessed: 7 February 2022).

European Parliament (2011). Directive 2011/36/EU of the European Parliament and of the Council of 5 April 2011 on preventing and combating trafficking in human beings and protecting its victims, and replacing Council Framework Decision 2002/629/JHA.

European Parliament (2017). *Human Trafficking: Nearly 16,000 Victims in the EU*. Available at: www.europarl.europa.eu/news/en/headlines/society/20171012STO85932/human-trafficking-nearly-16-000-victims-in-the-eu (Accessed: 29 January 2022).

Europol (2000). *Europol Annual Report*. Luxembourg: Europol. Available at: www.euro pol.europa.eu/cms/sites/default/files/documents/europol_annual_report_2000.pdf (Accessed 12 January 2022).

Europol (2017). *Serious and Organised Crime Threat Assessment: Crime in the Age of Technology*. The Hague: Europol. Available at: www.europol.europa.eu/cms/sites/ default/files/documents/socta2017_0.pdf (Accessed: 12 January 2022).

Evans, S. (2013). 'Sham marriage conspirators jailed by the courts after being rumbled by a registrar', *Wales Online*, 18 November [Online]. Available at: www.walesonl ine.co.uk/news/wales-news/sham-marriage-conspirators-jailed-courts-6316882 (Accessed: 20 January 2022).

Ewins, J. (2015). *Independent Review of the Overseas Domestic Workers Visa*. London: Home Office. Available at: https://assets.publishing.service.gov.uk/government/uploads/ system/uploads/attachment_data/file/486532/ODWV_Review_-_Final_Report_ _6_11_15_.pdf (Accessed: 24 January 2022).

Farley, M. (2004). '"Bad for the Body, Bad for the Heart": Prostitution harms women even if legalized or decriminalized', *Violence Against Women*, 10(10), pp. 1087–1125.

Farrell, A. and Fahy, S. (2009). 'The problem of human trafficking in the US: Public frames and policy responses', *Journal of Criminal Justice*, 37(6), pp. 617–626.

Farthing, D., Hodgson, J. and Lee, C. (2017). *Operation Shelter: Police Paid £10,000 to Child Rapist*. Available at: www.bbc.co.uk/news/uk-england-tyne-40504952 (Accessed: 9 February 2022).

FLEX, Focus on Labour Exploitation (2018). *Shaky Foundations: Labour Exploitation in London's Construction Industry*. FLEX. Available at: www.labourexploitation.org/ publications/shaky-foundations-labour-exploitation-londons-construction-sector (Accessed: 27 January 2022).

Francis, B., Humphreys, L., Kirby, S. and Soothill, K. (2013). *Understanding Criminal Careers in Organised Crime*, Research Report 74. Home Office. Available at: https:// assets.publishing.service.gov.uk/government/uploads/system/uploads/attachment_ data/file/246392/horr74.pdf (Accessed: 12 January 2022).

Franko, K. (2020). *The Crimmigrant Other: Migration and Penal Power*. Abingdon: Routledge.

Fryer, P. (1984). *Staying Power: The History of Black People in Britain*. London: Pluto Press.

Gadd, D. (2012). 'In-Depth Interviewing and Psychosocial Case Study Analysis', in Gadd, D., Karstedt, S. and Messner, S.F. *The SAGE Handbook of Criminological Research Methods*. London: Sage Publications, pp. 36–48.

Gadd, D. and Broad, R. (2018). 'Troubling recognitions in British responses to modern slavery', *British Journal of Criminology*, 58(6), pp. 1440–1461.

Gadd, D. and Dixon, B. (2011). *Losing the Race: Thinking Psychologically about Racially Motivated Crime*. London: Karnac.

Gallagher, A. (2017a). 'What's wrong with the Global Slavery Index?', *Anti-Trafficking Review*, (8), pp. 90–112.

Gallagher, A. (2017b). 'Whatever Happened to the Migrant Smuggling Protocol?', in McAuliffe, M. and Klein Solomon, M. (Conveners) *Ideas to Inform International Cooperation on Safe, Orderly and Regular Migration*. Geneva: IOM, pp. 105–109.

Gallagher, A. and Holmes, P. (2008). 'Developing an effective criminal justice response to human trafficking: Lessons from the front line', *International Criminal Justice Review*, 18(3), pp. 318–343.

Gallagher, P. (2019). 'Essex deaths: Number of migrants smuggled to UK in containers "on the rise"', *I news*, 23 October [Online]. Available at: https://inews.co.uk/ news/uk/migrants-smuggled-lorry-containers-rising-essex-354334 (Accessed: 14 January 2022).

Geringer-Sameth, E. (2015). *Why Does Including Modern Slavery in the S.D.G.s Matter?* Available at: https://blogs.lse.ac.uk/humanrights/2015/10/23/why-does-includ ing-modern-slavery-in-the-s-d-g-s-matter/ (Accessed: 7 February 2022).

Gill, A. and Harrison, K. (2015). 'Child grooming and sexual exploitation: are South Asian men the UK media's new folk devils?', *International Journal of Crime, Justice and Social Democracy*, 4(2), pp. 34–49.

Gilroy, P. (2004). *After Empire: Melancholia or Convivial Culture?* London: Routledge.

GLAA (2019). *Agricultural Industry: Headline Trends.* Available at: www.gla.gov.uk/media/ 5069/industry-profile-agriculture.pdf (Accessed: 27 January 2022).

GLAA (2021). *Conviction Totals.* Available at: www.gla.gov.uk/our-impact/conviction-totals/ (Accessed: 27 January 2022).

Goodey, J. (2008). 'Human trafficking: sketchy data and policy responses', *Criminology and Criminal Justice*, 8(4), pp. 421–442.

Gower, M. (2016). *Calls to Change Overseas Domestic Worker Visa Conditions.* (HC 2016 4786). London: House of Commons Library. Available at: http://researchbriefings. files.parliament.uk/documents/SN04786/SN04786.pdf (Accessed: 24 January 2022).

Grierson, J. (2017). 'Tens of thousands of modern slavery victims in UK, NCA says', *The Guardian*, 10 August [Online]. Available at: www.theguardian.com/world/ 2017/aug/10/modern-slavery-uk-nca-human-trafficking-prostitution (Accessed: 2 February 2022).

Guardian staff (2013). 'Oxford grooming gang: Profiles', *The Guardian*, 14 May [Online]. Available at: www.theguardian.com/uk/2013/may/14/oxford-grooming-gang-profiles (Accessed: 9 February 2022).

Guilbert, K. (2018). *H&M accused of failing to ensure fair wages for global factory workers.* Available at: www.reuters.com/article/us-workers-garment-abuse-idUSKCN1M4 1GR (Accessed: 27 January 2022).

Guild, E. and Barylska, A. (2021). 'Decent Work for Migrants? Examining the impacts of the UK frameworks of gangmasters legislation and modern slavery on working standards for irregularly present migrants', *Global Public Policy and Governance*, 1, pp. 279–299.

Hadjimatheou, K. and Lynch, J.K. (2017). '"Once they pass you, they may be gone forever": Humanitarian duties and professional tensions in safeguarding and anti-trafficking at the border', *British Journal of Criminology*, 57(4), pp. 945–963.

Hall, S., Clarke, J., Critcher, C., Jefferson, T. and Roberts, B. (1978). *Policing the Crisis: Mugging, Law and Order and the State.* London: Macmillan.

Hall, R. (2021). 'Donations to RNLI rise 3,000% after Farage's migrant criticism', *The Guardian*, 29 July [Online]. Available at: www.theguardian.com/world/2021/ jul/29/rnli-donations-soar-in-response-to-farages-migrant-criticism (Accessed: 2 February 2022).

Hall, S. (1980). *Drifting into a Law and Order Society.* London: Cobden Trust.

Hallett, S. (2016). '"An uncomfortable comfortableness": "Care", child protection and child sexual exploitation', *British Journal of Social Work*, 46(7), pp. 2137–2152.

Hansard (2019a). *Engagements: Volume 666: Debated on Wednesday 23 October 2019.* Available at: https://hansard.parliament.uk/Commons/2019-10-23/debates/ D3DCA636-3FA8-41A2-9EDB-E32E12970166/Engagements?highlight=trad ers%20human#contribution-4F04A12F-51CB-47BC-8D16-10D957A2DD41 (Accessed: 17 January 2022).

Hansard (2019b). *Major Incident in Essex: Volume 667: Debated on Monday 28 October 2019.* Available at: https://hansard.parliament.uk/Commons/2019-10-28/debates/4B217 694-62CB-4619-9A99-A810081808CD/MajorIncidentInEssex (Accessed: 17 January 2022).

Hennessy, P. (2012). 'Judges ordered to end "right to family life" farce', *The Telegraph,*
    7 April [Online]. Available at: www.telegraph.co.uk/news/uknews/law-and-order/
    9192270/Judges-ordered-to-end-right-to-family-life-farce.html (Accessed: 20
    January 2022).

HM Government (2014). *Modern Slavery Strategy.* London: HM Government. Available
    at: https://assets.publishing.service.gov.uk/government/uploads/system/uploads/
    attachment_data/file/383764/Modern_Slavery_Strategy_FINAL_DEC2015.pdf
    (Accessed: 11 January 2022).

HM Government (2015). *Historic Law to End Modern Slavery Passed.* Available at: www.
    gov.uk/government/news/historic-law-to-end-modern-slavery-passed   (Accessed:
    5 February 2022).

HM Government (2016). *Prime Minister Urges International Action to Stamp Out Modern
    Slavery.* Available at: www.gov.uk/government/news/pm-calls-for-global-action-to-
    stamp-out-modern-slavery (Available: 5 February 2022).

HM Government (2018). *Serious and Organised Crime Strategy.* London: HM Government.
    Available at: https://assets.publishing.service.gov.uk/government/uploads/sys
    tem/uploads/attachment_data/file/752854/SOC-2018-print.PDF (Accessed: 12
    January 2022).

HM Government (2019). *Independent Review of the Modern Slavery Act 2015: Final
    Report.* London: HM Government. Available at: https://assets.publishing.service.
    gov.uk/government/uploads/system/uploads/attachment_data/file/803406/
    Independent_review_of_the_Modern_Slavery_Act_-_final_report.pdf (Accessed
    5 February 2022).

HM Government (2019). *United Kingdom Labour Market Enforcement Strategy
    2019/20.* London: HM Government. Available at: www.gov.uk/government/
    publications/labour-market-enforcement-strategy-2019-to-2020 (Accessed:
    27 January 2022).

HM Government (2021a). *Nationality and Borders Bill: Explanatory Notes.* Available
    at: https://publications.parliament.uk/pa/bills/cbill/58-02/0141/en/210141en.pdf
    (Accessed: 16 February 2022).

HM Government (2021b). *New Plan for Immigration: Policy Statement.* Available at: https://
    assets.publishing.service.gov.uk/government/uploads/system/uploads/attachment_
    data/file/972517/CCS207_CCS0820091708-001_Sovereign_Borders_Web_Acc
    essible.pdf (Accessed: 16 February 2022).

HM Government (2021c). *UK Annual Report on Modern Slavery.* London: HM
    Government. Available at: https://assets.publishing.service.gov.uk/government/uplo
    ads/system/uploads/attachment_data/file/1033986/2021_UK_Annual_Report_on
    _Modern_Slavery.pdf (Accessed: 5 February 2022).

HM Government (n.d.). *Information for Persons Coming to the UK as an Overseas Domestic
    Worker.* Available at: https://assets.publishing.service.gov.uk/government/uploads/
    system/uploads/attachment_data/file/730783/Overseas_Domestic_Worker_applic
    ant_leaflet_2018_V2.1.pdf (Accessed: 24 January 2022).

HM Government (n.d.). *Overseas Domestic Worker Visa.* Available at: www.gov.uk/domes
    tic-workers-in-a-private-household-visa/domestic-workers-who-applied-before-
    5-april-2012 (Accessed: 24 January 2022).

HM Government (n.d.). *Overseas Domestic Worker Visa.* Available at: www.gov.uk/domes
    tic-workers-in-a-private-household-visa (Accessed: 24 January 2022).

HMICFRS, Her Majesty's Inspectorate of Constabulary and Fire and Rescue Services
    (2017). *Stolen Freedom: The Policing Response to Modern Slavery and Human Trafficking.*

HMICFRS. Available at: www.justiceinspectorates.gov.uk/hmicfrs/wp-content/uploads/stolen-freedom-the-policing-response-to-modern-slavery-and-human-trafficking.pdf (Accessed: 5 February).

Hobbs, D. (1997). 'Professional crime: Change, continuity and the enduring myth of the underworld', *Sociology*, 31(1), pp. 57–72.

Hobbs, D. (1998). 'Going down the glocal: The local context of organised crime', *The Howard Journal*, 37(4), pp. 407–422.

Hollway, W. and Jefferson, T. (2000). *Doing Qualitative Research Differently: Free Association, Narrative and the Interview Method*. London: Sage Publications.

Home Office (2004). *One Step Ahead: A 21st Century Strategy to Defeat Organised Crime*. London: The Stationary Office. Available at: https://assets.publishing.service.gov.uk/government/uploads/system/uploads/attachment_data/file/251075/6167.pdf (Accessed: 11 January 2022).

Home Office (2011). *Human Trafficking: The Government's Strategy*. London: HM Government. Available at: https://assets.publishing.service.gov.uk/government/uploads/system/uploads/attachment_data/file/97845/human-trafficking-strategy.pdf (Accessed: 11 January 2022).

Home Office (2013). *Draft Modern Slavery Bill*. London: Home Office. Available at: https://assets.publishing.service.gov.uk/government/uploads/system/uploads/attachment_data/file/266165/Draft_Modern_Slavery_Bill.pdf (Accessed: 19 February 2022).

Home Office (2014). *Modern Slavery Strategy*. London: HM Government. Available at: https://assets.publishing.service.gov.uk/government/uploads/system/uploads/attachment_data/file/383764/Modern_Slavery_Strategy_FINAL_DEC2015.pdf (Accessed: 11 January 2022).

Home Office (2017). *Modern Slavery Awareness & Victim Identification Guidance*. London: Home Office. Available at: https://assets.publishing.service.gov.uk/government/uploads/system/uploads/attachment_data/file/655504/6.3920_HO_Modern_Slavery_Awareness_Booklet_web.pdf (Accessed: 20 January 2022).

Home Office (2020). *National Referral Mechanism Statistics UK, End of Year Summary, 2019*. London: HM Government. Available at: https://assets.publishing.service.gov.uk/government/uploads/system/uploads/attachment_data/file/876646/national-referral-mechanism-statistics-uk-end-of-year-summary-2019.pdf (Accessed: 5 February 2022).

Home Office (2021a). *2021 UK Annual Report on Modern Slavery*. London: HM Government. Available at: https://assets.publishing.service.gov.uk/government/uploads/system/uploads/attachment_data/file/1033986/2021_UK_Annual_Report_on_Modern_Slavery.pdf (Accessed: 16 February 2022).

Home Office (2021b). *Research and Analysis: Issues Raised by People Facing Return in Immigration Detention*. Home Office. Available at: www.gov.uk/government/publications/issues-raised-by-people-facing-return-in-immigration-detention (Accessed: 16 February 2022).

Home Office (2021c). *New Plan for Immigration*. Available at: www.gov.uk/government/consultations/new-plan-for-immigration (Accessed: 7 February 2022).

Home Office (2021d). *Modern Slavery: National Referral Mechanism and Duty to Notify Statistics UK, End of Year Summary, 2020*. London: Home Office. Available at: https://assets.publishing.service.gov.uk/government/uploads/system/uploads/attachment_data/file/970995/modern-slavery-national-referral-mechanism-statistics-end-year-summary-2020-hosb0821.pdf (Accessed: 5 February 2022).

Home Office (2021e). *Immigration Act 2014: Marriage and Civil Partnership Referral and Investigation Scheme: Statutory Guidance for Home Office Staff*. London: Home Office. Available at: https://assets.publishing.service.gov.uk/government/uploads/system/uploads/attachment_data/file/974164/marriage-civil-prtnr-referral-v2.0.pdf (Accessed: 20 January 2022).

Home Office (2022). *Modern Slavery: National Referral Mechanism and Duty to Notify Statistics UK, End of Year Summary, 2021*. London: Home Office. Available at: www.gov.uk/government/statistics/modern-slavery-national-referral-mechanism-and-duty-to-notify-statistics-uk-end-of-year-summary-2021/modern-slavery-national-referral-mechanism-and-duty-to-notify-statistics-uk-end-of-year-summary-2021 (Accessed: 9 March 2022).

Home Office/FOCO (2018). *Forced Marriage Unit Statistics 2017*. London: Home Office/Foreign and Commonwealth Office. Available at: https://assets.publishing.service.gov.uk/government/uploads/system/uploads/attachment_data/file/730155/2017_FMU_statistics_FINAL.pdf (Accessed: 21 January 2022).

Home Office and Patel, P. (2021). *Press Release: Alarming Rise of Abuse within Modern Slavery System*. Available at: www.gov.uk/government/news/alarming-rise-of-abuse-within-modern-slavery-system (Accessed: 16 February 2022).

House of Commons (2019). *Fixing Fashion: Clothing Consumption and Sustainability*. HC 1952. Available at: https://publications.parliament.uk/pa/cm201719/cmselect/cmenvaud/1952/1952.pdf (Accessed: 19 February 2022).

House of Commons Home Affairs Committee (2013). *Child Sexual Exploitation and the Response to Localised Grooming: Second Report of Session 2013–14*. London: Stationary Office. Available at: https://publications.parliament.uk/pa/cm201314/cmselect/cmhaff/68/68i.pdf (Accessed: 9 February 2022).

Howard, N. (2017). 'Of *Coyotes* and *Caporali*: How Anti-Trafficking Discourses of Criminality Depoliticise mobility and exploitation', in Piotrowicz, R., Rijken, C. and Uhl, B.H. (eds.) *Routledge Handbook of Human Trafficking*. London: Routledge, pp. 511–525.

Howard, N. (2019). 'Neither predator nor prey: What trafficking discourses miss about masculinities, mobility and work', *Anthropology Today*, 35(6), pp. 14–17.

Hulland, L. (2020). 'We escaped modern slavery and have big dreams for the future – but thousands more like us need help', *i news*, October 13 [Online]. Available at: https://inews.co.uk/news/long-reads/modern-slavery-stolen-lives-human-trafficking-and-slavery-in-britain-today-interviews-712477 (Accessed: 22 January 2022).

Human Rights Watch (2018). *The Hidden Cost of Jewellery*. Available at: www.hrw.org/report/2018/02/08/hidden-cost-jewelry/human-rights-supply-chains-and-responsibility-jewelry (Accessed: 19 February 2022).

Hyland, K. (2018). *Letter to Theresa May*, 4 May. Available at: https://assets.publishing.service.gov.uk/government/uploads/system/uploads/attachment_data/file/708125/20180504_IASC.PDF (Accessed: 16 February 2022).

IASC (2020). *Independent Anti-Slavery Commissioner Annual Report 2019–2020*. London: Stationary Office. Available at: www.antislaverycommissioner.co.uk/media/1461/ccs207_ccs0520602790-001_iasc_annual-report-2019-2020_e-laying.pdf (Accessed: 7 February 2022).

IASC (2021). *Independent Anti-Slavery Commissioner: Annual Report 2020–2021*. London: Stationary Office. Available at: https://assets.publishing.service.gov.uk/government/uploads/system/uploads/attachment_data/file/1001984/CCS207_CCS0521518548-002_IASC_20pt.pdf (Accessed: 16 February 2022).

ICAI (2020). *The UK's Approach to Tackling Modern Slavery through the Aid Programme: A Review*. London: Independent Commission for Aid Impact. Available at: https://icai.independent.gov.uk/wp-content/uploads/ICAI-modern-slavery-review_FINAL.pdf (Accessed: 7 February 2022).

Immigration Act 1971, *c. 77*. Available at: www.legislation.gov.uk/ukpga/1971/77/contents (Accessed: 17 January 2022).

Immigration Act 2014, *c. 22*. Available at: www.legislation.gov.uk/ukpga/2014/22/contents/enacted (Accessed: 2 February 2022).

Immigration Act 2016, *c. 19*. Available at: www.legislation.gov.uk/ukpga/2016/19/contents/enacted (Accessed: 2 February 2022).

Immigration and Asylum Act 1999, *c.33*. Available at: www.legislation.gov.uk/ukpga/1999/33/contents (Accessed: 20 January 2022).

Inman, P. (2020). 'Boohoo must take fashion more seriously after factory scandal', *The Guardian*, 8 July [Online]. Available at: www.theguardian.com/business/2020/jul/08/boohoo-fashion-factory-retailer-uk (Accessed: 27 January 2022).

Intelligence Reform and Terrorism Prevention Act 2004. Available at: www.dni.gov/index.php/ic-legal-reference-book/intelligence-reform-and-terrorism-prevention-act-of-2004 (Accessed: 7 February 2022).

International Labor Rights Forum (2018). *Taking Stock: Labor Exploitation, Illegal Fishing and Brand Responsibility in the Seafood Industry*. Washington: International Labor Rights Forum. Available at: https://laborrights.org/sites/default/files/publications/Taking%20Stock%20final.pdf (Accessed: 27 January 2022).

Isiugo-Abanihe, U.C. (1985). 'Child fosterage in West Africa', *Population Development Review*, 11(1), pp. 53–73.

Jay, A. (2014). *Independent Inquiry into Child Sexual Exploitation in Rotherham 1997 – 2013*. Available at: www.rotherham.gov.uk/downloads/download/31/independent-inquiry-into-child-sexual-exploitation-in-rotherham-1997---2013 (Accessed: 9 February 2022).

Jefferson, T. (2008). 'Policing the crisis revisited: The state, masculinity, fear of crime and racism', *Crime, Media, Culture: An International Journal*, 4(1), pp. 113–121.

Joint Committee on Human Rights (2021). *Legislative Scrutiny: Nationality and Borders Bill (Part 5) – Modern Slavery*. Available at: https://committees.parliament.uk/committee/93/human-rights-joint-committee/news/160035/nationalities-and-borders-bill-risks-failing-victims-of-modern-slavery/ (Accessed: 7 February 2022).

JRF, Joseph Rowntree Foundation (2012). *Experiences of Forced Labour in the UK Food Industry*. York: Joseph Rowntree Foundation. Available at: www.jrf.org.uk/sites/default/files/jrf/migrated/files/forced-labour-food-industry-full.pdf (Accessed: 27 January 2022).

Kalayaan (2019). *The Overseas Domestic Worker visa – keeping migrant domestic workers visible, legal and able to seek assistance from the authorities*. Kalayaan. Available at: www.kalayaan.org.uk/wp-content/uploads/2019/03/How-the-ODW-visa-prevents-trafficking-and-exploitation-position-statement-for-MSU.pdf (Accessed: 24 January 2022).

Kay Hoang, K. (2015). *Dealing in Desire: Asian Ascendancy, Western Decline, and the Hidden Currencies of Global Sex Work*. Oakland, CA: University of California Press.

Keeble, J., Fair, A. and Roe, S. (2018). *An Assessment of Independent Child Trafficking Advocates: Interim Findings: Research Report 101*. London: Home Office. Available at: https://assets.publishing.service.gov.uk/government/uploads/system/uploads/attachment_data/file/730098/assessment-of-independent-child-trafficking-advocates-horr101.pdf (Accessed: 9 February 2022).

Kenway, E. (2021). *The Truth About Modern Slavery*. London: Pluto Press.

Kerr, J., Patel, R., Lovbakke, J., Paskell, C., and Barnard, M. (2017). *Responding to child sexual abuse and exploitation in the night-time economy*. NatCen Social Research. Available at: www.csacentre.org.uk/documents/responding-to-child-sexual-abuse-and-exploitation-in-the-night-time-economy/ (Accessed: 5th April 2022).

Keo, C., Bouhours, T., Broadhurst, R. and Bouhours, B. (2014). 'Human trafficking and moral panic in Cambodia'. *The ANNALS of the American Academy of Political and Social Science*, 653, pp. 202–224.

Kleemans, E. (2014). 'Theoretical perspectives on organised crime', in Paoli, L. (ed.) *Oxford Handbook of Organised Crime*. Oxford: OUP, pp. 32–52.

Kleemans, E. and De Poot, C. (2008). 'Criminal careers in organised crime and social opportunity structure', *European Journal of Criminology*, 5(1), pp. 69–98.

Krieg, S.H. (2009). 'Trafficking in human beings: The EU approach between border control, law enforcement and human rights', *European Law Journal*, 15(6), pp. 775–790.

Larsen, J. and Diego-Rosell, P. (2017). *2017 Insight Series: Using surveys to measure modern slavery*. Walk Free Foundation. Available at: https://cdn.walkfree.org/content/uploads/2020/10/06153808/02-Insight-Series-171201_FNL.pdf (Accessed: 7 February 2022).

Latour, B. (1993). *We Have Never Been Modern*. London: Harvester Wheatsheaf.

Lawrence, F. (2017). 'How big brands including Sports Direct unwittingly used slave labour', *The Guardian*, 8 August [Online]. Available at: www.theguardian.com/global-development/2017/aug/08/how-big-brands-including-sports-direct-unwittingly-used-slave-labour (Accessed: 27 January 2022).

LeBaron, G. and Rühmkorf, A. (2019). 'The domestic politics of corporate accountability legislation: Struggles over the 2015 UK Modern Slavery Act', *Socio-Economic Review*, 17(3), pp. 709–743.

Levenkron, N. (2007). *"Another delivery from Tashkent": Profile of the Israeli trafficker*. Tel Aviv: Hotline for Migrant Workers. Available at: https://hotline.org.il/wp-content/uploads/Another_Delivery_From_Tashkent_Eng.pdf/ (Accessed: 9 September 2021).

Levy, J. and Jakobsson, P. (2014). 'Sweden's abolitionist discourse and the law: Effects on the dynamics of Swedish sex work and on the lives of Sweden's sex workers', *Criminology and Criminal Justice*, 14(5), pp. 593–607.

Lightowlers, C., Broad, R. and Gadd, D. (2022). 'Temporal measures of modern slavery victimisation'. *Criminology and Criminal Justice*. Available at: https://journals.sagepub.com/doi/pdf/10.1177/17488958221094988 [online]

Lord, N. and Broad, R. (2018). 'Corporate failures to prevent serious and organised crimes: Foregrounding the "organisational" component', *European Review of Organised Crime*, 4(3), pp. 27–52.

Maher, S. (2018). 'Out of West Africa: Human Smuggling as a Social Enterprise', *The Annals of the American Academy of Political and Social Science*, 676(1), pp. 36–56.

Mai, N. (2010). *The Psycho-Social Trajectories of Albanian and Romanian 'Traffickers'*. ISET/London Metropolitan University. [Online]. Available at: www.academia.edu/1237559/The_Psycho_Social_Trajectories_of_Albanian_and_Romanian_Traffickers_2010 (Accessed: 31 January 2022).

Mai, N. (2012). *Normal: Real Stories from the Sex Industry* (2012). Directed by Nicola Mai Available at: https://vimeo.com/50289487

Mai, N. (2016). '"Too much suffering": Understanding the interplay between migration, bounded exploitation and trafficking through Nigerian sex workers' experiences', *Sociological Research Online*, 21(4), pp. 159–172. [Online]. Available at: https://journ als.sagepub.com/doi/abs/10.5153/sro.4158 (Accessed: 28 January 2022).

Malik, K. (2018). 'We're told 84% of grooming gangs are Asian. But where's the evidence?' *The Guardian*, 11 November [Online]. Available at: www.theguardian.com/commentisfree/2018/nov/11/84-per-cent-of-grooming-gangs-are-asians-we-dont-know-if-that-figure-is-right (Accessed: 9 February 2022).

Marcus, A., Horning, A., Curtis, R., Sanson, J. and Thompson, E. (2014). 'Conflict and agency among sex workers and pimps: a closer look at domestic minor sex trafficking', *The ANNALS of the American Academy of Political and Social Science*, 653(1), pp. 225–246.

Marcus, A., Sanson, J., Horning, A., Thompson, E. and Curtis, R. (2016). 'Pimping and profitability: Testing the economics of trafficking in Street Sex Markets in Atlantic City, New Jersey', *Sociological Perspectives*, 59(1), pp. 46–65.

Martin, A-C., Bucktin, C., Byrne, P. and White, S. (2019). 'Tragic Vietnamese migrant "was kicked out of Britain" before dying in Essex lorry', *The Mirror*, 27 October [Online]. Available at: www.mirror.co.uk/news/uk-news/tragic-vietnamese-migr ant-was-kicked-20738392 (Accessed: 10 January 2022).

Maskens, M. (2015). 'Bordering intimacy: The fight against marriages of convenience in Brussels', *The Cambridge Journal of Anthropology*, 33(2), pp. 42–58.

Meikle, J. (2014). 'Peterborough gang jailed for sexual assaults', *The Guardian*, 20 February [Online]. Available at: www.theguardian.com/uk-news/2014/feb/20/peterborough-child-sex-gang-sentenced (Accessed: 9 February 2022).

MEN, Manchester Evening News (2013). *Dead at 15 – care girl who sold body to buy heroin*. Available at: www.manchestereveningnews.co.uk/news/local-news/dead-at-15---care-girl-986640 (Accessed: 9 February 2022).

Messinger, I. (2017). 'Viewpoint: marriages of convenience in times of crises', *Discover Society*, 44. [Online]. Available at: https://discoversociety.org/2017/05/02/viewpoint-marriages-of-convenience-in-times-of-crises/ (Accessed: 21 January 2022).

Modern Slavery Act 2015, c.30. (2022). Available at: www.legislation.gov.uk/ukpga/2015/30/contents/enacted (Accessed: 17 January 2022).

Modern Slavery Act 2015, c.30. Available at: www.legislation.gov.uk/ukpga/2015/30/contents/enacted (Accessed: 17 January 2022).

Mowat, L. (2016). 'EXCLUSIVE: Sham marriages have increased by almost 850% and authorities "are overwhelmed"', *Express*, 28 February [Online]. Available at: www.express.co.uk/news/uk/648025/Sham-marriages-increased-by-almost-850-and-authorities-are-overwhelmed-warns-MP (Accessed: 20 January 2022).

Nair, P. (2017). *Protest against Deliveroo's 'exploitation' of gig economy workers scheduled.* Available at: www.growthbusiness.co.uk/protest-against-deliveroos-drivers-explo itation-gig-economy-workers-2549643/ (Accessed: 27 January 2022).

National Audit Office (2017). *Reducing Modern Slavery*. London: Home Office. Available at: www.nao.org.uk/wp-content/uploads/2017/12/Reducing-Modern-Slavery.pdf (Accessed: 5 February 2022).

National Police Chiefs' Council (2016). *Police scale up operations into modern slavery.* Available at: https://news.npcc.police.uk/releases/police-scale-up-response-to-mod ern-slavery (Accessed 10 February 2022).

Nationality and Borders Bill. 2021. (HL Bill 82, 2021–2022). Available at: https://bills. parliament.uk/publications/44307/documents/1132 (Accessed: 2 February 2022).

NCA (2016). *National Referral Mechanism Statistics – End of Year Summary 2015.* National Crime Agency. Available at: https://nationalcrimeagency.gov.uk/who-we-are/publi cations/364-national-referral-mechanism-statistics-end-of-year-summary-2015/file (Accessed: 4 February 2022).

NCA (2017). *National Referral Mechanism Statistics – End of Year Summary 2016.* National Crime Agency. Available at: www.antislaverycommissioner.co.uk/media/1133/ 2016-nrm-end-of-year-summary.pdf (Accessed: 4 February 2022).

NCA (2018). *National Referral Mechanism Statistics – End of Year Summary 2017.* National Crime Agency. Available at: https://nationalcrimeagency.gov.uk/who-we-are/publi cations/159-modern-slavery-and-human-trafficking-national-referral-mechanism- statistics-annual-report-2017/file (Accessed: 4 February 2022).

NCA (2019). *National Referral Mechanism Statistics – End of Year Summary 2018.* National Crime Agency. Available at: https://nationalcrimeagency.gov.uk/who-we-are/publi cations/282-national-referral-mechanism-statistics-end-of-year-summary-2018/file (Accessed: 4 February 2022).

NCA (2020). *National Strategic Assessment of Serious and Organised Crime.* London: NCA. Available at: www.nationalcrimeagency.gov.uk/who-we-are/publications/437- national-strategic-assessment-of-serious-and-organised-crime-2020/file (Accessed: 12 January 2022).

New, S.J. (2015). 'Modern slavery and the supply chain: The limits of corporate social responsibility?' *Supply Chain Management,* 20(6), pp. 697–707.

Newell, S. (2020). *Histories of Dirt: Media and Urban Life in Colonial and Postcolonial Lagos.* North Carolina: Duke University Press.

Newsam, M. and Ridgway, G. (2019). *Independent assurance review of the effectiveness of multi-agency responses to child sexual exploitation in Greater Manchester: Part One: An assurance review of Operation Augusta.* Greater Manchester: Imprana Ltd and GKR Partnerships Ltd. Available at: www.nagalro.com/_userfiles/pages/files/operation_ augusta_january_2020_digital_final.pdf (Accessed: 9 February 2022).

Nicot, M. and Kopp, B. (2018). 'Policy perspective', *The Annals of The American Academy of Political and Social Science,* 676(1), pp. 223–225.

Norfolk, A. (2011). Revealed: conspiracy of silence on UK sex gangs, *Sunday Times,* 5 January, p. 1.

NPCC, National Police Chiefs' Council (2016). *Police Scale Up Operations into Modern Slavery.* Available at: https://news.npcc.police.uk/releases/police-scale-up-response- to-modern-slavery (Accessed 10 February 2022).

Nye, C. (2017). *The Real Reason Why British Workers Won't Pick Fruit.* Available at: https:// theconversation.com/the-real-reasons-why-british-workers-wont-pick-fruit-80152 (Accessed: 27 January 2022).

O'Connell Davidson, J. (2014). 'Let's go outside: bodies, prostitutes, slaves and worker citizens', *Citizenship Studies,* 18(5), pp. 516–532.

O'Connell Davidson, J. (2015). *Modern Slavery: The Margins of Freedom.* London: Palgrave Macmillan.

Office for National Statistics (2020a). *Modern Slavery in the UK: March 2020.* Office for National Statistics. Available at: file://nask.man.ac.uk/home$/Downloads/ Modern%20slavery%20in%20the%20UK%20March%202020.pdf (Accessed: 4 February 2022).

Office for National Statistics (2020b). *Dataset: Modern Slavery in the UK – Appendix Tables*. Office for National Statistics. Available at: www.ons.gov.uk/peoplepopulat ionandcommunity/crimeandjustice/datasets/modernslaveryintheukappendixtables (Accessed: 4 February 2022).

Orchiston, A. (2016). 'Precarious or protected? Evaluating work quality in the legal sex industry', *Sociological Research Online*, 21(4), pp. 173–187. [Online]. Available at: https://journals.sagepub.com/doi/10.5153/sro.4136 (Accessed: 29 January 2022).

Osbourne, S. (2019). 'Essex lorry horror: 39 found dead in Bulgarian lorry – police murder probe launched', *Express*, 23 October [Online]. Available at: www.express. co.uk/news/uk/1194418/thurock-lorry-39-bodies-found-murder-investigation-essex-police (Accessed: 10 January 2022).

Paoli, L. (2002). 'The paradoxes of organised crime', *Crime, Law and Social Change*, 37, pp. 51–97.

Paoli, L. and Fijnaut, C. (2006). 'Organised crime and its control policies', *European Journal of Crime, Criminal Law and Criminal Justice*, 14(3), pp. 307–327.

Pearce, J.J. (2011). 'Working with trafficked children and young people: Complexities in practice', *British Journal of Social Work*, 41(8), pp. 1424–1441.

Petrunov, G. (2014). 'Human trafficking in Eastern Europe: the case of Bulgaria', *The ANNALS of the American Academy of Political and Social Science*, 653(1), pp. 162–182.

Philips, N. (2015). 'Private Governance and the Problem of Trafficking and Slavery in Global Supply Chains', in Waite, L., Craig, G., Lewis, H. and Skrivankova, K. (eds.) *Vulnerability, Exploitation and Migrants: Insecure Work in a Globalised Economy*. Basingstoke: Palgrave Macmillan, pp. 15–27.

Phoenix, J. (2009). 'Frameworks of Understanding in Regulating Sex for Sale: Prostitution Policy and Reform in the UK', in Phoenix, J. (ed.) *Regulating Sex for Sale: Prostitution Policy Reform in the UK*. Bristol: Bristol University Press, pp. 1–28.

Phoenix, J. (2018). 'A commentary: Response to Weitzer "Resistance to sex work stigma"', *Sexualities*, 21(5–6), pp. 740–742.

Pitcher, J. (2015). 'Sex work and modes of self-employment in the informal economy: diverse business practices and constraints to effective working', *Social Policy and Society*, 14(1), pp. 113–123.

Pitcher, J. and Wijers, M. (2014). 'The impact of different regulatory models on the labour conditions, safety and welfare of indoor-based sex workers', *Criminology and Criminal Justice*, 14(5), pp. 549–564.

Policing and Crime Act 2009, c.26. Available at: www.legislation.gov.uk/ukpga/2009/26/ contents (Accessed: 28 January 2022).

Poynting, S., Noble, G., Tabar, P. and Collins, J. (2004). *Bin Laden in the Suburbs: Criminalising the Arab Other*. Sydney: Sydney Institute of Criminology Series.

Press Association (2014). 'Manchester trafficking ring "sold pregnant woman into sham marriage"', *The Guardian*, 13 November [Online]. Available at: www.theguardian. com/uk-news/2014/nov/13/human-trafficking-manchester-arrested-sham-marri age (Accessed: 21 January 2022).

Proceeds of Crime Act 2002, c.29. Available at: www.legislation.gov.uk/ukpga/2002/29/ contents (Accessed: 17 January 2022).

Reuter, P. (1983). *Disorganized Crime: The Economics of the Visible Hand*. Cambridge, MA: MIT Press.

Reuter, P. (1985). *The Organisation of Illegal Markets: An Economic Analysis*. Washington, DC: US Department of Justice.

Ridge, T. (2013). '"We are in this together?" The hidden costs of poverty, recession and austerity policies on Britain's poorest children', *Children and Society*, 27(5), pp. 406–417.

Riley, E. (2018). 'Sainsbury's gang who made over £500,000 by arranging sham marriages between Asian immigrants and Eastern European brides face jail', *Daily Mail*, 27 March [Online]. Available at: www.dailymail.co.uk/news/article-5550125/Gang-500-000-arranging-sham-marriages-facing-jail.html (Accessed: 20 January 2022).

Robinson, M. (2019). 'Hunt for Vietnamese gang lord behind Essex migrant tragedy: Police identify millionaire people-smuggler boss "Mr Truong" after his thugs threaten victims' families for speaking out', *Mail*, 30 October [Online]. Available at: www.dailymail.co.uk/news/article-7629207/Hunt-Vietnamese-gang-lord-Essex-migrant-tragedy-Police-identify-millionaire-Mr-Truong.html (Accessed: 10 January 2022).

Rugman, J. (2019). 'Vietnamese communities undeterred from UK migration – despite lorry deaths', *Channel 4 News*, 30 October [Online]. Available at: www.channel4.com/news/vietnamese-communities-undeterred-from-uk-migration-despite-lorry-deaths (Accessed: 11 January 2022).

Salvation Army (n.d.). *Ever seen him at a car wash?* Available at: www.salvationarmy.org.uk/modern-slavery/spot-signs-modern-slavery-car-wash (Accessed: 27 January 2022).

Sanchez, G. (2014). *Human Smuggling and Border Crossings*. London: Routledge.

Sanchez, G. (2020). *Beyond Militias and Tribes: The Facilitation of Migration in Libya*. EUI Working Papers, RSCAS, Migration Policy Centre. Available at: https://cadmus.eui.eu/handle/1814/66186 (Accessed: 12 January 2022).

Sanders, T. (2004). 'A continuum of risk? The management of health, physical and emotional risks by female sex workers', *Sociology of Health and Illness*, 26(5), pp. 557–574.

Sanders, T. (2005). *Sex Work: A risky business*. Cullompton: Willan Publishing.

Sanders, T., Scoular, J., Campbell, R., Pitcher, J. and Cunningham, S. (2018). *Internet Sex Work: Beyond the Gaze*. London: Palgrave MacMillan.

Sarfaty, G. (2015). 'Shining light on global supply chains', *Harvard International Law Journal*. 56(2), pp. 419–563.

Savage, C. and Williams, T. (2018). 'U.S. seizes Backpage.com, a site accused of enabling prostitution', *New York Times*, 7 April [Online]. Available at: www.nytimes.com/2018/04/07/us/politics/backpage-prostitution-classified.html (Accessed: 29 January 2022).

Scarpa, S. (2020). 'UN Palermo trafficking protocol eighteen years on: A critique', in Winterdyk, J. and Jones, J. (eds.) *The Palgrave International Handbook of Human Trafficking*. Cham: Palgrave Macmillan, pp. 623–640.

Segrave, M. (2009). 'Human trafficking and human rights', *Australian Journal of Human Rights*, 14(2), pp. 71–94.

Sen, S. and Nair, P.M. (2004). *A Report on Trafficking in Women and Children in India, 2002–2003*. New Delhi: Institute of Social Science/National Human Rights Commission/UNIFEM. Available at: https://nhrc.nic.in/sites/default/files/ReportonTrafficking.pdf (Accessed: 7 February 2022).

Serious Organised Crime and Police Act 2005, *c. 15*. Available at: www.legislation.gov.uk/ukpga/2005/15/contents (Accessed: 17 January 2022).

Sexual Offences Act 2003, *c. 42*. Available at: www.legislation.gov.uk/ukpga/2003/42/contents (Accessed: 2 February 2022).

Sexual Offences Act 1956, *c. 69*. Available at: www.legislation.gov.uk/ukpga/Eliz2/4-5/69/contents (Accessed: 28 January 2022).

Shen, A. (2016). 'Female perpetrators in internal child trafficking in China: An empirical study', *Journal of Human Trafficking*, 2(1), pp. 63–77.

Shen, A. (2016). 'Motivations of women who organized others for prostitution: Evidence from a female prison in China', *Criminology and Criminal Justice*, 16(2), pp. 214–232.

Shoal Collective (2017). 'DSEI: A supermarket for state surveillance and border wars', *libcom.org blog*, 3 September. Available at: https://libcom.org/news/dsei-supermar ket-state-surveillance-border-wars-04092017 (Accessed: 11 January 2022).

Shuker, G. (2018). 'Foreword', in the APPG on Prostitution and the Global Sex Trade. *Behind Closed Doors: Organised sexual exploitation in England and Wales*. London: APPG, pp. ii. Available at: www.appg-cse.uk/wp-content/uploads/2018/05/Behind-clo sed-doors-APPG-on-Prostitution.pdf (Accessed: 29 January 2022).

Siddique, H. (2019). 'Tesco withdraws Christmas cards from sale after forced labour claims', *The Guardian*, 22 December [Online]. Available at: www.theguardian.com/ business/2019/dec/22/tesco-halts-production-at-chinese-factory-over-forced-lab our-claims-christmas-cards?sa=X&ved=2ahUKEwj1-7j88vjmAhXiV98KHU_w CfUQ0Y8FMAl6BAgEEAQ (Accessed: 27 January 2022).

Silverman, B. (2014). *Modern Slavery: an application of Multiple Systems Estimation*. Home Office. Available at: www.gov.uk/government/uploads/system/uploads/atta chment_data/file/386841/Modern_Slavery_an_application_of_MSE_revised.pdf (Accessed: 4 February 2022).

Silverman, B. (2020). 'Multiple-systems analysis for the quantification of modern slavery: classical and Bayesian approaches', *Statistics in Society*, 183(3), pp. 691–736.

Smith, L., Pettifor, T., Beattie, J. Martin, A.C., Fricker, M. and Byrne, P. (2019). 'Chinese "snakehead" gang hunted over deaths of 39 migrants in Essex lorry', *The Mirror*, 24 October [Online]. Available at: www.mirror.co.uk/news/uk-news/chinese-snakehead-gang-hunted-over-20719114 (Accessed 11 January 2022).

Smithers, R. (2019). 'Workers exploited at farms supplying UK supermarkets: report', *The Guardian*, 10 October [Online]. Available at: www.theguardian.com/busin ess/2019/oct/10/workers-exploited-at-farms-supplying-uk-supermarkets-report (Accessed: 27 January 2022).

Spencer, J. and Broad, R. (2012). 'The "groundhog day" of the human trafficking for sexual exploitation debate: New directions in criminological understanding', *European Journal on Criminal Policy and Research*, 18(3), pp. 269–281.

Spicer, D. (2018). *Joint Serious Case Review Concerning Sexual Exploitation of Children and Adults with Needs for Care and Support in Newcastle-upon-Tyne*. Newcastle: Newcastle Safeguarding Children Board and Newcastle Safeguarding Adults Board. Available at: www.newcastle.gov.uk/sites/default/files/Final%20JSCR%20Report%20160 218%20PW.PDF (Accessed: 9 February 2022).

Spicer, J. (2021). 'The policing of cuckooing in "County Lines" drug dealing: An ethnographic study of an amplification spiral', *British Journal of Criminology*, 61(5), pp. 1390–1406.

Stephens, K. (2019). *'Asian Grooming Gangs': Media, State and the Far Right*. Available at: www.irr.org.uk/news/asian-grooming-gangs-media-state-and-the-far-right/ (Accessed: 9 February 2022).

Stevens v Christy [1987] Cr. App. R. 249, DC

Stop the Traffik (2018). *Sex Trafficking Vs Sex Work: Understanding the Difference*. Available at: www.stopthetraffik.org/sex-trafficking-vs-sex-work-understanding-difference/ (Accessed: 28 January 2022).

Street Offences Act 1959, *c.57*. Available at: www.legislation.gov.uk/ukpga/Eliz2/7-8/57/contents (Accessed: 28 January 2022).

Sullivan, B. (2010). 'When (some) prostitution is legal: The impact of law reform of sex work in Australia', *Journal of Law and Society*, 37(1), pp. 85–104.

Summers, H. (2018). 'Thousands enslaved in forced marriages across UK, investigation finds', *The Guardian*, 28 May [Online]. Available at: www.theguardian.com/global-development/2018/may/28/thousands-enslaved-in-forced-marriages-across-uk-investigation-finds (Accessed: 20 January 2022).

Sunderland, J. (2019). *No Escape from Hell: EU Policies Contribute to Abuse of Migrants in Libya*. Available at: www.hrw.org/report/2019/01/21/no-escape-hell/eu-policies-contribute-abuse-migrants-libya (Accessed 11 January 2022).

Sykes, G. and Matza, D. (1957). 'Techniques of Neutralisation: A theory of delinquency', *American Sociological Review*, 22(6), pp. 664–670.

Tade, O. (2019). 'Why Nigerian women in Oyo state use child domestic workers', *The Conversation*, 27 October [Online]. Available at: https://theconversation.com/why-nigerian-women-in-oyo-state-use-child-domestic-workers-123890 (Accessed: 24 January 2022).

Tade, O. and Aderinto, A. (2012). 'Factors influencing the demand for domestic servants in Oyo State, Nigeria', *International Journal of Child, Youth and Family Studies*, 4(1), pp. 521–545.

Tapsfield, J. (2020). 'Boris Johnson launches drive to "cut the head off the snake" of criminal gangs as he takes personal charge of Whitehall taskforce', *Mail Online*, 15 January [Online]. Available at: www.dailymail.co.uk/news/article-7889355/Boris-Johnson-vows-cut-head-snake-criminal-gangs.html (Accessed: 9 February 2022).

Thompson, F. (2022). 'Record number of suspected modern slavery victims in UK', *The Independent*, 3 March [Online]. Available at: www.independent.co.uk/news/uk/home-office-government-vietnamese-border-force-b2027579.html?r=1542&s=08 (Accessed: 8 March 2022).

Travis, A. (2014). 'UK axes support for Mediterranean migrant rescue operation', *The Guardian*, 27 October [Online]. Available at: www.theguardian.com/politics/2014/oct/27/uk-mediterranean-migrant-rescue-plan (Accessed 11 January 2022).

Trussell Trust (2021). *Trussell Trust data briefing on end-of-year statistics relating to use of food banks: April 2020 – March 2021*. Available at: www.trusselltrust.org/wp-content/uploads/sites/2/2021/04/Trusell-Trust-End-of-Year-stats-data-briefing_2020_21.pdf (Accessed: 16 February 2022).

Tufail, W. (2015). 'Rotherham, Rochdale, and the racialised threat of the "Muslim Grooming Gang"', *International Journal for Crime, Justice and Social Democracy*, 4(3), pp. 30–43.

Turnbull, N. and Broad, R. (2020). 'Bringing the problem home: The anti-slavery and anti-trafficking rhetoric of UK non-government organisations', *Politics*, pp. 1–16. [Online]. Available at: https://journals.sagepub.com/doi/pdf/10.1177/0263395720962402 (Accessed: 2 February 2022).

United Nations (2004). *United Nations Convention Against Transnational Organized Crime and The Protocols Thereto*. Vienna: UNODC. Available at: www.unodc.org/documents/middleeastandnorthafrica/organised-crime/UNITED_NATIONS_CONVENTION_AGAINST_TRANSNATIONAL_ORGANIZED_CRIME_AND_THE_PROTOCOLS_THERETO.pdf (Accessed 12 January 2022).

United Nations (2011). *Guiding Principles on Business and Human Rights: Implementing the United Nations "Protect, Respect and Remedy" Framework*. Geneva: United Nations.

Available at: www.ohchr.org/documents/publications/guidingprinciplesbusinesshr_en.pdf (Accessed: 27 January 2022).

United Nations (2015). *Sustainable development: The 17 goals*. Available at: https://sdgs.un.org/goals (Accessed 4 February 2022).

United Nations (2017). *Unlawful death of refugees and migrants*. United Nations General Assembly Seventy-Second Session, 15th August 2017. Available at: https://undocs.org/A/72/335 (Accessed: 12 January 2022).

UN News (2021). *Nigeria: Traumatized, abducted schoolchildren need rehabilitation – independent rights experts*. Available at: https://news.un.org/en/story/2021/03/1086242 (Accessed: 24 January 2022).

UN University (2021). *Developing freedom: The sustainable development case for ending modern slavery, forced labour and human trafficking*. UN University Centre for Policy Research. Available at: https://nottingham-repository.worktribe.com/index.php/preview/6392872/DevelopingFreedom_MainReport_WebFinal.pdf (Accessed: 4 February 2022).

US Department of State (2004). *Trafficking in Persons Report*. US Department of State. Available at: https://2009-2017.state.gov/documents/organization/34158.pdf (Accessed: 4 February 2022).

US Department of State (2017). *Trafficking in Persons Report*. US Department of State. Available at: www.state.gov/wp-content/uploads/2019/02/271339.pdf (Accessed: 21 January 2022).

US Department of State (2020). *Trafficking in Persons Report 20th Edition*. US Department of State. Available at: www.state.gov/wp-content/uploads/2020/06/2020-TIP-Report-Complete-062420-FINAL.pdf (Accessed: 4 February 2022).

van Duyne, P. and Vander Beken, T. (2009). 'The incantations of the EU organised crime policy making', *Crime, Law and Social Change*, 51(2), pp. 261–281.

Vere van Koppen, M. and De Poot, C. (2013). 'The truck driver who bought a café: Offenders on their involvement mechanisms for organized crime', *European Journal of Criminology*, 10(1), pp. 74–88.

Vere van Koppen, M., De Poot, C., Kleemans, E. and Nieuwbeerta, P. (2010). 'Criminal trajectories in organised crime', *British Journal of Criminology*, 50(1), pp. 102–123.

Villacampa, C. and Torres, N. (2019). 'Human trafficking for criminal exploitation: Effects suffered by victims in their passage through the criminal justice system', *International Review of Victimology*, 25(1), pp. 3–18.

Walby, S., Apitzsch, B., Armstrong, J., Balderston, S., Follis, K., Francis, B., Kelly, L., May-Chahal, C., Rashid, A., Shire, K., Towers, J., and Tunte, M. (2016). *Study on the gender dimension of trafficking in human beings: Final Report*. Luxembourg: European Commission. Available at: file://nask.man.ac.uk/home$/Downloads/study_on_the_gender_dimension_of_trafficking_in_human_beings._final_report.pdf (Accessed: 31 January 2022).

Walker, P. (2016). 'Briton who made wife live like slave is first to be jailed for domestic servitude', *The Guardian*, 1 April [Online]. Available at: www.theguardian.com/uk-news/2016/apr/01/man-made-wife-live-like-slave-domestic-servitude-faces-jail (Accessed: 24 January 2022).

Walk Free Foundation (2016). *The Global Slavery Index 2016*. Perth: The Minderoo Foundation. Available at: https://respect.international/wp-content/uploads/2018/07/The-Global-Slavery-Index-2016-Walk-Free-Foundation.pdf (Accessed: 7 February 2022).

Webb, S. and Burrows, J. (2009). *Organised immigration crime: a post-conviction study*, Research Report 15. Home Office. Available at: www.gov.uk/government/uplo ads/system/uploads/attachment_data/file/116629/horr15-report.pdf (Accessed: 12 January 2022).

Weitzer, R. (2007). 'The social construction of sex trafficking: ideology and institution-alisation of a moral crusade', *Politics and Society*, 35(3): pp. 447–475.

Weitzer, R. (2018). 'Resistance to sex work stigma', *Sexualities*, 21(5–6), pp. 717–729.

Werbner, P. (1990). *The Migration Process: Capital, Gifts and Offerings among British Pakistanis*. Oxford: Berg Publishers.

Whitehead, J., Jackson, J., Balch, A. and Francis, B. (2019). 'On the unreliability of mul-tiple systems estimation for estimating the number of potential victims of modern slavery in the UK', *Journal of Human Trafficking*, 7(1), pp. 1–13.

Whitty, N. (2011). 'Human rights as risk: UK prisons and the management of risk and rights', *Punishment and Society*, 13(2), pp. 123–148.

Williams, A. (2016). 'Babysitter who married a Nigerian immigrant in a sham marriage is jailed for six months as judge says her crime 'struck at the heart of the immigra-tion system'', *Daily Mail*, 11 January [Online]. Available at: www.dailymail.co.uk/ news/article-3393663/Babysitter-married-Nigerian-immigrant-sham-marriage-jai led-six-months-judge-says-crime-struck-heart-immigration-system.html (Accessed: 20 January 2022).

Windle, J., Moyle, L. and Coomber, R. (2020). '"Vulnerable" kids going country: chil-dren and young people's involvement in county lines drug dealing', *Youth Justice*, 20(1–2), pp. 64–78.

Woodiwiss, M. and Hobbs, D. (2009). 'Organised Evil and the Atlantic Alliance: Moral panics and the rhetoric of organised crime policing in America and Britain', *British Journal of Criminology*, 49(1), pp. 106–128.

World Health Organization (2011). *Child-fosterage promises and trafficking in children for domestic work in Nigeria: issues and implications for policy*. World Health Organization. Available at: https://apps.who.int/iris/bitstream/handle/10665/70575/WHO_ RHR_HRP_11.05_eng.pdf (Accessed: 24 January 2022).

World Vision (2012). *Tainted Technology: Forced and child labour in the electronics industry*. Available at: http://campaign.worldvision.com.au/wp-content/uploads/2013/04/ Forced-and-child-labour-in-the-technology-industry-fact-sheet.pdf   (Accessed: 27 January 2022).

Wray, H. (2015a). 'The 'Pure' Relationship, Sham Marriages and Immigration Control', in Miles, J., Mody, P. and Probert, R. (eds.) *Marriage Rites and Rights*, Oxford: Hart Publishing, pp. 141–165.

Wray, H. (2015b). '"A thing apart": Controlling male family migration to the United Kingdom', *Men and Masculinities*, 18(4), pp. 424–447.

Wray, H. (2015c). 'Spousal Migration, Gender and UK Immigration Law'. Available at: http://bordercriminologies.law.ox.ac.uk/spousal-migration-gender/ (Accessed: 21 January 2022).

Wright, R. (2019). 'Truck deaths highlight UK's lucrative people smuggling networks', *Financial Times*, 13 November [Online]. Available at: www.ft.com/content/06996 e9a-000c-11ea-be59-e49b2a136b8d (Accessed 11 January 2022).

Yeo, C. (2021). *Welcome to Britain: Fixing Our Broken Immigration System*. London: Biteback Publishing.

Young (2007). *The Vertigo of Late Modernity*. London: Sage.

Zhang, S. (2011). 'Woman pullers: pimping and sex trafficking in a Mexican Border City', *Crime, Law and Social Change*, 56(5), pp. 509–528.

Zhang, S. (2013). 'Snakeheads and the Cartwheel Network: Functional Fluidity as Opposed to Structural Flexibility', in Morselli, C. (ed.) *Crime and Networks*. London: Routledge, pp. 126–158.

Zhang, S. and Chin, K-L. (2002). *The Social Organization of Chinese Human Smuggling-A Cross National Study*. San Diego, CA: San Diego State University.

Zhang, S, and Chin, K-L. (2015). 'Swim against the Tide: Using Qualitative Data to Build a Theory on Chinese Human Smuggling', in Miller, J. and Palacios, W. (eds.) *Qualitative Research in Criminology Advances in Criminological Theory*. New Brunswick, NJ: Transaction, pp. 215–237.

Zhang, S., Sanchez, G. and Achilli, A. (2018). 'Special editors' note', *The ANNALS of the American Academy of Political and Social Science*, 676(1), pp. 6–15.

Index